Outsiders and Insiders

Studies of World Literature in English

Norman Cary,
General Editor

Vol. 1

PETER LANG
New York • San Francisco • Bern • Baltimore
Frankfurt am Main • Berlin • Wien • Paris

Michael Harris

Outsiders and Insiders

Perspectives of Third World Culture in British and Post-Colonial Fiction

PETER LANG
New York • San Francisco • Bern • Baltimore
Frankfurt am Main • Berlin • Wien • Paris

Library of Congress Cataloging-in-Publication Data

Harris, Michael.
Outsiders and insiders : perspectives of Third World culture in British and post-colonial fiction / Michael Harris.
p. cm. — (Studies of world literature in English ; v. 1)
Includes bibliographical references.
1. Commonwealth of Nations fiction (English)—History and criticism. 2. Literature, Comparative—Commonwealth of Nations (English) and English. 3. Literature, Comparative—English and Commonwealth of Nations (English). 4. English fiction—History and criticism. 5. Developing countries in literature. 6. Culture conflict in literature. 7. Imperialism in literature. 8. Colonies in literature. I. Title. II. Series.
PR9084.H27 1992 823'.9109321724—dc20 91-28482
ISBN 0-8204-1668-1 CIP
ISSN 1043-8580

Die Deutsche Bibliothek-CIP-Einheitsaufnahme

Harris, Michael:
Outsiders and insiders : perspectives of third world culture in British and post-colonial fiction / Michael Harris.—New York; Berlin; Bern; Frankfurt/M.; Paris; Wien; Lang, 1992
(Studies of world literature in English ; Vol. 1)
ISBN 0-8204-1668-1
NE: GT

Cover Design by Jim Brisson.

The paper in this book meets the guidelines for permanence and durability of the Committee on Production Guidelines for Book Longevity of the Council on Library Resources.

Printed in the United States of America.

Contents

Acknowledgements

I am delighted to have the opportunity of acknowledging the many people who helped and inspired me in the writing of this book. The project would never have been begun were it not for Albert Wertheim, who gave me advice, help, and encouragement on occasions too numerous to mention. I would also like to express my gratitude to Patrick Brantlinger and Donald Gray who gave me their time, assistance and guidance at every stage of the writing process. To Al, Pat, and Don, I am deeply grateful, and only hope I can carry their example forward through my work with my own students.

I have learned a great deal from discussions with my students about British and post-colonial literature. I would like to give special thanks to my Literature of South Africa class at the University of Notre Dame (Spring 1987), my Literature of the Third World class at Stetson University (Spring 1989), my Post-Colonial Literature class at Grinnell College (Fall, 1989), and my Post-Colonial Fiction class here at Central College (Fall, 1991). My students' insights have enriched my understanding of the fiction I treat in this study, and I greatly appreciate them for their perceptions.

Friends and colleagues in various places have also contributed much to my understanding and appreciation of British and post-colonial literature, and various so-called Third World cultures. I should mention Manthia Diawara, Clement Ndulute, Sashi Panthi, Bes Bahadur Kumar, James Naremore, Lewis Miller, Emile Snyder, Ellen Smith, Peter Walshe, Malusi Mpumlwana, Joseph Buttigieg, G. D. Killam, Kenneth Ramchand, Valerie and Roger Vetter, Jim Zaffiro, Mary Stark, and Walter Cannon. These individuals, and many others, have enabled me on more than one occasion to think out-loud and use them as sounding boards for trial ideas. I have also benefitted greatly from their ideas and views.

I would also like to thank the Research and Development Committee at Central College for its generous assistance in allowing me to complete this project. Without the committee's help, the publication of this study would not have been possible. The people at the Central College Computer Center have been wonderful in helping me put this book together. Thanks are due to Deb Rooda, Peggy Vanden Berg, Carol Van Weelden, and to the Director of the Center, Lee Vande Voort. Members of the staff of the Geisler Learning Resource Center have also been generous in helping me track down sources and locate information: I should especially mention Keith Eiten, Lois Smith, and Joan Reitz.

I would like to thank Diana Brydon, editor of *World Literature Written in English*, and John Barnes, editor of *Meridian*, for permission to use revised versions of earlier published articles.

I also wish to acknowledge the following writers, publishers and literary agents who have granted me permission to quote from their copyrighted texts: Brandt & Brandt for *Island in the Sun* (Copyright 1955 by Alec Waugh); Elspeth Huxley and Heather Jeeves for *A Thing to Love*; Faber and Faber for *Wild Conquest*; Andrew Lownie and the Estate of Joyce Cary for *Mister Johnson*; the Octopus Publishing Group Library for *Things Fall Apart*; Heinemann Educational Books for *A Grain of Wheat*; and George Lamming for *In the Castle of My Skin*.

Finally, I owe a special debt of thanks to my wife, Kimberly Koza, who has been a constant inspiration and support during the various stages of my work on this study. I deeply appreciate her encouragement and understanding, as I do the innate curiosity and energy of my two sons, Lech and Will. I hope some of the open-mindedness and generosity of these three special people carries over into this book.

For Kim, Lech, Will, and Al

It is rare for us to find ourselves in books, but in our own books we were able to find and define our lives.

Patricia Grace, *Potiki*

Introduction

Early British colonial writers, like H. Rider Haggard and Rudyard Kipling, served the important purpose of introducing readers to worlds and cultures entirely different from their own. In "Kipling's Place in the History of Ideas," Noel Annan shows how Kipling's primary concern with the inner workings of societies, as opposed to individuals, became a way of depicting not only Indian society but English society as well. "And what should they know of England who only England know?" asked Kipling, implying that to know one's own culture and society, one must first experience a contrasting culture and society (Carrington, 227). Kipling, Haggard, and other British colonial writers, such as Forster, Orwell, and Leonard Woolf, often wrote about the clash between alien cultures brought on by British imperialism. Of course, the British writers described colonial territories from an outsider's point of view. In more recent years, however, indigenous Third World writers like Chinua Achebe, George Lamming, and Salman Rushdie have shown the reader another side of this confrontation, and thus have pointed up the limitations of the British fiction. Since the British writers reflect the colonizer perspective on the clash of cultures, their chief concern is usually with their English characters. The subject peoples and their homeland typically perform the role of an exotic background. The limitations of British fiction set in "the tropics" thus speak eloquently about the ethnocentric nature of the British Empire itself.

That empire was largely founded by explorers, adventurers, and commercial traders, many of whom became legendary figures in British history.[1] Robert Clive, a clerk in the East India Company, was instrumental in England's colonization of India when he led a military victory over the French at the Battle of Plassey in 1757. Other commercial developers and adventurers, like Cecil Rhodes in southern Africa, Frederick Lugard in Nigeria, and Hugh Cholmondeley Delamere in Kenya, played important roles in later British colonization on the African continent. Although the British government initially kept a safe distance from these adventurers and their questionable aims and practices, it later adopted many of their early dreams and ambitions to justify colonial expansion. British commercial companies modeled after the East India Company established economic footholds in various "undeveloped" areas throughout the world. And the English government in most cases provided the companies with protection to ensure free trading rights. Eventually the government took the natural step of establishing administrative, colonial control over those areas in which British trading companies were involved, as the government did in India in 1857.

As a result of the way in which British colonial control was established in scattered, faraway places, the Empire was from the beginning remarkably decentralized. As the Empire expanded, the British became increasingly aware of the difficulty, if not impossibility, of adopting a single standard by which to rule all its colonies. By the time the African colonies of Nigeria, Kenya, Uganda, and the Gold Coast were established, Britain had adopted the policy of "indirect rule," in which colonial rule was filtered through the decree of traditional, native rulers. In this way, the colonizers maintained control while preserving the local social and political system to which the indigenous people were accustomed. The British, of course, held the power of selecting the leader and deposing him when and if they saw fit. Unlike the relatively smooth and efficient rule in India, indirect rule in the African colonies often met obstacles. A power vacuum existed in pre-colonial India which the British could conveniently fill, but the unification of diverse African peoples under colonial rule proved more difficult. As a result, in the African colonies and later in India and the West Indies as well, British colonial rule came to be seen as an imposition of an alien system of government on unwilling, indigenous peoples.

The romantic era of the explorers and adventurers was followed by the mundane administrative work of civil servants whose unromantic duty it was to keep the imperial machine running smoothly. Both of these colonial eras are well represented in British fiction. Rider Haggard's *King Solomon's Mines*, for instance, celebrates the exploits of early explorers and adventurers through the portrayal of romantic characters like Allan Quatermain and Sir Henry Curtis. By contrast, later fiction, such as Kipling's *Kim*, Joyce Cary's *Mister Johnson*, and Alec Waugh's *Island in the Sun*, portrays civil servants carrying out their routine task of administering out-of-the-way colonies.

In the administration of the colonies, it was perhaps inevitable that notions of racial and ethnic superiority, always latent in the colonizing process, would surface. Part of the British self-justification for administration of an increasingly large and diverse Empire was a belief in their own superiority as administrators and, similarly, in the superiority of England as a civilization. Missionaries, who followed the adventurers and commercial traders to remote parts of the Empire, especially to Africa, conveyed their belief in the superiority of Christianity to indigenous religions, which were deemed false and heretical. As a result, the Empire came to be seen through its own eyes as serving a humanitarian as well as a strategic and economic purpose. Moreover, the success of the Evangelical Movement in the early nineteenth century in abolishing first the slave trade and then slavery throughout the colonies lent added moral credibility to the Empire. Even many of the early opponents of imperialism in England thus came to accept the idea of Empire as an altruistic mission which their country seemed destined to fulfill. And clearly, writers like Haggard and Kipling explicitly endorsed the idea that in colonizing the "new-caught, sullen peoples/Half devil and half child," as Kipling put it, the English were actually serving and helping the needy (Howe, 602). Clearly, these writers as well as many others serving the Empire were either unaware of or chose to overlook what Edward Said has described in *Orientalism* as the "paradox that a Western conquest of the Orient was not conquest after all, but liberty" (172).

Once begun, the Empire seemed to grow of its own accord. After the Berlin Conference in 1884-85, almost the entire continent of Africa was divided up among the European powers. By that same time, virtually all of the Indian subcontinent had also come under British rule. Toward the end of the nineteenth century, the golden era of the Empire, British colonial control extended to every continent in the world; the English ruled one-quarter of the globe and over one-quarter of the world's population. Many of the additions to the Empire were acquired in treaties. As a result of the Congress of Vienna in 1814-15, which marked the end of the Napoleonic Wars, England gained colonies in southern Africa, Ceylon, and Malta. And later, as a result of the Treaty of Versailles following World War I, Palestine, Iraq, and Tanganyika were added.

Once the huge British Empire was established and its administrative machinery set in motion, it became increasingly obvious that the British had only a vague sense of direction. The basic plan was to keep the imperial machinery turning: to maintain the status quo. As a result of British colonial institutions—most importantly school, church, and government—an educated, indigenous middle class emerged. That class became most prominent in India but eventually appeared in the other colonies as well. It did not, however, behave the way the British expected. Rather than being satisfied with its advances, this anglicized group became dissatisfied with the limited opportunities offered under colonial society. Nevertheless, for a long while, the British took advantage of the gap between the newly educated class and the uneducated, peasant majority to solidify its ruling position. Certainly one generally successful colonial policy which transcended geographic setting was that of divide-and-rule. To consolidate their power, the British effectively played upon already existent religious differences in India, tribal differences in Africa, and color and ethnic differences in the West Indies. The colonizers quickly realized that keeping the colonized people divided amongst themselves would prevent internal alignments seeking to abrogate rule by a foreign power.

But the Empire did not always run smoothly, as British colonial fiction by writers such as Orwell, Cary, Elspeth Huxley, and Alec Waugh bears testimony. Indeed, throughout the nineteenth century, there were violent flare-ups, labor strikes, and organized revolts in various areas of the Empire. In 1857, the shockingly violent Sepoy Mutiny occurred in India as a result of a rumor that animal grease, anathema to Hindu and Muslim soldiers, was used in soldiers' cartridges. The West Indian colonies had a long history of slave revolts and labor strikes. In 1865, laborers' grievances in Jamaica boiled over into violence in the Morant Bay Uprising, and British troops were called in from England to quell the revolt. In Kenya, a colonial ban on a traditional female circumcision rite led to native resistance and clashes between the colonial authorities and the subject people. These and other isolated instances of revolt by the colonized people were put down, but, at the very least, they signalled the beginning of a concerted resistance throughout the colonies to imperial domination.

The gradual development and improvement of communications had much to do with the eventual dissolution of the Empire. As a result of improved communications, the uprisings by various groups came to seem less isolated and eventually formed a pattern. Mohandas Gandhi played such an influential role in what came to be known as the decolonization movement that he might be called not only the father of India but also the father of the nationalization which eventually swept through and transformed all the colonies. First in South Africa and then in his native India, Gandhi proved to be an excellent organizer. The defiance of British decree in India had a "bandwagon effect" on the other colonies, where Gandhi's successes were applauded and emulated. The Gandhi-led mass burning of British-made cotton clothing and the concerted refusal to buy

British-produced salt were blows against an unfair colonial monopoly over Indian goods. Ali Mazrui, the African scholar and writer, has stated that during decolonization and afterward, Indian "influence on African thought has been significant" (123). An important example of this influence was Kwame Nkrumah, the leader of the Gold Coast, who consciously adopted Gandhi's tactics in his own country's independence movement. The effect of these acts of defiance was like a fire which burned throughout the Empire and which the British were finally unable to extinquish or control.

Although the bandwagon effect held true in many colonies, there were exceptions to this general pattern. Perhaps the most important exception was southern Africa. There the situation was complicated not only by the British colonial presence, but also by a large group of Dutch settlers, the Afrikaners, who had first arrived in 1652. After breaking off ties with their European homeland, the Afrikaners overran various indigenous southern African peoples and eventually came into conflict with the British colonists. The long-standing conflict between the British and the Afrikaners culminated in the Boer War of 1899-1902, which the British won, but only at the price of thousands of soldiers and a considerable dampening of national morale. Many historians, in fact, consider the Boer War as the British Waterloo, signaling a downward turning-point in the Empire's fortunes.[2] Ten years after the war, in a sudden reversal of policy characteristic of the Empire, the two sides signed a treaty and the British returned the land they had earlier fought so hard to win. In 1910, the four territories of southern Africa were consolidated into the self-governing Union of South Africa which has retained power under a minority white rulership to the present day.

World War I and World War II brought important changes to the Empire, and especially to relations between colonizer and colonized. The nationalization movement in India became much stronger after World War I. Gandhi, for instance, on board an ocean liner returning to India from England in 1914, noticed an almost total lack of social intercourse between British and Indian passengers. "The reason for this," Gandhi recalls in his autobiography, "was, I think, to be found in the conscious or unconscious feeling at the back of the Englishman's mind that he belonged to the ruling race, and the feeling at the back of the Indian's mind that he belonged to the subject race" (360). As a result of the "European War," the colonized people found themselves on a new, more self-conscious footing with their colonial rulers, and both seemed to realize that as a result of the war things would never be the same. World War I, in effect, removed the Europeans from their pedestal, demonstrating that the colonizers had grave problems of their own at home. In the African colonies, where British rule was a much shorter and more recent phenomenon, the independence movements began in earnest only after World War II. The two world wars, in general, served as an introduction to the outside world for many of the colonized men conscripted to fight under British command overseas. Moreover, the colonized soldiers' wartime experience allowed them to see their rulers for the first time as equals and without all their colonial trappings. Following the wars, illusions about the colonizers' moral ascendancy and their civilization's superiority were irreparably damaged.

The transition of power was peaceful in most but not all of the colonies. Frantz Fanon, in his classic study of colonial dynamics, *The Wretched of the Earth*, states that following World War II, no colonial power was "capable of adopting the only form of contest which [had] a chance of succeeding, namely, the prolonged establishment of large forces of occupation" (74). Faced with little choice, England and other European colonial powers in most cases relinquished colonial rule willingly and as expediently as possible. India gained its independence in 1947 without serious incident, although the partition of the colony into two separate countries following independence led to sectarian violence. In 1957, the Gold Coast became the first African colony to gain independence, adopting the name of a great, pre-colonial African civilization, Ghana. Nigeria followed in 1960. In Kenya, however, where many British colonists hoped to settle permanently, an entirely different situation unfolded. There, the British colonial authorities went to great length to discourage the growing independence movement, and finally declared a state of Emergency in 1952. The result was the Mau Mau Revolt, a bloody civil conflict creating a rift in the country between loyalists to the British and the Mau Mau rebels. Although the revolt was put down, it accelerated the drive for independence and prompted the British realization that Kenya was no longer a "white man's country," as it had come to be known. The West Indies, where independence movements were marked by a series of labor strikes and riots, eventually followed the example of India and the African colonies. Jamaica and Trinidad became independent in 1962, and Barbados followed in 1966.

The British relinquishment of rule did not suddenly erase the effects of decades of colonial domination. In most cases, British influence and institutions, such as the English language, a Parliamentary form of government with heads of state determined by election, and the British legal system, remained long after the colonizers left. Architecture, religion, education, and social customs were other areas affected by the British colonial intervention. Even today in many former colonies, a strong background in English language, literature, and history remains a key component of the standard educational curriculum. Moreover, to satisfy the educational requirements at many schools, students must pass an examination which is drawn up and graded in England. And the result, of course, of generations of students matriculating through a British-modeled school system is a continuation of ideals and goals established by the Empire.

In *The Wretched of the Earth*, Frantz Fanon defines a *national culture* as "the whole body of efforts made by a people in the sphere of thought to describe, justify, and praise the action through which that people has created itself and keeps itself in existence" (233). And Ngugi wa Thiong'o, the Kenyan novelist and playwright, has a similar, all-encompassing definition for the term *culture*: "a way of life fashioned by a people in their collective endeavor to live and come to terms with their total environment. It is the sum of their art, their science and all their social institutions, including their system of beliefs and rituals" (*Homecoming*, 4). It is this all-encompassing, indigenous culture which has suffered the most damage in the wake of British colonialism. In order to demonstrate their own superiority and thus to justify their colonial presence, the British had to demonstrate repeatedly the inadequacy and inferiority of the native culture and institutions of the colonized people. And certainly the fractured cultural identity engendered by the colonial encounter has remained a problematic legacy in former colonies.

A remarkable by-product of the decolonization movement has been the outpouring of literature written in English by indigenous writers from these same former British colonies. Although this literature has taken the form of poetry, drama, and fiction, perhaps most impressive has been the output in fiction, and in particular, the novel. Writers from diverse, formerly-colonized areas have adapted the Western form of the novel to suit their own purpose: to relate life in their region from the inside, as it is experienced by those who live there. Long interpreted from the outside by writers and travelers from the "mother country," these areas of the so-called Third World have now found their own unique voice.

One of the leading voices in this new body of writing, alternatively called post-colonial literature, Commonwealth literature, and Third World literature, is that of Chinua Achebe from Nigeria. Achebe's literary output includes five novels which as a group chronicle Nigeria's recent history, from the pre-colonial era through colonization to a problematic independence. Through his writing, Achebe has called into question the portrayal of Africa by earlier British colonial writers, such as John Buchan and Joyce Cary. Although post-colonial fiction, in general, is marked by great diversity, many other writers from such disparate areas as India, Africa, the West Indies, and the Pacific have also employed tactics similar to Achebe's. They have often reconstructed their country's colonial history, and, in doing so, have offered a striking, alternative view to the one conveyed in earlier British fiction. These writers have, in short, opened up a dialogue with their colonial predecessors, contesting the latter's authority to pass judgment on a people and culture about which they knew very little.

Peter Abrahams, a Coloured writer from South Africa now living in Jamaica, has, like Achebe, been an important influence on many later post-colonial writers, especially those from Africa. In *Wild Conquest*, Abrahams reconstructs the historical conflict between the Matabele, an indigenous southern African people, and the Afrikaners who encroach on Matabele territory in search of a homeland following their Great Trek. In his realistic portrait of southern African history, Abrahams calls into question Rider Haggard's portrayal of southern Africa in his "African romances," such as *King Solomon's Mines*. Ngugi wa Thiong'o, the Kenyan novelist, has also been critical of representations of his country in British literature such as Isak Dinesen's *Out of Africa* and Elspeth Huxley's *A Thing to Love*. In such novels as *Weep Not, Child*, *A Grain of Wheat*, and *Petals of Blood*, Ngugi has provided an insider's view of Kenyan history and, in particular, of the Mau Mau Revolt and post-independence. George Lamming, a writer of mixed African and British ancestry from the West Indian island of Barbados, has similarly recreated the colonial past of his island home, consciously responding to portraits of the West Indies in valorized English literary works, such as *The Tempest* and *Robinson Crusoe*. And in a similar way, *Midnight's Children*, by the Indian writer Salman Rushdie, recaptures Indian history from independence to the present. Like other Third World writers, Rushdie implicitly calls into question the outsider's account of India to be found in such British works as Kipling's *Kim* and Forster's *A Passage to India*.

Not every post-colonial writer, however, writes fiction that falls into this recognizable pattern. Two examples which immediately come to mind are the Indian writer, R. K. Narayan, and the Trinidadian writer, V. S. Naipaul. Narayan's novels and stories, often set in the fictional South Indian town of Malgudi, attempt neither to recreate Indian history nor to respond to British literary predecessors. Naipaul, likewise, represents an entirely different case. A prolific writer of both fiction and non-fiction, Naipaul has often been out-spokenly critical of attempts by formerly colonized Third World countries to achieve a unified and satisfactory nationhood. The existence of these exceptions points to the possibility that these disparate geographical regions are simply too unique and distinct to be compared to one another in global terms. There are a significant number of writers, moreover, who would seem to occupy an intermediary position between the British and post-colonial writers. The group of liberal white South African writers, including Alan Paton, Nadine Gordimer, and J. M. Coetzee, for instance, seems to belong racially-speaking to the British colonial tradition, and yet they frequently write in protest against the white South African regime and in favor of the cause of the indigenous, black South African people.

One might easily question the validity of the wholesale grouping of such a diverse body of writing under the single heading of post-colonial literature. Do India, the African nations, and the West Indies have enough in common to make a comparison of their literatures fruitful? It seems clear that the writers of these countries play an important role in the resurrection of a national culture damaged by European colonial domination. Their individual national cultures, nevertheless, seem to have little in common. Furthermore, although the pattern of colonial history in each of these countries is similar, the effect of British colonialism on their cultures varies. Indian civilization, for instance, stood up relatively well to the onslaught of colonial domination. African societies, on the other hand, seem to have been more deeply affected, and yet there, too, many cultural traditions and institutions remain intact. In the West Indies, by contrast, the indigenous people and their culture were completely erased and replaced with a transplanted African slave population and, later, with indentured laborers from India and China. Unlike the ancient, resilient Indian culture which goes on today much like it did before the *Raj*, contemporary West Indian culture is a direct product of colonialism.

One might also question the validity of grouping together all the British writers who wrote about the colonies under the single, and perhaps misleading, heading of "British colonial fiction." Some of these writers, for instance, were clearly more in favor of the Empire than others. What do writers as diverse as Kipling, Haggard, Conrad, Orwell, Leonard Woolf, Cary, Elspeth Huxley, Isak Dinesen, Alec and Evelyn Waugh, and Graham Greene really have in common besides their occasional use of a British colony as a fictional setting? Do not, for instance, writers such as Kipling and Forster actually represent opposite poles in their attitudes towards India; and isn't, in fact, Forster's *A Passage to India* intended as an answer to what the author perceived as Kipling's imperialistic stance in works like *Kim* and the Indian stories? In short, aren't these writers' intentions and attitudes too much at variance to place them together in a single category?

Perhaps one impulse for grouping these various writers under the same heading of British colonialism lies in their writing itself. Many of these writers, both British outsider and indigenous insider, adopt as their primary focus the relations between the colonizer and the colonized. Their language, settings, narrative structures, and characters reflect their fascination with the Empire and its effects upon colonizer and colonized alike. There are, moreover, a host of commentators on colonialism from a variety of disciplines who implicitly assume connections between the various formerly-colonized countries. Gandhi, for instance, linked these various colonized countries together in his many writings on the subject of colonialism. Gandhi's statement that colonialism is "a perpetual insult for it assumes that the outsider has the right to rule the insiders who cannot rule themselves" (61) is characteristic of distinctions made by many writers and scholars who concern themselves with the phenomenon of colonialism. Frantz Fanon's *The Wretched of the Earth* and *Black Skin, White Masks*, which grew out of the author's experience in the Algerian War of Independence against the French, also establish explicit links between those people throughout the world who have been dominated by colonial rule. Albert Memmi, a Jewish writer who grew up in French Tunisia, makes similar inferences about the colonial compartmentalization of people in *The Colonizer and the Colonized* and *Dominated Man*. Moreover, Dominique Mannoni, who looks at the colonial phenomenon from a European colonizer's viewpoint in *Prospero and Caliban*, uses language and terminology strikingly similar to these other writers. Although he views the situation from a European perspective, Mannoni also sets up a paradigm between colonizer and colonized in colonial Madagascar in order to explain the various psychological motivations of each side.

This study attempts to test the validity of the colonizer-colonized distinction. Can one talk about "the colonial encounter" in reference to such diverse regions as India, Africa, and the West Indies, and, if so, what are the points of similarity? Perhaps it is necessary to make certain qualifications in order to speak of a generalized colonial experience applicable to all these areas: that British colonial interests in each area were not the same; that the nature of the colonizer-colonized relations might have differed in different areas; or that the degree of disruption of the indigenous society surely varied from one region to the next. In each of the five chapters of this study—on India, Southern Africa, West Africa, East Africa, and the West Indies—my aim is to seek similarities among the various colonial encounters while remaining open to the unique circumstances and history of each region.

The study is arranged in such a way as to reflect the geopolitical evolution of the British Empire. The five British novels form a roughly chronological sequence from Rudyard Kipling's *Kim* and H. Rider Haggard's *King Solomon's Mines* to the later treatments of the Empire in Joyce Cary's *Mister Johnson*, Elspeth Huxley's *A Thing to Love* and Alec Waugh's *Island in the Sun*. There is a perceptible change among these works in the British writers' attitudes toward the Empire which surely reflects historic developments of the times, including an overall shift in the British public's attitude toward the country's imperial endeavor. Nevertheless, these writers have in common a detached outsider's perspective of the colonized people and their culture which is later countered in the fiction by post-colonial writers dealing with the same era in retrospect. This point is made by Raymond Williams in *The Country and the City* where he draws a distinction between the portrayals by British and post-colonial writers of the colonial experience:

> We are already familiar with the work of Englishmen who experienced the tensions of [the colonizing] process: E. M. Forster's *A Passage to India*, Orwell's *Burmese Days*, Joyce Cary's important African novels *Aissa Saved*, *The African Witch*, *Mister Johnson*. Characteristically these are liberal ways of seeing the experience, in the critical and self-questioning generation after Kipling. But we have only to go across to the Indian and African and West Indian writers to get a different and necessary perspective (285).

To achieve this "different and necessary perspective," this study juxtaposes paradigmatic novels by a British and a post-colonial writer to examine the differing perceptions of colonizer and colonized. Chapter One, entitled "The Example of India," pairs two contrasting views of India: Rudyard Kipling's *Kim* and Salman Rushdie's *Midnight's Children*. The chapter on India forms a cornerstone of the study, for one of my chief premises is that India played a key role in the decolonization process which began with Gandhi's nonviolent noncooperation movement in the early twentieth century, accelerated in the aftermath of the two World Wars, and eventually succeeded in dismantling the Empire. India's independence, achieved in 1947, thus served as an example to the other colonies throughout the world which followed suit with independence movements of their own. The selection of the two novels for this chapter was based on the appearance of Salman Rushdie's dazzling novel, *Midnight's Children*, which clearly attempts to convey the Indian experience from an Indian's point of view. Rushdie's novel represents a response to all British fiction set in India, but especially to Kipling as the chief purveyor of the British colonial experience in India. Comparing Kipling's *Bildungsroman* masterpiece, *Kim*, with Rushdie's treatment of the coming of age of a young Indian boy, born in the same hour as his country, thus enabled me to underscore the contrast between the outsider and insider perspectives.

Chapter One is thus designed to demonstrate the importance of India's role in the global decolonization movement. Taken together, Kipling's *Kim* and Rushdie's *Midnight's Children* cover a broad spectrum of Indian history: from the heyday of the British *Raj* through independence to the present. Chapter Two, "Adventure and Conquest," has a much narrower historical focus: the period in southern African history when indigenous Africans vied with Europeans for the future ownership of the land. The two novels dealt with in this chapter, H. Rider Haggard's African romance, *King Solomon's Mines*, and Peter Abrahams' historical novel, *Wild Conquest*, treat this early phase in southern African history in different ways. Haggard's romance represents the idealization of colonialism as an exotic adventure, whereas Abrahams' novel is one of the earliest efforts by an indigenous South African to recast the historical moment when possession of the land passed from black Africans to white Afrikaners.

Chapters Three and Four trace continuing developments of the Empire as they unfold in West and East Africa. Chapter Four, "The Cultural Clash," develops some of the concerns of the fictional treatments of southern Africa in Chapter Two, showing the inevitable consequences of colonial domination. The two novels included in this chapter, Joyce Cary's seriocomedy, *Mister Johnson*, and Chinua Achebe's tragic novel, *Things Fall Apart*, illustrate the contrasting British and indigenous perspectives on the establishment of formal colonial control in Nigeria and its effect on the native traditions and institutions of the Nigerian people. Chapter Four, "The Struggle for Independence," moves forward roughly fifty years to colonial Kenya during the Mau Mau conflict when indigenous Kenyans took up arms against both British and fellow Kenyans in an effort to gain their independence and self-determination. The two novels included in this chapter, Elspeth Huxley's *A Thing to Love* and Ngugi wa Thiong'o's *A Grain of Wheat*, render contrasting portrayals of this bloody historical conflict between a demand for national freedom and a desire to preserve the Empire.

Chapter Five, "The Demise of Empire," concludes the main part of the study, moving to the West Indies at a time several years after the Mau Mau conflict in Kenya. The two novels selected for this chapter, Alec Waugh's *Island in the Sun* and George Lamming's *In the Castle of My Skin*, both deal in a partly allegorical way with a West Indian island on the verge of decolonization. The tense situation described in both novels demonstrates the reverberating effect on the relatively isolated West Indian islands of events like India's successful drive for independence and the Mau Mau revolt in colonial Kenya. The indigenous islanders long for their own self-determination and threaten the colonizers with disorder and violence. Waugh and Lamming give illuminatingly conflicting perspectives of this historic period. Waugh shows the reader how the British colonizer perceives the breakup of Empire, and Lamming demonstrates the effect of the same events on the indigenous islanders, in particular, a nine-year old boy coming of age in his native Barbados, which is languishing under England's crumbling colonial rule.

Several recent critical studies and anthologies have appeared which demonstrate the interrelationships of African and Afro-Caribbean or Afro-American literature.[3] What this study offers is an exploration of the interconnections of the fiction coming out of a much broader, diverse group of regions. I have deliberately included fiction from several different areas of Africa, including southern Africa, as well as India and the West Indies in an attempt to seek connections among Third World countries which may share little except a period of history under British colonial rule. Westerners' views, in general, of so-called Third World countries have long been dictated by commentators from the West. As a result, Westerners are often surprised by what they find when they actually go to those countries, frequently discovering a dimension which Western writers and correspondents have been unable to convey. It is this additional dimension to these countries—the side that only an indigenous commentator can know and portray—that post-colonial writers reveal in their fiction. Rather than providing the final "truth" about the Third World, post-colonial anglophone literature rectifies an imbalance created by the earlier British colonial portrayal of an increasingly vital part of the world. In addition to giving us a more accurate representation of Third World peoples and cultures, this fiction also paradoxically enables us to have a more balanced perspective of the British imperial endeavor.

As Abdul R. JanMohamed has argued, in "order to appreciate [British colonial fiction and ideology] thoroughly, we must examine them in juxtaposition to . . . the anglophone fiction of the Third World, which originates from British occupation and which . . . is establishing a dialogic relation with colonialist fiction" (Gates, 103).

The great value of this emerging anglophone literature for Western readers is the opportunity to be taken to parts of the world previously unseen or only partially seen. Besides exploring the contrasting views of British outsider and indigenous insider, this study seeks connections among these disparate parts of the world, and poses a question. Is there finally enough similarity between these areas and their colonial history to make such a broad study fruitful? In the study's conclusion, I hope to offer an answer to that question.

Chapter I
The Example of India: Rudyard Kipling and Salman Rushdie

Rudyard Kipling's *Kim*

Rudyard Kipling was born in Bombay in 1865. His father was a principal of an art school as well as an artist. In *Kim*, Kipling was to use him as a model for the curator at the Lahore Museum, whom the lama calls "the Wise One" in the "House of Wonders." At age six, Kipling was taken to England by his parents; his next six years there, spent attending boarding school, were very unhappy ones, and this experience of misery in childhood never left him. As Kipling stated in "Baa Baa Black Sheep," an autobiographical story dealing with this period in his life, "when young lips have drunk deep of the bitter waters of Hate, Suspicion, and Despair, all the Love in the world will not wholly take away that knowledge" (*Twenty-One*, 96). At the age of seventeen, Kipling returned to India with his parents and sister, the "family square" complete and secure again. Undoubtedly one can see the contrast between his positive childhood memories of India and his miserable early years in England in the idealization of India in *Kim* as a boy's wonderland. Kipling found work on *The Civil and Military Gazette*, an English newspaper in Lahore and, after a year, transfered to Allahabad, where he did editing work for a larger newspaper, *The Pioneer*. This was the same Allahabad newspaper to which Gandhi refers in his *Autobiography* as "an opponent of Indian aspirations" (168).

Kipling wrote many stories and poems for the newspapers. His readership was Anglo-Indian: train-passengers, civil servants and their families, soldiers, and government officials. *Departmental Ditties* (1886) was followed by the enormously popular book of short stories, *Plain Tales from the Hills* (1888). Both of these were published in cheap editions which could be bought in railway stations for a few rupees apiece, and served as excellent amusement for an Anglo-Indian's journey across the tedious landscape of India. Kipling's parents arranged for the publication of these early works in London, and it happened that upon his return to England at the age of twenty-four, Kipling was famous. This fame, however, proved to be more a hindrance than a help to his artistic development. Advised by W. E. Henley not to let his sudden overwhelming popularity cause his decline as a writer, he set himself to write a novel. *The Light that Failed* (1890) was well-received by the public, but many critics doubted its merits. With all the pressures of fame descending on him, Kipling suffered a nervous breakdown and was advised to travel. He embarked on a journey which took him to South Africa, Australia, New Zealand, and a last visit to India. Indeed, by the age of thirty, he had visited every continent in the world, a fact which has led one critic to see in Kipling's compulsive traveling and difficulty in settling down a sign of his being, like a number of later British and American writers, a "rootless man" searching for meaning (Harrison, 18).

After marriage, Kipling and his wife settled in Vermont, where they spent four happy years. It was here that Kipling wrote one of his best short stories about India, "The Bridge Builders," as well as the novel, *Kim* (1901), which was his last fictional portrayal of India. Written at a turning-point in his life, after his fiercely active political involvement in the Boer War situation and after the death of his oldest daughter, *Kim* was therapy for Kipling, a nostalgic return to his happy childhood years in India. At a time when his name was a public commodity, he sought the anonymity of the obscure bazaar boy in "great, gray, formless India" (*Kim*, 97). After a falling-out with his wife's brother in a highly publicized court case, Kipling and his wife returned to England. From this time until his death, Kipling lived mainly in England although he still traveled a great deal. From 1900 to 1908, the Kiplings spent the winter months as special guests of Cecil Rhodes in a home in South Africa which Rhodes had built for them. In 1907, Kipling won the Nobel Prize for Literature, becoming the first British writer to do so. In 1936, after a protracted illness, Kipling died; he was buried in the Poets' Corner in Westminister Abbey.

Kipling's dramatic rise to fame can in part be explained by his position in history. Even more than most writers, Kipling was a man of his times; there was a strong connection between his personal history and England's national history, for he reached the height of his fame at the same time England was at the heyday of its imperial power. Kipling's attitudes, expressed in his fiction, were similar to the popular attitudes held by many English of his time. His writing appealed to the general reader rather than to an elite literary world. Kipling's fall in popularity was only a little less dramatic than his rise, for as England's role as an imperial power waned following the Boer War and World War I, the popular sentiments of the country shifted away from Kipling and imperialism. After World War I, for many people in England, Kipling seemed to represent what they most wanted to put behind them and forget.

Judgments by fellow writers both chronicled and aided Kipling's loss of popularity. E. M. Forster's *A Passage to India,* conceived in part as an answer to Kipling's "imperialism," came out in 1924. George Orwell's critical essay "Rudyard Kipling" appeared in 1942, and further served to undermine Kipling's literary standing. As he had ridden a historic wave to fame, Kipling was victimized by history when his staunchly held views fell out of popular favor. More favorable critical appraisals by T. S. Eliot and others have partially restored Kipling's literary standing, but his ballads and short stories still draw a mixed response. In many ways, it appears Kipling will always be chained to history and, to some extent, will always be known as the chronicler of imperial England.

Kipling called *Kim* "nakedly picaresque and plotless—a thing imposed from without" (*Something of Myself,* 245). Indeed, the wanderings of Kim and Teshoo Lama recall those of Don Quixote and Sancho Panza or Huck Finn and Jim. *Kim* is also quite similar to another work of Twain's, *The Prince and the Pauper*, written in 1892, just nine years before *Kim*. Kipling's crusty, knowing narrative voice is not so very different from Twain's. Like *The Prince and the Pauper*, *Kim* involves a case of mistaken identity. The first time we encounter Kim in the novel, he is a rough-and-tumble bazaar boy, "burnt black as any native" (5). However, like the pauper who becomes a prince, Kim soon has to grapple with what it means to be a Sahib instead of a lowly bazaar urchin. *Kim* presents the British view of colonialism in miniature; from common citizens, the British in India found themselves transformed into royalty and treated like princes by the indigenous people. One might say *Kim* is about living up to the responsibilities implied in inheriting a higher social position than one had ever dreamed possible. Surely that was also the British situation during the height of the Empire.

Like *The Prince and the Pauper*, *Kim* possesses a fairy tale quality. The setting for Kim's adventures in the Great Game and his travels with Teshoo Lama in his Search is a sanitized India, a land of adventure, mystery, romance, and intrigue. Though there is some violence in the novel, the "Little Friend of the Stars," as Kim is called, is immune to any harm. As Kim's horoscope promises, there is to be honor in his future, and Kipling utilizes India's reputed national expertise in astrology to give his central character the protection of the stars. The emphasis on magic, the occult, and astrology is connected with two important aspects of *Kim*. First, the novel gives a portrait of India as a mysterious land in which people believe in magic and witchcraft and in which astrology is widely practiced and used in most important social ceremonies. In connection with this image of India, Kipling said, "All kinds of magic are out of date, and done away with except in India, where nothing changes in spite of the shiny, toy-scum stuff that people call 'civilization'" (*Plain Tales*, 266).[1] Second, the magic and the occult in *Kim* are also connected with the novel as a boys' adventure tale, involving mystery, intrigue, and danger. As a story of an English boy's exotic experiences abroad, *Kim* is solidly in the romantic tradition of G. A. Henty, Rider Haggard, and Robert Louis Stevenson.

As the main character of a *Bildungsroman*, Kim makes a successful passage from boyhood to manhood, and it is telling how in Kipling's novel Kim's process of maturation parallels the process of his Anglicization. As Father Victor tells Kim when he is being sent off to a school for Anglo-Indian children: "They'll make a man o' you, O'Hara, at St. Xavier's—a white man" (119). Although Kim seems quite self-sufficient and even worldly-wise when we first meet him—the narrator tells us Kim "had known all evil since he could speak" (7)—he is wild and undisciplined, not recognizably different from the other street-wise, low-caste boys thronging the bazaar.

Frantz Fanon, in *The Wretched of the Earth*, defines the colonial world as "a world divided into compartments" (31); the colonizer establishes boundaries and distinctions between himself and the colonized, and he enforces strict territorial separation. As Fanon explains, in the colonial world, "the first thing which the native learns is to stay in his place, and not to go beyond certain limits" (41). At the outset of *Kim*, one realizes that this colonial compartmentalization has been broken down. The native-born orphan of Irish parentage has been thoroughly assimilated into Indian society, with no recognizable harm done to his character. On the road as the lama's *chela*, Kim can easily pass for a low-caste Hindu boy, but this situation changes as the novel progresses. Early in the narrative, Kim is sent on a mission of intrigue, bearing a message from Mahbub Ali to Creighton Sahib, which is the boy's first bit of work for the Secret Service, though he doesn't know this at the time. Having delivered his message, Kim lies hidden in the grass, peering at the mysterious Englishman's bungalow, observing the off-limits world of the Sahibs from the point-of-view of a native Indian. It is only later that Kim consciously transforms himself into a Sahib and can view a compartmentalized colonial world from the other side.

Early in the novel, Kipling suggests that Kim is living a charmed existence, that he is somehow extraordinary and special. In what way is he special? The different characters who serve as Kim's father figures might answer that question differently. To the lama, Kim is the one fated to serve as *chela*, a combination apprentice and servant, destined to accompany him in his Search. Without this particular *chela*, the River of the Arrow, the goal of the lama's spiritual quest, will never be found. To Mahbub Ali and Creighton Sahib, Kim's special quality involves his intimate knowledge of India and his proven ability to survive and fend for himself in the underground world of intrigue, mystery, and danger ever-present in the "India" of this novel. This quality makes him ideally suited for Secret Service work in the Great Game. As Mahbub Ali says of Kim, using the horse-trading spy lingo only he and Creighton Sahib can understand: "only once in a thousand years is a horse born so well fitted for the Game as this our colt" (168). Kim knows India as well, if not better, than the native Indians themselves. He has mastered the art of begging, an important survival skill in India. "'A master beggar art thou,' purred the priest approvingly. 'Not the cunning of forty years could have done better'" (52). Kim's skills draw startled praise from native Indians. Two views of Kim—the *chela* and the secret agent—represent the two sides of his character, his two selves, which he must finally integrate by means of an identity crisis. And Kim's changing perspective of India as he travels across the country becomes a reflection of his changing view of himself.

"India is to England what the western frontier is to America," Marshall McLuhan wrote in an essay on Kipling and Forster in 1944 (334). In *Kim*, India is a huge playground, a young boy's paradise where adventure, intrigue, and a variety of pleasurable sensations are ever at hand. A country of endless variety and mystery, "great gray, formless India" is a land which embodies "the happy Asiatic disorder" (67). Unlike England, India can offer the young boy myriad delights of pure sensation: "bustling and shouting, the buckling of belts, and beating of bullocks and creaking of wheels, lighting of fires and cooking of food, and new sights at every turn of the approving eye" (76). India is also a land of wide-open expanses, similar to the American "wild west," a testing ground where a young man can fulfill himself and prove his manhood. In *Kim*, there is a contrast between the order and conformity enforced at school, and the entirely different, useful kind of education that can be gained on the Road, accompanying Mahbub Ali on his secret journeys during the school holidays. Kipling suggests that the common happenings in the daily life of a school lad in India are beyond any adventure available to young boys growing up in England. As the narrator tells us, "The mere story of [the St. Xavier's school boys'] adventures, which to them were no adventures, on the road to and from school would have cropped a Western boy's hair" (125). This "waning of adventure" in England is one of three chief themes Patrick Brantlinger finds in the "imperial Gothic" subgenre, made popular by Kipling, Haggard, Stevenson and others during the nineteenth century (253). To find "adventure," the young male must go to a place like India, where he can paradoxically both escape Victorian restraints and achieve maturity. The beauty of India for Kipling is thus that it is not "civilized" in the sense that England is. India is a raw, tortuous place, where in order to survive and endure, a young boy must become a man quite quickly.

Kim has been perceived as unique in British colonial fiction in its open, non-judgmental treatment of a colonized culture and people. Abdul JanMohamed, for instance, calls *Kim* "a positive, detailed, and nonstereotypic portrait of the colonized that is unique in colonialist literature" (Gates, 97). Such a view seems improbable, however, on a close reading of the novel. Unlike his rounded portrayal of Kim, Kipling's Indian characters are almost all flat stereotypes, unchanging caricatures etched permanently into the Indian landscape. They are, moreover, portrayed as variations of two basic, seemingly contradictory types. On the one hand, many of the natives Kim and the lama encounter in their Search are simple and down-to-earth: naive, afraid of offending the gods, charitable, superstitious. Though not himself Indian (he is from Tibet), the lama also falls into this stereotypic category of the simple Oriental peasant. An example of this figure in *Kim* is the angry farmer Kim and the lama run afoul of when crossing his fields during the Search. The farmer shouts at them not to trample his crops and calls them "shameless beggars" (45), but is instantly pacified when he approaches close enough to recognize the lama as a holy man and not a common beggar. To amend his hasty remarks, the farmer offers them milk and a meal. "I—I would not draw evil upon myself—or my crops" (46). Though Kim wishes to make the man feel guilty, the lama quickly forgives him and blesses his fields, gently admonishing the farmer, "Beware not to judge men too hastily" (46).

Another example of the simple, superstitious native is the group of "coolies" who serve as porters for the Russian and the Frenchman on their excursion into the hills. In a miniaturization of imperialism, the Russian makes a grab at the lama's chart of the Wheel of Life, which he is unwilling to sell to them, and in the confusion that ensues, the Russian strikes Teshoo Lama. Kim reacts by attacking the Russian, but the superstitious porters react differently, fleeing from the scene. The narrator explains: "They had seen sacrilege unspeakable, and it behoved them to get away before the Gods and devils of the hills took vengeance" (242). After they have run a safe distance away, the porters stop to argue whether or not they should return to exact justice upon the holy man's attacker. They are uncertain what the gods would have them do and fear drawing divine wrath upon themselves. As one porter expresses it: "Our cattle will be barren—our wives will cease to bear! The snows will slide upon us as we go home!" (243) Finally, the lama convinces them not to seek revenge, else they might be "re-born as a rat, or a snake under the eaves—a worm in the belly of the most mean beast" (244).

Kipling clearly views the simple, naive native character positively and affectionately. This character represents the old, traditional India, "those who hold by the use of their forefathers" (67). Though this Indian is portrayed as being mired in superstition and ignorance, Kipling presents his honesty and piety in an appealing way, as if this figure represents a backward and yet an admirable way of life. This affectionate, paternal portrayal of the innocent, simple villager going about life in centuries-old traditional ways runs consistently through all of Kipling's Indian fiction. We can see other examples of this native figure in Bukta in "The Tomb of His Ancestors," Purun Bhagat from *The Jungle Books*, and Gunga Din.

A second stereotypic Indian character prevalent in *Kim* is the treacherous, avaricious native, given to underhanded dealings with others. Mahbub Ali, though his role in the novel is a positive one, is an example of such an Indian character. The Hindu priest whom Kim and the lama meet in the Ressaldar's village is another example. The priest makes an outward show of friendliness, inviting the lama to stay the night in his home. Kim, however, suspecting the priest to be a thief, takes care to conceal the lama's money, and the next morning, the priest is cold and distant because "he had wasted some opium on a man who carried no money" (54). Another example of this duplicitous character is the native who breaks into and searches Mahbub Ali's stall, and later, disguised as a *faquir*, plots with another to kill Mahbub. In both cases, Kim helps Mahbub escape the trap and later the two men are arrested by an English police officer.

It is through this second stereotypic character that Kipling projects the image of India as a land of danger and treachery, "the motif of the Orient as insinuating danger," as Edward Said puts it. "Rationality is undermined by Eastern excesses, those mysteriously attractive opposites to what seem to be normal values" (57). Other untrustworthy, treacherous Indian characters are the jealous Hindu boy at Lurgan Sahib's shop who tries to poison Kim; the money-lender whom Kim and the lama meet on the train to Umballa; and the Woman of Shamlegh who hates Sahibs and whose snare of lust Kim avoids. The devious and treacherous native figure is connected with Kipling's portrayal of India as a lawless, dangerous land and with *Kim* as a boy's adventure tale. These two Indian stereotypes—the simple, ignorant peasant and the underhanded, shrewd native—seem to be contradictory and incompatible, and yet somehow they are the same. In the India of this novel, innocent peasants turn into secret agents or subversives. Danger and intrique are omnipresent, but hidden, subterranean, on the same level on which the Great Game is played. In *Kim*, a large part of the appealing mystery of India, along with the strange customs and beliefs of the people, is this world of intrigue and danger hidden just below the surface, which Kim finds so exciting and stimulating.

A third, less visible stereotypic Indian character in Kipling's fiction is the simple villager's opposite, the progressive representative of the new India from Bengal, like Hurree Chunder Mookerjee in *Kim* and Grish Chunder De from "The Head of the District." The progressive Indian appears rarely in Kipling's fiction and of them all, Hurree Chunder Mookerjee fares the best. Even so, Kim takes more than half the narrative to accept Hurree as other than "a Calcutta-taught Bengali" whom it would be fun to "outface and down-talk" (217). The reader gets the impression that Kipling found the idea of the new India somewhat disturbing. He singles out for criticism Indians who are viewed as too progressive or too closely imitative of the English. It is clear that in portraying his Indian characters, Kipling's prejudices come into play. He preferred Muslims to Hindus, though the latter make up eighty-five per cent of India's population, and he favored the naive, servile, non-threatening native, like Bukta or Teshoo Lama, over the ambitious, well-informed native who might possess leadership qualities and thus be a threat to the Empire.

As partner to Kim in Kipling's picaresque narrative, the lama is a perplexing character. He is not an Indian, but is rather a Tibetan Buddhist priest, who has come to India to undertake a pilgrimage, following the Buddha's footsteps. He is more of an outsider in India than Kim, and although Kim accompanies him out of a sense of curiosity and adventure, the lama desires his *chela*'s companionship out of need for help and guidance in his pilgrimage. The lama believes Kim's service to him is part of his fate, that perhaps in a former life, he helped Kim, and therefore the latter has now returned to repay him. Although the narrator doesn't directly contradict the lama's view, he implies that many of the lama's notions and ideas are fantastic. After Kim successfully begs money from the Amritsar courtesan—the narrator tells us in his knowing way that "ladies of that persuasion . . . were generous"—the lama solemnly states that "beyond doubt it was a nun" (34).

If Kim is seen in the novel as a man-child, then the lama is a child-man. In contrast to the curator of the Lahore Museum, who is an authoritative, paternal figure, the lama exhibits a child-like wonder at the museum relics and curios. Although his childishness is part of his attractive simplicity and spirituality as a character, it is also part of his helplessness and need for Kim. Kim is strongly attached to the lama and willingly serves him, but it is clear that Kim has no intention of following the lama's path of the Middle Way. The lama's view of external events is shown to be a muddled one. Whereas he perceives himself as guiding Kim "upon the Way," Kim actually has little understanding of or interest in the heady stuff of the lama's "teachings":

> "Just is the Wheel, swerving not a hair! Learn the lesson, *chela*."
>
> "It is too high for me," Kim muttered. (252)

In contrast to the lama's abstractions, the earthy Woman of Shamlegh more accurately expresses Kim's sentiments when, in the face of the lama's solemn pronouncements, she asks: "Since when have men and women been other than men and women?" (262).

The lama's main function in the novel is to serve as Kim's foil. Kim is quick-witted and practical, fast to see and take advantage of opportunity; he enjoys the pleasures of action and sensation, and as such, is the representative of the West; he is in the same mold as Tarvin in *The Naulahka*, the fast-talking Western businessman. Teshoo Lama is the representative of the East, embodying the religious, spiritual values of Buddhism, and, as such, is Kim's opposite in every way. Unlike the youthful, adventurous Kim, the lama is a philosopher who persistently avoids the pleasureable sensations of life; he lives largely the life of the mind and the spirit, seeking unity with the Great Soul, nirvana, free of desires that bind man to the corporeal world of illusion. Although righteous in his living, it is clear that the lama knows nothing of the ways of this world, and that he needs someone to guide him and take care of him. Perhaps here Kipling is making a case for India's need for England. It is more than coincidence that the other representatives of the East, characters who are actually Indian, also seem needy and incomplete. Though the Afghan Mahbub Ali and the Bengali Hurree Chunder Mookerjee are characters more like Kim—practical, quick-witted, and worldly—there is finally something they lack that Kim has, and that is a sense of duty and responsibility. The reader gets the impression that for both Mahbub and Hurree, employment in the British Secret Service has meant not only a rise in status and respectability, but a beneficial check on bad tendencies. One can easily see Mahbub giving himself over to horse-stealing and Hurree uselessly aping any Englishman who happens to cross his path. What the lama lacks in practical, worldly wisdom, Mahbub and Hurree lack in discipline and restraint. In all three cases, the British connection seems to be a favorable one. The implication is that all of these various Indian (or Asian) characters need some outside force to help control their country's borders, to keep law and order, and to assume responsibility for their people.

In direct contrast to the lama's child-like state is Kim's passage from boyhood to manhood and acceptance of the responsibility entailed in becoming a Sahib. Early in the novel, Kim has only unpleasant associations with being a Sahib, most of which have to do with compulsory attendance at the Umballa school. He sees the order and tame conformity demanded of the students in school in direct opposition to the chaotic sensations and freedom of the Road. Kim repeatedly tells Teshoo Lama that he has no intention of becoming a Sahib. As the narrative progresses, however, over a period of three years in which Kim is in school and the lama continues his pilgrimage, the young orphan begins to perceive the advantages in becoming a Sahib, or, as Said puts it, "Kipling's White Man," who possessed "the certain knowledge that he belonged to . . . a long tradition of executive responsibility towards the colored races" (226).

At first, the still undisciplined Kim associates the process of Anglicization with the opportunity for adventure and excitement in the Great Game. It is only later that he becomes aware of another aspect involved in becoming a Sahib and playing the Great Game: the sense of duty and responsibility demanded of the players. It is at this later point that Kim decides that the *madrissah*, or school, for which the lama pays his tuition, serves an important function. As Kim tells Mahbub Ali, whose own skepticism of a school education indicates his lack of judgment: "I see my road all clear before me to a good service. I will stay in the *madrissah* until I am ripe" (136). Kim has finally realized that his education at St. Xavier's is instrumental for his future Secret Service role in the Great Game. As the narrator tells us: "St. Xavier's looks down on boys who 'go native altogether.' One must never forget that one is a Sahib, and that some day, when examinations are passed, one will command natives" (126).

We see practically all of the native Indian characters through Kim's relations or interaction with them, and it is here that their innate innocence, gullibility, and superstitiousness are most evident. Kim's usefulness to the Secret Service lies in his intimate knowledge of the natives and of how to play on their weaknesses. Three characters besides the lama whom Kim is able to manipulate successfully are the Ressaldar, Kamjoh the Jat, and the Woman of Shamlegh. The Ressaldar's weakness is his nostalgia for his youthful days as a soldier when he distinguished himself during the Mutiny through his courage and unswerving loyalty to the British. The Ressaldar literally worships the British officer Sahibs under whom he served in the Mutiny, and Kim is able to play upon this. Kim convinces the Ressaldar of his magical, prophetic powers—which are actually those of the Hindu priest who cast his horoscope—by describing Creighton Sahib in such detail that the Ressaldar is convinced of the accuracy of the boy's prophecy of war. In their dialogue, whenever either refers to Creighton Sahib with a pronoun, it is capitalized as if the officer were divine. Kim also plays on the superstitions and gullibility of Kamjoh the Jat, whose starving child Kim cures with the "magic" of beef bouillon and quinine. Although Kim's saving of the child is a mark of his compassion and of his ongoing transformation from irresponsible child to responsible adult, it is also a way for him to manipulate the Jat's view of him as a "miracle-worker." Later, Kim is able to procure food for himself and the lama by employing the services of the servile Kamjoh. Still later on the train, Kim uses the threat of evil charms effectively to silence the naturally garrulous Jat whose indiscretion almost gives away the identity of Kim's fellow agent, E23.

Kim is also able to manipulate the Woman of Shamlegh, who is none other than Lispeth from the short story of that name in *Plain Tales From the Hills*. In order to send Lispeth on a message-carrying errand to the Babu, he promises to make a charm for her. Kim gives his name as "the Son of the Charm," and Lispeth is immediately taken in: "Ai! Truly! Truly! By a magician—who is like a Sahib" (256). Kipling's characterization of the Woman of Shamlegh is a revealing one. As in the short story, Lispeth is fiery, seductive, and sexually eager for a Sahib. She is a stereotype of the sexually frank, yet morally depraved hill-woman. After trying unsuccessfully to get Kim to stay with her, she becomes abusive and claims never to have believed in his powers to make charms or curses; instead, she reveals, "I thought it was my Sahib come back, and he was my God" (263). Like the dangerous, enticing Sitabhai in *The Naulahka*, we have the fiery, passionate, sexually insatiable Indian woman setting her snare for the white Sahib, who narrowly and fortunately is able to overcome the temptation. Salman Rushdie has said that "Kipling's Indian women . . . are (at best) the cause of trouble and danger for men" (*IH*, 78). Variations on this stereotype can be found in much Anglo-Indian fiction, as in Paul Scott's characterization of Mrs. Bhoolabhoy in *Staying On*. Lispeth's male counterparts—embodiments of lust or at least of lack of sexual restraint—are found in the characterizations of Nana Sahib in G. A. Henty's *Rujub the Juggler* and the Nawab in Ruth Jhabvala's *Heat and Dust*. It is this stereotype based on British sexual fantasy that Forster ridicules in *A Passage to India*, when Adela imagines that Aziz takes sexual advantage of her in the caves, only to retract her story as false later in court. Kipling, however, far from questioning this stereotype, uses it to further his theme of Kim's growth into manhood. Though Kim doesn't stay with Lispeth, he is flattered by her desire for him and takes it as further proof that he is now a man. As he leaves Shamlegh, he thinks, "At least she did not treat me as a child" (266).

Of all the Indian characters whose gullibility and superstition Kim skillfully manipulates, Teshoo Lama is the most thoroughly fooled. Early in the novel, after Bennet and Victor reveal the fact that Kim is a Sahib and must be taken away from him, the lama seems to realize he's been fooled by the boy's disguise artistry: "Ah, *chela*, thou hast done a wrong to an old man because my heart went out to thee" (93). Kim, however, convinces him that he had no idea that the prophecy of the Red Bull on the field of green would lead him to be captured by the Sahibs. Based on his limited experience of Sahibs—up to this point, he has only met one, "the Wise One" in the House of Wonders—Teshoo Lama decides to support Kim's education at St. Xavier's. It is at this point that Kim begins to live a double life in relation to the lama.

Teshoo Lama waits patiently for his *chela* to gain a Sahib's education and return to him, because he believes that only with Kim's guidance will he find the River of the Arrow. However, what the lama doesn't know is that Kim's education is to serve as preparation for a Secret Service career in the Great Game, played against enemies of the British Empire inside and outside India's borders. The lama sees the journey with Kim and "the Dacca physician" into the hills as a segment of their pilgrimage brought about by his own personal desires, which he later repents. What the gullible lama never discovers is that their journey is a spy mission, that the incident in which the Russian strikes him across the face and he temporarily loses sight of the Way is not accidental, but related to the true purpose of the spy mission, and that Kim and "the Dacca Physician," who is really Kim's fellow agent, Hurree Chunder Mookerjee, are not fellow pilgrims but agents of the British Government Secret Service. His temporary loss of the Way due to the altercation with the Russian is a source of anguish and distorted self-awareness for the lama—"'A brawler and a swashbuckler upon the hillsides was I.' Kim bit back a smile" (259)—but it is clear that Teshoo Lama's understanding of the incident and that of Kim and Hurree are widely divergent. The lama's "enlightenment" is shown to be no different than self deception, as he remarks ironically, "The blow was a sign to me, who am no better than a strayed yak, that my place is not here. Who can read the Cause of an act is half-way to Freedom!" (261) In this scene, we can see clearly the function of the lama's flat, dimensionless character as the focus of Kim's conflict between duty and love, which is at the heart of this novel, just as the dichotomy of East and West embodied Kipling's own conflict between his emotional attachment to India and his intellectual commitment to the British Empire.

Finally in *Kim*, order prevails, as it always does in Kipling's fiction. Man must obey the inexorable dictates of the Law and follow his chosen path. Kipling's Law can assume different forms, and often it seems to imply not only the temporal laws of the British Empire, which Kim helps to carry out, but also the eternal, spiritual laws, which the lama obeys. By the novel's end, Kim has joined the British Secret Service. As Mowgli in *The Jungle Book* must finally leave the animal kingdom and return to the world of man, so Kim must finally leave his boyhood wonderland and take up the responsibilities entailed in becoming a Sahib. As a carefree boy, Kim embraced the excitement and chaos of India on the Grand

Trunk Road, but finally he must choose, not between the Wheel and the Great Game, because he never actually followed the lama's teachings, but between the chaotic irresponsibility of the Road and the order and responsibility involved both in the Great Game and in the teaching of his secular mentors, Mahbub Ali and Creighton Sahib. It is clear that, the theme of *rapprochment* notwithstanding, Kipling subscribes to the novel's oft-repeated view, "Once a Sahib, always a Sahib" (109). Stated another way, Kim's progress in this novel is to leave spiritual fulfillment to the East and the lamas of this world and to embrace the physical world of action, responsibility, and duty to one's country.

Vinobha Bhave, the famous Indian statesman, once said that people in the West "have developed the head; the heart did not keep pace. With us it was the opposite—it was with the development of the heart that we have been concerned in India" (Meyers, 42). We see a similar view in *Kim*. What Kim learns from India, from his travels with the lama, is the power of love. By the last chapter, Kim has learned a great lesson from his attachment to the all-too-human lama, even though this lesson doesn't seem to affect his future with the Secret Service. Teshoo Lama is in need of guidance through this "great and terrible world" (39), but Kim, too, is shown to be in need of guidance. Kim's failing or "sin" is that of pride, the pride of a Sahib, the pride of a prince who too quickly forgets he was once a pauper. Here, Kipling is certainly making a statement about England's imperial rule over India. The bond of love that grows between Kim and Teshoo Lama is the ideal relationship of colonizer and colonized, if such can be said to exist. As in "Recessional" and "The Man Who Would Be King," in this last chapter, Kipling gives an implicit warning about what would happen to the Empire should it forfeit its moral authority. Here, India is more than a playground or a training ground in which the young Kim can selfishly pursue his own personal fulfillment. Rather, India, with its teeming masses of humanity, is a country that somehow still bares a human face, a land and culture whose human values can still give one that miraculous thing—fulfillment. More "civilized" and "developed" countries in the so-called First World have abandoned the very simple, human values which a poor country like India has had no choice but to hold onto. It is this human face of India in the novel that has its beneficial, humanizing effect on Kim.

Salman Rushdie's *Midnight's Children*

Salman Rushdie was born in Bombay in June, 1947, two months before India won its independence. His parents, affluent, middle-class Moslems, did not immediately move to Pakistan following the Partition of India. Rushdie has said in an interview that his parents "were certainly not of the Pakistani persuasion. They belonged to that group of Indian Moslems who wanted to stay and then they gradually changed their minds" (Kaufman, 22). Since most of their relatives had already settled in Pakistan, Rushdie's parents also finally made the decision to leave India, which they carried out in 1964. One year later, the Indo-Pakistani War broke out. Three years before their planned exodus, his parents had sent fourteen-year old Salman to England and enrolled him at Rugby. Rushdie graduated from Rugby and stayed in England to attend university, graduating from King's College, Cambridge. After graduation, he worked as an advertising copywriter in London, and also wrote fiction.

At Rugby, Rushdie was forced to make an early transition from an Eastern to a Western way of life and to learn quickly certain facts about an Indian's position in England. Coming from a wealthy family and a recently emancipated colony, Rushdie was, by his own admission, self-important and snobbish about his position in the world, and thus, "perfect English public school material" (Kaufman, 22). In this connection, there seem to be similarities between the author at this time and young Saleem, in *Midnight's Children*, who envisions for himself a central role in world events. However, Rushdie soon came to understand first-hand his position as an outsider in England; he realized he didn't belong and that he would never be permitted to enter English society. Nevertheless, he now looks back on his experience in England as beneficial:

> I think the central mistake was not being foreign, but being bad at games, which are the heart of the public school ethic. If I'd been able to bat elegantly at cricket and play field hockey, I would have been accepted by my peers, been captain of the eleven and grown up as a kind of ultrarightist Indian businessman. (Kaufman, 23)

Rushdie turned to fiction as a means of self-expression. In 1975, his first novel, *Grimus*, was published and met with mixed reviews. Six years later, *Midnight's*

Children was released to critical acclaim in both England and the United States, and was awarded the Booker McConnell Prize. Like *Grimus*, *Midnight's Children* is a highly imaginative novel which blends the comic and the tragic. But unlike Rushdie's first novel, a work of science fiction fantasy set in a mythic America at some undetermined time, *Midnight's Children* is firmly rooted in history and invokes a strong sense of India as a unique country. In this case, Rushdie's fictional return to his native land was a fruitful one.

Since the appearance of *Midnight's Children*, one might say that Rushdie's career has taken off, though it has proceeded in a way he neither intended nor foresaw. He has written two more novels, *Shame* (1983), which takes Pakistan as its setting, and *The Satanic Verses* (1989), the controversial, best-selling magical realist text about the lives of two Muslims who "emigrate" from India to England. Rushdie's view of himself as belonging to three countries—India, Pakistan, and England—thus manifests itself in the settings of his three major novels.[2] Rushdie has also written an account of a trip to Nicaragua, *The Jaguar's Smile: A Nicaraguan Journey* (1987); an allegorical fantasy for children, *Haroun and the Sea of Stories* (1990); and a book of essays and reviews, *Imaginary Homelands* (1991). At present, Rushdie remains in hiding, presumably somewhere in London, as a result of a death warrant placed on him by Iran's Ayatollah Khomeini, following the publication of *The Satanic Verses*, a work many Muslims find blasphemous.

Midnight's Children takes its readers beyond the halcyon days of the British *Raj*, during which Kipling's narrative is set, to the moment of India's independence from England and the multitude of problems the country faced following its long history of invasion, domination, and foreign rule. Although Rushdie's narrative traces the Aziz family back to around 1915, it is clear that his focus is upon India after independence. The main character, Saleem Sinai, shares the exact birthday of the country—midnight, August 15, 1947—and a series of correspondences is established between Saleem's personal and India's recent history. The disillusion, confusion, and disappointment Saleem experiences as an individual reflect the state of the country following its long-sought independence.

Midnight's Children is a much more complicated work than most fiction written about India. Rushdie's narrative moves back and forth in space and time between Saleem's present life with Padma, "the dung lotus," and the convoluted story of his past life that he is telling her. Saleem looks back ironically on himself as a younger man, and like the recent history of his country, his life has been filled with turbulence, catastrophe, and sudden changes, both good and bad. In addition to Saleem, *Midnight's Children* involves a deliberately bewildering, vast array of characters who surface and unexpectedly resurface throughout a narrative that is spread over a multiplicity of locations. In short, Rushdie's novel portrays an India that defies comprehension and neat categorization. Unlike the static, monolithic portrait of colonial India we get in Kipling's *Kim*, Rushdie's post-colonial India is greater than the sum of its many parts: a vast, complex country whose long history bears out its own unexpected resolutions, and whose people have shown a genius for survival and revitalization.

Kim can be seen as a neat justification of the British Empire in India. By imposing British notions of civilization, order, and progress on India's "decadent civilization," the British believed they could change the course of things for the better and create a higher standard of life for the people of India. In his novel about life in post-colonial India, Rushdie suggests that rather than improving life in India, the British only created a new set of problems and difficulties for the people to face. Kipling portrays the movement on the Grand Trunk Road as incessant, chaotic, and exciting, but nothing comes of it. The ceaseless activity of the people is all ferment without order or direction. He implies that history is made only by Sahibs; India is static. Rushdie, on the other hand, portrays post-colonial India as swept up in continual change—Independence, Partition, wars with China and Pakistan, the birth of Bangladesh, the rise and fall and return of Indira Gandhi, the rise and fall and near-return of Rajiv Gandhi, industrialization and modernization—which is indeed chaotic but which also has its own underlying direction and order. In *Kim*, the job of the Sahibs is to impose order on the chaos of India. Rushdie suggests that life is by definition chaotic and that we often exaggerate our ability to determine or alter the course of human events.

Although Richard Cronin has labeled Rushdie an "outsider" (6) in regard to India, Rushdie as author clearly identifies with India and the East in this novel. Rushdie has said in an interview, "English fiction set in India—Kipling, Forster—has only been about what happened to the West when it went East. The language, contents and tone have never reflected how Indians experience India" (Smolowe, 56). The contents of *Midnight's Children* at times suggest an awareness of Kipling's Indian fiction: *Kim*, "the Soldiers Three" stories, or "Wee Willie Winkie." Rushdie's narrative contains a Pakistani version of the soldiers three, an Indian street-singer named Wee Willie Winkie, and a main character who presents an illuminating contrast to Kipling's Irish orphan, Kim. There are other points of comparison between *Kim* and *Midnight's Children* as well. Like *Kim, Midnight's Children* bears similarities to Mark Twain's *The Prince and the Pauper* written in 1891, nine years before *Kim*. Rushdie, however, gives Twain's tale a moral significance directly contrary to Kipling. Kim, like the pauper who comes to realize he is actually a prince, has to grapple with what it means to be a Sahib, instead of a lowly bazaar urchin. Saleem, of low birth, swapped in the cradle with an aristocratic Indian infant, is brought up as a prince, but must finally accept a diminutive version of himself, his true low-birth inheritance. *Kim* reflects the British inheritance of a position of respect, responsibility, and administrative duty. *Midnight's Children* reflects the Indian emphasis on acceptance: of one's position both in society and in the cosmos, of one's inexorable fate, as well as of the post-colonial Indian need to find unity amidst diversity. Echoing Saleem's search for identity is a nation's search for unity; Saleem's effort throughout most of the narrative is to unify and organize the Midnight's Children Conference, the 581 children who, like himself, were born in India during the hour of midnight, August 15, 1947.

Points of comparison notwithstanding, Rushdie's actual response to Kipling's portrayal of India lies more in the structure and style of the novel than in any direct parodying of elements in Kipling's work. Rushdie works primarily in the surrealist, or magical realist, or what one critic calls the "fantastic realist" (Cronin, 15), tradition of Gunter Grass' *The Tin Drum* and Gabriel Garcia Marquez's *One Hundred Years of Solitude*. An example of Rushdie's surrealistic mode is his character Tai Bibi who, at 512 years of age, is "the oldest whore in the world" (308). Other examples are Saleem's nocturnal, telepathic communication with the other Midnight Children (with whom he holds conferences in his mind) and the thousands of offspring sired by Saleem's rival, Shiva. The author feels no need to justify realistically or explain these phenomena in his narrative: they are simply part of his fictional mode. Here Rushdie implies that the realistic mode alone cannot capture a sense of India, a "country which is itself a sort of dream" (118). India is more than fact: it is a "mythical land, a country which would never exist except by the efforts of a phenomenal collective will—except in a dream we all agreed to dream" (112).

Although the story of Saleem and his illusory "dream of saving the country" (413) comprises a large part of *Midnight's Children*, it is India, not Saleem, that finally emerges at the center of the narrative. As Rushdie has explained, the portrayal of Saleem is intertwined with that of a number of other characters:

> When I started writing, I just tried to explain one life, and it struck me more and more that, in order to explain this life, you had to explain a vast amount of material which surrounded it, both in space and time. In a country like India, you are basically never alone. The idea of solitude is a luxury which only rich people enjoy. For most Indians, the idea of privacy is very remote. So it seemed to me that people lived intermingled with each other in a way that perhaps they don't anymore in the West, and that it was therefore idiotic to try and consider any life as being discrete from all other lives (Durix, 22-23).

As in Raja Rao's *Kanthapura*, the community or country is emphasized, rather than the individual, who is only part of the group. In Rao's novel, the village of Kanthapura overshadows the story of Moorthy, the leader of the resistance movement opposing colonial exploitation. Moreover, like Anita Desai's *Clear Light of Day*, Kamala Markandaya's *Nectar in a Sieve*, and Bharati Mukherjee's *The Tiger's Daughter*, there is an emphasis on the achievement of unity through acceptance in Rushdie's novel. Though Desai's, Markandaya's, and Mukherjee's concern is with a family unit whereas Rushdie's is with the entire country in its recent history, the theme of unity amidst diversity is central to all four novels.

One of the main differences between *Midnight's Children* and British fiction set in India, such as *Kim*, *A Passage to India*, and *Heat and Dust*, lies in Rushdie's presentation of an Indian family. The Indian characters we know in British fiction are almost always individuals; we rarely see them functioning as part of a family unit. Yet the family is obviously a central part of Indian society. We remember the Indian characters in *Kim*, Mahbub Ali or Hurree Chunder Mookerjee or the Tibetan Teshoo Lama, all of whom are conveniently presented without the burdensome ties of family. In *A Passage to India*, Aziz is a widower with children, but they are elsewhere; likewise, we meet the Hindu Godbole as a public figure, an individual, rather than as a family man. In *Heat and Dust*, the Nawab is also presented as free from family ties (with the exception of his mother), conveniently available for an affair with Olivia. In portraying their Indian characters as representative individuals of an alien culture, the British writers not only emphasize the exoticism of India, but also show that their perception was often conditioned by their Western cultural orientation, with its emphasis on individualism as opposed to the priority placed upon community in the East. Rushdie, on the other hand, minimizes the Indian characters' exoticism and mystery by humanizing them and depicting them within an understandable family context.

In *Midnight's Children*, we are introduced to Saleem's entire family, beginning with the presentation of his maternal grandparents, Aadam and Naseem Aziz, who represent Saleem's Kashmiri roots. The characterization of Saleem is imbedded in the interrelationships of the Sinai family; Rushdie takes pains to show how these family members affect and influence each other, or, as Saleem puts it, "leak into" each other. As the large cast of characters grow older, we watch as each new family splits off and goes its own way, but we remain in touch with each, especially focusing on the three Aziz sisters, Alia, Mumtaz, and Emerald, and their brothers, Hanif and Mustapha. Indeed, even after it is discovered that Saleem's blood-type is different and that he is not a rightful member of the family, he is not disowned, because, as he tells us, "In a kind of collective failure of imagination, we learned that we simply could not think our way out of our pasts" (118).

A typical scene involving Saleem's grandparents serves to place the Indian family in an understandable context and to humanize the Indian characters. Early in the novel, we learn that Saleem's grandfather first met his grandmother on a professional call, when, as a physician, he visited her in response to her complaint of stomach ache. Here, Rushdie clearly makes fun of the Muslim custom of *purdah*, the seclusion of women. On this visit, Aadam is only able to see his future wife's stomach through a small hole cut in the middle of a sheet, which her father orders held up in front of her. On successive visits, only those areas which are infirm—a shoulder, a finger, a foot, etc.—can be viewed, or, if necessary, touched by Aadam. In this way, Saleem's grandfather is shown to fall in love with his wife piecemeal, a process later duplicated by Saleem's mother, who gradually learns section by section to love her husband. Although the scene is rendered comically, it represents a celebration of Indian family life, rather than a form of criticism or satire. Moreover, Aadam's piecemeal introduction to his future wife is also the equivalent of the narrative technique of the novel: attempting to see the whole of India by examining its parts. Saleem as narrator is aware of the impossibility of this narrative undertaking, but its failure only proves Rushdie's point: ultimately, India is larger than the sum of its many parts.

The idea of the exotic, strange, and foreign assigned to India in *Kim* is turned around in *Midnight's Children*, where English things and customs become the objects and subjects of curiosity and incredulity. The Sahibs' appearance is strange—they are seen as "the pink conquerors" (69)—and they are viewed as having numerous peculiarities. A primary example of the Indian cultural perspective in *Midnight's Children* is the strange condition the Englishman Methwold imposes upon selling his four houses to the Sinais and several other Indian families as Independence day is approaching and the British are planning their exit from India. Methwold's condition, "that the houses be bought complete with every last thing in them, that the entire contents be retained by the new owners" (95), is farcical, but it enables Rushdie to explore stunningly his cross-cultural topic. Saleem's father thinks only of the low price put on the houses, but the other new Indian tenants are filled with shock and outrage at such a condition, and also at the numerous puzzling English things that are now to become part of their lives. Here we have enacted an aspect of decolonization which Fanon describes in *The Wretched of the Earth*: "In the period of decolonisation, the colonised masses mock at [the colonisers'] very values, insult them, and vomit them up" (35). Saleem's mother is scandalized by "pictures of old Englishwomen everywhere," with no place to hang the traditional photo of her father. Saleem's mother is also shocked at the new bathroom arrangements her family must adapt to: "for two months we must live like those Britishers? You've looked in the bathrooms? No water near the pot. I never believed, but it's true, my God, they wipe their bottoms with paper only!" (96).

Methwold's injunction is finally a marvelous echo of the British legacy: that India retain forever the stamp of its British occupation. Here we have the transference and imposition of British order on Indian society, and the Indian families find the arrangement odd and not to their liking. Nevertheless, however much they are unaccustomed to these new articles and thus distrust and dislike them, Rushdie shows that the new tenants are not immune to the "subtle magic of Methwold's Estate" (100). Rushdie puts forward the explanation that irrational habit, something set in motion in time, does not easily die, and soon the families have adopted Methwold's habitual six o'clock cocktail hour, the use of English accents, the operation of kitchen gadgets, and the playing of the pianola. Rushdie suggests that we over-emphasize the power of the conscious mind; that certain things live on whether we will them or not. The British legacy—architecture, customs, language—is a living part of India. Although the British *Raj* is a thing of the past, the spirit of the British in India is still very much alive, one side among many of the "many-headed monster" (71) which is India. However, Methwold's legacy involves more than just his estate; we later come to learn that *he*, not the street-singer Wee Willie Winkie, is Saleem's actual father. On the individual level, then, Rushdie affirms that England, through Saleem's genes, will remain forever as a part of India.

In *Kim*, we see Kim's passage from boy to man, from native to Sahib; the Kim we know at the start is not the same Kim we find at the novel's conclusion. However, the other characters, primarily Indians, are static: products, even types, who remain unchanged throughout the narrative. In *Midnight's Children*, Saleem also undergoes the passage from boy to man, but he is not the only character going through change. Every character in *Midnight's Children* is revealed as enmeshed in the process of becoming. As Saleem says, "Transformation without end" (239). Cyrus-the-great, Saleem's boyhood friend, becomes Lord Khusro Khusrovhand, a great spiritual leader; Saleem's sister, "the Brass Monkey," becomes the famous Pakistani recording artist, Jamila Singer; Nadir Khan, the rhymeless, lank-haired poet and first husband of Saleem's mother, is transformed into the Communist leader, Qasim the Red; and Mary Pereira, the family ayah, becomes Mrs. Braganza, manager Begum of Braganza Pickles, Ltd. Likewise, Saleem's father and mother are depicted dynamically, as they go through the ups and downs of an evolving life. It literally takes Saleem's father a lifetime to fall in love with his wife, and we see this process unfold gradually in the narrative. Saleem's mother, Mumtaz Aziz, is likewise transformed by her husband into Amina Sinai. And in the last days of his life, Saleem's grandfather, an avowed agnostic, is transformed into a visionary who sees God.

Rushdie's vision is one of life in flux, constantly moving and changing, never the same, and his interest is in all his characters and their changes. In this connection, one might think of the works of R. K. Narayan, especially *The Guide* and *The English Teacher*, in which the transformational potential of characters seems practically infinite. Narayan's "guide" begins as a common tout, the kind who swarms around tourists at Indian railway stations, but by the novel's end, he's a spiritual guru, a leader of his people. Native characters in Indian anglophone fiction are frequently portrayed as going through change, adapting to shifting circumstances, caught up in the process of becoming. Like their country, these characters find themselves in a position in which they have to change and transform themselves repeatedly, to absorb setbacks and assimilate new influences, to survive and to continue living.

The image of India evolving, in the process of change, in *Midnight's Children*, is antithetical to Kipling's view of an India "full of holy men stammering gospels in strange tongues; . . . as it has been from the beginning and will continue to the end" (36). The India we see in *Midnight's Children* is dynamic. Throwing off the British in 1947 brought immediate, drastic change. Following Independence, the Partition created three countries where there had previously been one. Moreover, since Independence, India has embarked on a process of industrialization and modernization which Rushdie portrays as disturbing. In its rush to modernize, India seems to forget its roots and betray its ancient inheritance. Rushdie's portrayal of India's modernization resembles Garcia Marquez's *One Hundred Years of Solitude*, in which there is gradual change in the Colombian village of Macondo, from the fading out of the visits of the alchemist Melquiades and his traveling troupe of magicians to the sudden appearance of the junk-salesmen who begin to make annual trips to the village to sell the strange new gadgetry they bring in from the outside world. As in Garcia Marquez's fictional Colombian world, so in Rushdie's India something is lost and a heavy price is paid by the country in its headlong rush to modernize. We see this particularly in the Widow's systematic dissolution of the Midnight Children's Conference and the destruction of the Magicians' Ghetto, where Saleem takes up residence. In India's determination to forge a new "reality" befitting its role in the twentieth century, it has sacrificed its "dream," its magical, irrational sense of infinite possibility.

If Kipling portrays India as a land of mystery, fantasy, and magic, then in one sense we might say that Rushdie simply carries that image much further. Kipling's method is to give an example of an incredible happening and then to have his British characters shake their heads and exclaim "Powers of Darkness below!"[3] or, as in several Kipling stories, the British character quotes Hamlet: "There's more in heaven and earth than is dreamt of in your philosophy, Horatio."[4] Rushdie's method is to fuse the worlds of magic and reality. Magical events, such as Saleem's invisibility in Parvati's wicker basket, are not justified or explained, but rather presented as part of the everyday world of India. In Rushdie's surreal technique, the fantastic is described as if it were the matter-of-fact and the everyday. In a surreal episode, typical in *Midnight's Children* and similar to the kind found in a Garcia Marquez narrative, Saleem's parents fall on hard times after the Partition; Ahmed Sinai's financial resources are frozen in a Bombay bank in what appears to be a deliberate act of reprisal by the Hindu majority against the Muslims remaining in India. Lost in grief and hopelessness, unable to carry out the plan of moving the family to Pakistan, Ahmed takes to drink, but Saleem's mother, whose assiduity is inherited by her son, passes one day by the Mahalaxmi

Racecourse and gets a sudden idea. Although she knows nothing about horses, she bets the family's meager remaining finances on "mares known not to be stayers to win long races . . . jockeys because she liked their smiles" and "won and won and won" (139-40), finally earning enough money to pay for a good lawyer and eventually to win the court case and unfreeze the family assets. This improbable scene is typical of Rushdie's narrative. Yet, despite its improbability, this scene aptly conveys Rushdie's point: India's traditional strength lies in its people's great ability to improvise, overcome setbacks, and rely on faith. Whereas Ahmed Sinai is the rational schemer whose business ventures are all failures, his wife relies upon time-honored Indian intuition and faith, and thus her streak of luck at the racetrack averts family disaster.

Rushdie supports the "reality" of India as magical realm by showing the unreality of India as political entity. Rushdie maintains suspense in his chronicle of modern India by intermittently dropping in the two words, "tick tock," reminding us that not only is time incessant but, in the case of recent Indian history, incendiary. Through the nightmarish experiences of the Indo-Pakistani War of 1965 and the Bangladesh War of 1971, the nearer the narrative approaches the present, the more uncertain, haphazard, and incomprehensible events appear. Whereas the early narrative account of Saleem's grandfather, Aadam Aziz, is rendered in relatively straightforward and chronological prose, Saleem's narrative of his own adulthood seems always on the verge of falling apart. The sense of impending collapse is also echoed and embodied in Saleem's physical self: he gives us periodic reports that his body is breaking apart; and at the novel's conclusion, that is literally what happens. India and Saleem's family thus come full circle. As his grandfather came to know his wife and life by piecing fragmentary views together, so at the end the wholeness of a life falls apart into fragments.

Rushdie portrays the 1965 Indo-Pakistani War, fought over the disputed territory of the Rann of Kutch, as unreal and incomprehensible. Although Saleem is not directly involved in the fighting, he hears about events through the first-hand experience of his ill-fated cousin, Zafar. Rushdie portrays the war through the far-flung reports coming from both India and Pakistan of casualties inflicted on the other side. The so-called "facts" of the war are at least as fantastic as events in the Ghetto of the Magicians: "In the first five days of the war Voice of Pakistan announced the destruction of more aircraft than India had ever possessed; in eight days, All-India Radio massacred the Pakistani Army down to, and considerably beyond, the last man" (339). In those days, Saleem shows, the real and fantastic were quite literally the same: "Nothing was real, nothing certain" (340). Saleem later describes the Emergency of 1975 as a "time which damaged reality so badly that nobody ever managed to put it together again" (420). In Rushdie's narrative, the transformation of India is taking it more and more away from its ancient, spiritual, mythical roots toward a confusing, grotesque, modern reality in which governmental lies, distortions, and cover-ups cloud the perception and understanding of external events. The "old dark priapic forces of ancient, procreative India" (176) are giving way to modern progress.

Maintaining his "central role" in recent Indian history, Saleem is conscripted into the Pakistani Army during the 1971 Bangladesh War, even though his personal allegiance is to India. Due to his sensitive nose, which can sniff out evil omens as well as land mines, Saleem serves as tracker for three Pakistani soldiers, Ayooba, Shaheed, and Farooq, parodic characters based on Kipling's "soldiers three," Mulvaney, Ortheris, and Learoyd. Unlike Kipling's affectionate portrayal of a British soldier's life, Rushdie's portrayal of the three Pakistani soldiers reveals the nightmarish aspect of war: all three soldiers are killed, after being lost in the jungle of the phantasms, the Sundarbans. Of the group, Saleem alone survives the war, due to a fortuitous loss of memory. If some of the occult happenings in India seem hard to believe, Saleem as narrator suggests that the reader should consider "the great ballooning fantasy of history" (345). From his happy childhood, in which he could telepathically communicate with the other Midnight Children, Saleem is ushered continuously into "an adulthood whose every aspect grew daily more grotesque" (345).

Rushdie's Midnight Children are the embodiments of the magic, life, hope, and dream of India. Not only does Rushdie suggest that children are quite literally India's future and thus the preservation of India's traditional strength and values, but in a larger sense he implies that losing the wonder and mystery of childhood is like losing life itself. Rushdie's is a poetic vision. In his novel, the sterilization of the Midnight Children is the draining of hope for all of India. Saleem's happy childhood—the chaotic sensations, the sense of magic, multiplicity, freedom, and infinite possibility—is linked with India; his problematic adulthood is associated with Pakistan where he lives with the all-too-adult Uncle Zulfikar whose catch-phrase, "Let's get organized!" rings throughout his "dull, lifeless house" (285). Saleem's maturation process takes him from his magical ability to communicate telepathically with the Midnight Children to the "adult" experiences of conflict during the Indo-Pakistani War and the Bangladesh War, and to an exaggerated, systematic effort to control national life during the Emergency. And yet, through it all, he remains optimistic, perhaps hopelessly so. Between Shiva's dualistic principles of Them or Us, kill or be killed, Saleem envisions a life-giving "third principle": childhood. But, in a post-colonial India bent on transforming itself into a modern, industrial power at any cost, childhood "dies; or rather it is murdered" (256).

A significant line repeated throughout the novel is "What can't be cured must be endured" (187): in Saleem's life-story, "cures" prove to be his undoing, doctors are villains, and hospitals are places of evil. Saleem's accidents, first in the washing-closet and then on the bicycle, give him severe sinus stoppage and a concussion resulting paradoxically in his telepathic communicative abilities. His mind becomes an internal version of All-India Radio, a medium through which he can reach the other Midnight Children. Saleem's aberrational, gigantic cucumber-nose, his mark of deficiency in the external world, is the locus of his extraordinary internal, psychic powers. Part of "the odour of failure" (73) of Saleem's father, Ahmed Sinai, is due to his inability to follow his own nose or rely upon his own instinct and intuition. Ahmed is a reasoner, but his rationalizing constantly leads him to disaster. Saleem realizes that his nose, which is sensitive to outside omens of good and evil, is his gift.

It is in the hospital, where the doctor "cures" him of sinus stoppage, that Saleem loses his telepathic ability, the source of his communication with the other Midnight Children. Rushdie places a high value on the unique and the aberrational. Saleem's son's huge ears, which make him resemble the elephant-headed Hindu god Ganesh, are the source of his strange power—he is "omni-audient" and can absorb all sound. The Midnight Children themselves are described as "the grotesque aberrational monsters of independence, for whom a modern nation-state could have neither time nor compassion" (434). We can see in Rushdie's negative portrait of doctors a criticism of India's national policies of modernization and industrialization along western lines. As a nation, India is applying "cures" that will leave it permanently wounded.

Though there are numerous dualities in *Midnight's Children*, Rushdie's vision goes beyond "harsh dichotomies" (335), as Marshall McLuhan labelled the dualism in Kipling's fiction. *Midnight's Children* is a novel of acceptance: although Saleem as character longs for a central role in his country's history and, like his mother, wants to carry the responsibilities of the world on his own shoulders, Saleem as narrator looks upon his younger self through wiser, more experienced, accepting eyes. Saleem suffers an identity crisis which leads him to the goal of his life-long search: the answer to the question which has plagued him throughout the entire narrative:

> Who what am I? My answer: I am the sum total of everything that went before me, of all I have been seen done, of everything done-to-me. I am everyone everything whose being-in-the-world affected was affected by mine. (383)

Saleem makes the same point another way: "To understand just one life, you have to swallow the world" (109).

Unlike Kim, who finally aligns himself with England as an agent of the power that proposes to order or at least control the confusing Indian "muddle," Saleem gives up his long effort to effect change and shape the course of events, and instead embraces the complex, chaotic multiplicity of his country. Rushdie implies that rather than creating or forging a personal identity, one must discover and accept an already given identity. At the end of the narrative, Saleem remembers his ayah's song—"Anything you want to be, you can be; you can be just what all you want" (253)—and calls it "the greatest lie of all" (46). More acted upon than acting, Saleem concludes, "From ayah to Widow, I've been the sort of person *to whom things have been done*; but Saleem Sinai, perennial victim, persists in seeing himself as protagonist" (237). Saleem's past efforts to order and organize—not only the Midnight Children's Conference, but also India as a whole—have all ended in disaster; by accepting things as they are and his appointed role in the flux of life, he finds contentment. The strong suggestion in *Midnight's Children* is that, like Saleem's favorite childhood game of Snakes and Ladders, life creates its own resolutions, and human effort to the contrary makes little difference. "For every snake, a ladder will compensate" (141), argues Saleem the mature narrator. One of the most surprising resolutions of the novel comes after the Widow has apparently exterminated the Midnight Children. The unforeseen, unplanned "ladder" turns out to be the thousands of children Shiva has begotten during his career as war hero, all of whom have inherited the supernatural powers and sense of hope and possibility embodied in all the Midnight Children. Thus, Rushdie finally implies that, contrary to the reader's expectation, India's ancient power is not extinct but only transformed into new incarnations.

Even though there are similarities between *Midnight's Children* and works by other Indian writers, such as Raja Rao, Anita Desai, Kamala Markandaya, Bharati Mukherjee, and R. K. Narayan, there is also something which sets this novel apart and it has to do with the portrait of India it contains. Rushdie has said in an interview that, "it seemed amazing to me that when you looked at the literature that had been produced about India, it seemed dated and delicate, and I wondered why these dainty, delicate books were being written about this massive, elephantine place" (Kaufman, 22). *Midnight's Children* is an ambitious novel which is not always successful; it tries to capture not only the life of a character, but the life of a vast, populous country through its recent turbulent history. Although it may have occasional lapses, the novel succeeds in a way not usually attempted by anglophone Indian writers: it gives the reader a sense of the enormous vitality of India. In much Indian anglophone fiction, there is a meditative, philosophic quality with which we traditionally associate "ancient India." In *Midnight's Children*, Rushdie takes the language popularized by Hindi cinema with its street-slang, fast pace, melodrama, romance, and action, and fuses it into his narrative to render a surprisingly modern, energetic India. Though Saleem encounters more than his share of hardship, his narrative never flags. The headlong narrative drive, constantly planting hints of things to come in the chapter or chapters to follow, the sheer energy and vibrancy of the language, and the deft handling of the chronology, moving forward and backward in time, make this novel extraordinary and brilliantly render a view of another side of India: the chaotic hustle and bustle, the ceaseless energy and variety of its people, and its great promise for the future.

Midnight's Children shares with other works by so-called Third World writers the embodiment of a strong hope for the future. Even though the personal life-story of Saleem, Rushdie's persona, is one of self-delusion, disappointment, and failure, Rushdie himself is not pessimistic about the future of India, for he has explained:

> The optimism of the book seems to me to lie in its "multitudinous" structure. It's designed to show a country with an almost endless capacity for generating stories, events, new ideas, and constantly renewing, rebuilding itself. In the middle of that you have one rather tragic life. The two have to be seen together. And simply to say that the book despairs is to see it in too linear a way (Durix, 23).

Indeed, what Saleem leaves to the world in the form of his son is a distinct sign of hope for a better future for India. Aadam Sinai has the appearance of the elephant-headed god of good luck, the Remover of Obstacles, Ganesh. As a child with "omni-audient" ears, Aadam hears all, but refuses to utter one sound, convincing his parents that they are in "the presence of one of the earth's most implacable wills" (423). Born during the Emergency, he is more cautious than his father; "but when he acts, he will be impossible to resist." His father sees him as "stronger, harder, more resolute" (425) than himself, though certainly in the course of this long narrative, Saleem has endured more than would seem humanly possible. Above all, it is Aadam's first word, "Abracadabra," finally uttered after his father takes him to Bombay, that signifies his possession of the proven Indian ability to transform, to adapt and remain vital in a constantly changing world.

Chapter II
Adventure and Conquest: Rider Haggard and Peter Abrahams

Rider Haggard's *King Solomon's Mines*

Rider Haggard first went to southern Africa in 1874 at the age of eighteen. The eighth of ten children, Haggard made an unimpressive start in life—doing poorly in numerous schools and failing the Army examinations—before he was accepted on the staff of Sir Henry Bulwer, the new Lieutenant-Governor of Natal, as wine steward. Although Rider's father, William Haggard, a lawyer, was convinced his eighth child was "only fit to be a greengrocer," Rider adapted well to life in southern Africa and was rapidly promoted in the new British colonial administration (Higgins, 4). At the age of twenty-one, Haggard was appointed Registrar of the High Court, the youngest head of a British governmental department in southern Africa. He spent four years in his first and only tour of duty in southern Africa and got to know the country quite well. His youthful experiences provided him with wonderful material that he would draw upon in numerous works of fiction about southern Africa written after he returned to England.

In southern Africa, Haggard discovered a life of adventure and action he had previously never dreamed of in England. In 1876, he accompanied Sir Theophilus Shepstone in a trek from Natal to the interior of southern Africa to help carry out the British annexation of the Transvaal. It was Haggard who raised the Union Jack in the Transvaal for the first time. The open expansiveness of southern Africa appealed to Haggard's youthful sense of drama and adventure. As Court Registrar, his duties included "riding shotgun" for Judge John Kotze, the only magistrate in the Transvaal, on long journeys by wagon through hostile territory to various locales where the judge presided over hearings. During these journeys, Haggard and Judge Kotze were in constant fear of a Zulu attack. In a letter to a friend, Haggard wrote, "We had to sleep with a perfect armful of loaded guns and rifles of which I was more afraid than of the Kaffirs" (Higgins, 29). In a letter to his mother, however, he sounded a different note, resembling in tone his future literary creation, Allan Quatermain: "Do you know one quite gets to like this sort of life. It is a savage kind of existence but it certainly has attractions, shooting your own dinner and cooking it—I can hardly sleep in a house now, it seems to stifle one" (Higgins, 31). In his *Memoirs and Reminiscences* Judge Kotze later remembered Haggard as "emotional and much given to romancing," a young man who sometimes described "as fact what was mere fiction" (Higgins, 33).

During his time in southern Africa, Haggard began to gain a perspective on Britain's world position and he adopted strong opinions concerning the relationship between the British Empire and its subject peoples. Haggard was shocked and angry, for instance, to learn in 1876 of the massacre of 1500 British troops under Sir Bartle Frere at Isandhlwana in Zululand by a Zulu force led by Cetywayo, a descendant of Chaka. Later, in *King Solomon's Mines*, Haggard would portray the loyal Kukuana character, Umbopa, as having fought at Isandhlwana on the British side. In 1879, after four years in southern Africa, Haggard returned to England and was married a year later, after which he and his wife returned to southern Africa to take up ostrich farming. Just after their arrival, war broke out between the British and the Boers; Haggard, a partisan of the British imperial cause, took a keen interest in the conflict. As a result of the war, the British returned the Transvaal to the Boers, a concession which Haggard deplored. After the failure of Haggard's ostrich farm in a year's time, he returned home for good with his wife and baby son.

Back in England, Haggard began studying for the law, but also turned to writing articles about southern Africa for journals and newspapers. He felt that the British public misunderstood the situation in southern Africa, and was appalled to find out that some even considered the Zulu leader Cetywayo, who had dealt the British army its humiliating defeat at Isandhlwana, a noble chief. Haggard responded by writing *Cetywayo and His White Neighbours*, a polemical work published at his own expense, which portrayed Cetywayo as a bloodthirsty tyrant and argued that the British colonial policy in southern Africa was weak and ineffective. In 1885, after passing his final examination, Haggard became a barrister. By this time, he had also written and published two works of fiction, *Dawn* and *The Witch's Head*, neither of which sold well. Haggard's fortunes, however, changed dramatically after the publication in the same year of his third novel, *King Solomon's Mines*, a boys' adventure story set in southern Africa and modeled loosely on Robert Louis Stevenson's *Treasure Island*. Unlike Haggard's first two novels, *King Solomon's Mines* became a vastly popular work and sold well. During a remarkable period spanning the next seven years, Haggard wrote fifteen novels, including *She* (1887) and *Allan Quatermain* (1887).

Haggard's *King Solomon's Mines*, published under unusual circumstances in the history of book-printing, had a considerable impact on the English reading public. When the novel was published in 1885, printing presses in England were becoming increasingly mechanized and, as a result, books could be mass-produced. *King Solomon's Mines* first appeared in a cheap, one-volume edition rather than in the more expensive, three-volume, standard edition, and thus became affordable to a broad reading audience. Along with the book's mass-production went an unprecedentedly large advertising campaign. D. S. Higgins, in his biography, *Rider Haggard*, relates that large posters were put up all over London advertising Haggard's new novel as "THE MOST AMAZING BOOK EVER WRITTEN" (Higgins, 83). Whereas only five hundred copies of Haggard's first two novels were printed, eight thousand copies of *King Solomon's Mines* were printed in three months.

The timing of the novel's publication could not have been better. Like Kipling's fiction about India, *King Solomon's Mines* was written during the heyday of the British Empire; it expressed the spirit and interests of the age. The British reading public was hungry for fiction about the colonies in Africa. Upon publication of *King Solomon's Mines*, Haggard was immediately hailed as an innovative writer, and his novel was seen as an example of an exciting, new fiction breaking away from the predictable, conventional stories about English society set in familiar English locations. Andrew Lang, the influential critic, anthropologist and long-time friend of Haggard, commented on this bold brand of fiction:

> There has, indeed, arisen a taste for exotic literature; people have become alive to the strangeness and fascination of the world beyond the bounds of Europe and the United States. But that is only because men of imagination and literary skill have been the new conquerors, the Corteses and Balboas of India, Africa, Australia, Japan and the isles of the southern seas. All such writers . . . have, at least, seen new worlds for themselves; have

> gone out of the streets of the over-populated lands into the open air; have sailed and ridden, walked and hunted; have escaped from the fog and smoke of towns. New strength has come from fresher air into their brains and blood; hence the novelty and the buoyancy of the stories which they tell. Hence, too, they are rather to be counted upon among romanticists than realists, however real is the essential truth of their books (Street, 11).

Of his most popular novel, Haggard said, "*King Solomon's Mines* was written by me as an experiment in boys' books. It would be impossible for me to define where fact ends and fiction begins in the work, as the two are very much mixed up together" (Higgins, 71). With *King Solomon's Mines*, Haggard discovered his metier: the historical (or African) romance, or what one recent critic has called the "imperialist romance" (Patteson, 112). In this fictional form, used by Haggard in numerous other novels, a small party of Englishmen journey to Africa to seek, not only treasure and adventure, but signs of an ancient, white civilization which was said to have flourished in Africa during Biblical times and then somehow perished or was lost. The British experience in Africa has often been described in literature as a journey into the unknown which involves an encounter with "the Other," that is, the indigenous people. Modern examples of this journey motif are found in Joseph Conrad's *Heart of Darkness* and in Graham Greene's *Journey Without Maps* (1936), an autobiographical account of the author's trip on foot into the interior of West Africa. Frequently, in the literary framework of the journey, the reader sees the whole of Africa (the country is expanded into the continent) as a mysterious, exotic land; the native as a phenomenon of non-civilization, the "savage"; and the white Englishman as thc bold cxplorer penetrating the heart of a great mystery and afterwards returning to England (i.e. "civilization") a changed man. The journey is often spiritual as well as physical. Looking back on his own journey up the Congo, which formed the basis for *Heart of Darkness*, Conrad wrote: "Before the Congo, I was just a mere animal" (122). Similarly, Greene felt as if he had encountered a more primal form of life in Africa than he had ever experienced anywhere before.

Literary accounts in English of the white man's experience in southern Africa have also often taken the form of a journey into the unknown. Two early literary works concerned with journeys into southern Africa, besides Haggard's *King Solomon's Mines*, are G. A. Henty's *With Roberts to Pretoria* (1901), and John Buchan's *Prester John* (1910), both of which, like *King Solomon's Mines*, are romantic tales of adventure aimed primarily at a young male reading audience.

These three works, like those of Conrad and Greene, describe a journey and an encounter, but Haggard, Henty, and Buchan give their works an added twist so that the disorienting journey becomes a prolonged adventure and the encounter becomes a conflict or war in which the English hero battles savage forces and performs a crucial, heroic role in the cause of civilization.

Even though more recent fiction by white South African writers also often describes a journey, the dynamics of the setting and the encounter have changed. If we compare *King Solomon's Mines*, *With Roberts to Pretoria*, and *Prester John* with more recent novels by white South African writers, such as J. M. Coetzee's *Waiting for the Barbarians* (1980) and Nadine Gordimer's *July's People* (1981), both of which involve a journey into the "land of the barbarians," we see reflected the great change which has occurred in southern Africa in the last hundred years. In the novels by Gordimer and Coetzee, the main character is a white *native* of South Africa and that fact changes everything: there is no English homeland to which to return, and the opportunities for heroic adventure seem considerably diminished. The portrait of modern South Africa by the recent, native, white writer is thus not of an exotic land, but rather of an intolerable racial situation brought about by the South African government's policy of *apartheid*. Although Coetzee and Gordimer do not work in the same realist tradition as Conrad and Greene, their white characters are obviously changed profoundly by their environment, and learn something about themselves in the course of their journey. The earlier English writers working in the romantic tradition of the boys' adventure novel, like Haggard, Henty, and Buchan, by contrast, are less interested in their characters' heuristic response to Africa, and more interested in subtly affirming and even celebrating British imperialism.

Like Stevenson's *Treasure Island* (1883), *King Solomon's Mines* concerns a small group of Englishmen who travel to a foreign land in search of treasure. In *Treasure Island*, there is an English squire, a doctor, a captain, and young Jim Hawkins, the narrator, who comes of age in dealing with the adventures that befall him. Their counterparts in *King Solomon's Mines* are Sir Henry Curtis, a classical scholar; Captain John Good, a Royal Naval officer who has some medical training; Allan Quatermain, the narrator, a hunter with considerable knowledge and experience in Africa; and Umbopa, the servant, a native of Kukuanaland who seeks to regain the kingship of his people which is rightfully his. Although the quartet in *Treasure Island* successfully secure the sought-after treasure, they prove themselves to be above the common run of "gentlemen of fortune," as Long John

Silver describes himself and his fellow pirates (61). For example, Jim Hawkins learns about loyalty, responsibility, and the need for law and order in the course of the story. Similarly, in *King Solomon's Mines*, the Kukuana sorceress Gagool accuses Quatermain and company of materialistic aims: "And what came they for, the white ones, the terrible ones, the skilled in magic and all learning, the strong, the unswerving? What is that bright stone upon thy forehead, O king?" (122) Haggard takes pains, however, to show that the Englishmen have higher motives than mere materialistic gain. As Sir Henry Curtis tells Umbopa's translator: "Tell him that he mistakes an Englishman. Wealth is good, and if it comes in our way we will take it; but a gentleman does not sell himself for wealth" (127).

The actual motives of Quatermain, Curtis, and Good in journeying to Kukuanaland, which only one white man has previously reached, are manifold, and most of them have to do with Haggard's romantic portrait of southern Africa. As in *Treasure Island*, the element of the treasure hunt is always present in Haggard's narrative: the legendary wealth buried in King Solomon's mines is not revealed until the novel's end. The three Englishmen, however, are more than just "gentlemen of fortune"; they are red-blooded sportsmen, and in his novel, Haggard portrays southern Africa as a sportsmen's paradise, a land teeming with big game unknown in England. On the first day of their journey to King Solomon's mines, after spotting a giraffe, an elephant, and a lion, they decide to delay their journey in the interest of sport. As Sir Henry puts it, "It seems that we are in a paradise of game" (49). After bagging a total of nine elephants in what seems to be a few hours, they continue their journey. If Kipling portrays India in *Kim* as a boy's wonderland, a huge playground, then Haggard portrays southern Africa as a man's wonderland: a wide open frontier where an Englishman can test himself against wild game, the physical hazards of nature, and blood-thirsty savages whose primitive brand of warfare is a physical test of endurance.

In *Prospero and Caliban*, Dominique Mannoni talks about the "psychological satisfactions" of colonialism, and certainly we can see Quatermain, Curtis, and Good enjoying these pleasures of mastery in southern Africa (203). When Umbopa first accosts the white men in Durban about his desire to accompany them on their journey, they quickly agree, and though the matter is not discussed, all assume that the African will perform the role of servant, Man Friday with his three Robinson Crusoes. Like Kipling's characterization of the Ressaldar, who was loyal to the British in the Great Sepoy Mutiny, Umbopa is a loyal anglophile who fought on the British side against Cetywayo in the Zulu War.

Although he eventually proves himself to be of royal blood and the rightful king of Kukuanaland, it is clear after Umbopa joins the Englishmen that he is the retainer and they the royalty. Early on in the journey, Umbopa refers to his companions as "white men" rather than as "Inkosis" (chiefs), and Quatermain reprimands him for overstepping the bounds of his assigned role: "You forget yourself a little. Your words come out unawares. That is not the way to speak [to a white man]" (42). After his reprimand, Umbopa (who later, as king of the Kukuana, assumes his original name, Ignosi) is more careful to consult with "his advisors" before acting. He tells Quatermain, using the father-son language employed throughout the narrative, "Nay, my father, do thou speak, and let me, who am but a child in wisdom beside thee, hearken to thy words" (171). After the war breaks out, it is understood by all that the three white men will be the generals of each of the regiments and their commands heeded.

The restoration of Kukuanaland to its rightful rulership under Ignosi might seem to be a coincidental result of the journey, but it actually takes on major importance in the narrative. Although their stated purpose is to find Sir Henry's lost brother and to seek the legendary treasure hidden in King Solomon's mines, perhaps the real achievement of Quatermain and company is the overthrow of the usurping dictator Twala and the restoration of the land under Ignosi's enlightened leadership. Unlike the bestial Twala, whose annual witch-hunts provide an offering of human sacrifices to the Silent Ones, the "figures who sit in stone" outside the entrance to the mines and whom the Kukuana people worship, Ignosi has spent much of his life wandering in Natal, which in his words is the "land of wonders, where white people live," where for many years he "learned the wisdom of the white people" (125). In helping Ignosi regain power in Kukuanaland, Quatermain and company in effect establish a British colony. Before agreeing to participate in the war against Twala, Sir Henry makes Ignosi promise as king to govern in accordance with British notions of law and order. After defeating Twala, Ignosi declares his first act will be to kill Gagool and all other "witch doctors" (197). In other words, he will kill off the last remnant of African strength, memory, and religion, replacing them with the institutions of the white man.

Not only is southern Africa portrayed as a sportsman's paradise, but also as an El Dorado: abundant in precious minerals and natural resources with a climate far superior to the cold and fog in England. Sir Henry says that "in beauty, in natural wealth, and in climate I have never seen its like" (103). If Gagool's claim that an ancient white race originally settled the land is correct, then the intervention by Quatermain and company into the internal affairs of the Kukuanas can be seen as an important step to recovery of the land by the British as rightful owners. Haggard's aim, like that of John Buchan in *Prester John*, is to suggest an African past in which there was an advanced white civilization prior to the arrival of the present black inhabitants, thus invalidating the notion of a black nationalist Africa and legitimizing Britain's colonial interest in the area. Haggard's rewriting of southern African history thus proves consistent with Frantz Fanon's claim in *The Wretched of the Earth* that colonialism "turns to the past of the oppressed people and distorts, disfigures, and destroys it" (210). In *Gone Primitive*, Marianna Torgovnick finds that Edgar Rice Burroughs uses the same myth of an ancient white African civilization in his Tarzan series, and with similar effect: "The Tarzan novels gave enduring cultural life to the idea that civilizations in Africa were of white origin. They helped shape popular (mis)conceptions of Africa and its (non)past" (60).

Haggard's subject matter in *King Solomon's Mines*—the discovery of the remains of an ancient white civilization that inhabited Africa during Biblical times—was certainly influenced by the actual European discovery in 1872 of the ruins of Great Zimbabwe. At the time, many experts believed that the ruins dated back to Biblical times and were possibly in fact once part of an ancient civilization from which King Solomon took his legendary treasure. Later, after a number of archaeological excavations and studies, the history of the ruins at Great Zimbabwe was revised: they were dated around 900 A.D. and were found to have been part of a flourishing black African civilization. In *King Solomon's Mines*, however, Haggard used the discovery of the ruins to give credence to the theory that an advanced white race had originally inhabited Africa and then mysteriously perished.

Besides the oblique reference to Great Zimbabwe and brief references to the Zulu War, there are no historical allusions in *King Solomon's Mines*. The reader can infer that since the mysterious demise of the ancient white race, time has stood still in southern Africa, only to resume again since the white man's return. There is no mention in the novel how the black races first appeared there, but it is obvious from Haggard's portrayal of the Kukuana that their civilization has advanced little over this long period of time. *King Solomon's Mines* is thus a denial of the black man's history in southern Africa: the black races have simply occupied the remnants of the white civilization, with little idea of its operation. Since the disappearance of the white civilization, not only King Solomon's treasure but also the beautiful landscape and the bountiful wild game of Kukuanaland have been perfectly preserved. In *King Solomon's Mines*, Haggard wants to keep southern Africa a romantic adventureland, full of mystery and hidden treasure, far from the scars of history or the encroachment of civilization. He implies that the black races of Africa make no history; they exist on the level of animals, of little or no consequence in the ongoing march of white civilization.

Throughout *King Solomon's Mines*, the Englishmen are portrayed as being on a much higher plain of "civilization" than the Africans, who are repeatedly likened to animals. During the Englishmen's journey to Kukuanaland, the group runs out of water and faces certain death in the desert. One of their servants begins "sniffing the hot air for all the world like an old Impala ram who scents danger" and tells Quatermain, "I *smell* water" (73). Soon afterward, they discover "an undoubted pool of water" (75) which enables the group to survive the remainder of the journey across the desert. Quatermain as narrator remarks to the reader "what a wonderful instinct these wild-bred men possess" (73). The Africans' animalistic reliance upon instinct is double-edged, however, for this is what has apparently held them back from attaining a higher level of civilization.

Like many of the Indian characters in Kipling's *Kim*, Haggard's Kukuana show a lack of sophistication, an ignorance of the outside world, and a superstitious belief in magic and the supernatural. As Quatermain and company first enter Kukuanaland and encounter a band of Kukuana warriors, the latter see Good's eyeglass and false teeth and instantly believe the white intruders are gods. The head warrior apologizes to the "gods" for their menacing appearance:

> "I see that ye are spirits. . . . Pardon us, O my lords."
> "It is granted," I said, with an imperial smile. (95)

Quatermain relies upon the technological device of his rifle, which he tells the Kukuana warriors is a "magic tube," to convince them that he, Curtis, and Good come from another world. "We come from the stars, ask us not how. We come to see this land" (118). As in Kipling's "The Man Who Would Be King," Haggard renders a portrait of naive, gullible natives regarding white strangers as divine emissaries. Kipling intended his story as a warning about what could easily befall the British imperialist mission, but Haggard seems to have no such redeeming intention: he condones the trio's actions as necessary, and even laudable, survival tactics.

The Englishmen find all the people of Kukuanaland to be completely under the sway of the evil king Twala and the centuries-old sorceress Gagool. Twala is the antithesis of Ignosi. If Ignosi is an example of the ideal native who is resigned to the subservient position given to him by the colonial authority, then Twala is an example of what Frantz Fanon in *Black Skin, White Masks* describes as the "bad nigger"—huge, ugly, bestial, and savage—the dark Other whom the white man instinctively fears and distrusts (134). Twala is described in especially unflattering, racist terms as having "the most reprehensible countenace we had ever beheld. The lips were as thick as a Negro's, the nose was flat . . . and its whole expression was cruel and sensual" (115). Like Twala, Gagool is presented in animalistic, dehumanizing terms which befit her role as the embodiment of witchcraft and evil. She is initially mistaken for a "withered-up monkey" until Quatermain recognizes her countenance to be that "of a woman of great age, so shrunken in size it was no larger than that of a year-old child, and was made up of a collection of deep yellow wrinkles" (121). Further reinforcing the evil and strangeness of Twala, Gagool, and the other African characters, Haggard provides no humanizing sign of children or any family life in Kukuana society.

Since the indigenous people are portrayed as sheep incapable of thought and self-motivated action, and easily stirred into a blood-letting frenzy, the figure of the priest or priestess becomes potentially the most dangerous character of all. In British fiction set in Africa, African religion seems to have been especially denigrated. Conrad in *Heart of Darkness* and Buchan in *Prester John* both portray Africans involved in what they call "devil worship" and yet there is no historical evidence whatsoever that would indicate any African peoples engaging in a religious practice which exalts the devil. Haggard likewise caters to popular misconceptions about Africa rather than attempting to correct what was surely a distorted view of an entire continent. The most striking Kukuana character in Haggard's narrative is Gagool, the embodiment of Kukuana religion, which is seen as a form of witchcraft. Like Reverend John Laputa in *Prester John* and like the Blind Mullah in Kipling's story, "The Head of the District," Gagool is not only the high priestess of her people's religion, but also an agent of tyranny. She is a leader, and, like other native leaders in British colonial fiction, she is portrayed negatively. Like her counterparts in the fiction of Buchan and Kipling and like Haggard's priest Agon in *Allan Quatermain* and the ageless Ayesha in *She*, she is the representative of evil.

Since the boys' adventure tale is a male-oriented fictional form, it is not surprising that the figure of the evil religious leader would be a female: Gagool, the "mother of evil" (203). Likewise, the witch-finders who sniff out the king's enemies in Twala's annual witch-hunt are portrayed as female, old and gray like Gagool, and indeed trained in witchcraft by her. Moreover, the legend surrounding King Solomon's mines has it that years ago "a white man crossed the mountains, and was led by a woman to the secret chamber and shown the wealth, but before he could take it she betrayed him" (202). This misogynistic and anti-maternal element in *King Solomon's Mines* shows a western writer projecting his own perceptions and biases onto an alien culture. In *The Black Interpreters*, Nadine Gordimer has pointed out that in the West the relationship between mother and son is viewed as potentially destructive and she cites Proust and Lawrence as evidence of this view (6). In traditional African culture, however, the mother-son relationship is viewed as a special, nurturing bond which continues throughout the son's life and which is anything but destructive. By portraying the primary embodiments of evil as female and also as maternal figures, Haggard attributes a poisonous atmosphere to Kukuanaland and so justifies its overthrow by the Englishmen.

The Kukuana men in *King Solomon's Mines* are seen in a similarly stereotypical way as fearless warriors, unafraid of dying. After the war, in which the narrator informs us that over twenty thousand men were killed, Quatermain remarks to Ignosi that the latter's ascendancy to the throne has been a bloody one. The new Kukuana king responds, "Yes, but the Kukuana people can only be kept cool by letting the blood flow sometimes" (197). The narrator finds something to admire in the unthinking willingness of the Kukuana to enter into a battle in which they will likely be killed. Just before the start of the war, Quatermain looks at the faces of the Kukuana warriors and comments: "I could not even at that moment help contrasting their state of mind with my own . . . . Never before had I seen such an absolute devotion to the idea of duty and such a complete indifference to its bitter fruits" (176). In *Rule of Darkness*, Patrick Brantlinger lists "individual regression or going native" as a principal theme of the "imperial Gothic" subgenre, popularized by Haggard, Kipling, and others during the late nineteenth century. This "regression" is certainly an important feature of *King Solomon's Mines*. During the war, Quatermain, Curtis, and Good undergo a transformation similar to Umbopa's earlier metamorphosis from servant to king. During their journey to Kukuanaland, all three Englishmen make a partial change in adapting to their new environment and their servants give them African names: Macumazahn, Incubu, and Bougwan, respectively. Later, during the war, however, we see a complete transformation of the Englishmen into savage warriors. In Conrad's *Heart of*

Darkness, Kurtz undergoes a regression into primitive savagery as a result of his stay in Africa and it costs him his sanity. In *King Solomon's Mines*, however, we see Haggard's fundamental romanticism in his heroes' ability to change over from representatives of an advanced civilization to primitive warriors and back again, with benefits all around.

In the episode of the war, we clearly see Haggard's narrative as a fantasy of white male domination: taming the frontier, slaying savage foes by the hundreds, and conquering a formidable, dark enemy with outnumbered forces. The transformation of Sir Henry Curtis is especially evident, for he becomes literally a noble savage. As Curtis exchanges his trappings of civilization for a Kukuana war outfit, Quatermain remarks, "The dress was, no doubt, a savage one, but I am bound to say I never saw a finer sight than Sir Henry Curtis presented in this guise" (161). Quatermain, too, goes through a primitivization process: "my blood, which hitherto had been half-frozen with horror, went beating through my veins, and there came upon me a savage desire to kill and spare not" (176). At the war's end, Sir Henry, the biggest and strongest of the Englishmen, defeats Twala, the biggest and strongest of the Africans, by decapitating him with an axe. Clearly Haggard's objective in this episode is to identify Sir Henry with the barbarian-aristocratic, warlike "virtues," shared by "savages," while also paradoxically identifying him—the English "gentleman"—as one of the highest products of civilization.

In a letter to Kipling, Haggard once acknowledged that his novels were "too bloody for most tastes," and then added, "Piff! What is blood in Zululand?" (Cohen, *Record*, 76) Buchan in *Prester John* makes a similar reference to the supposed insensitivity of Africans: "[Kaffirs'] skins are insensible to pain" (145). J. M. Barrie, in a review of Haggard's novel, *Allan Quatermain*, in *The British Weekly* in 1887, voiced a common criticism of Haggard's adventure novels: "*Allan Quatermain* tells the story of three worthless old men, who go to Africa and slay their thousands of human beings. . . . It would have been a nobler part to stay at home and hire themselves out to butchers" (117). Certainly the depiction of war as a form of sport is a far cry from actual reports of the fighting in the Zulu War. As a member of the British medical corps in the first Boer War and the Zulu War, Gandhi had this to say about the latter:

> The Zulu "rebellion" was full of new experiences and gave me much food for thought. The Boer War had not brought home to me the horrors of war with anything like the vividness that the

> "rebellion" did. This was no war but a man-hunt, not only in my opinion, but also in that of many Englishmen with whom I had occasion to talk. To hear morning reports of the soldiers' rifles exploding like crackers in the innocent hamlets, and to live in the midst of them was a trial. (315)

There is obviously no close correspondence between Haggard's African "romance" and the actual Zulu War, "not so much," as Edward Said has put it, speaking of Western representations of the Orient, "because the language is inaccurate but because it is not even trying to be accurate" (71). Instead, Haggard and other colonial writers seek to portray their foreign subject in a manner that accommodates European preconceptions of African culture and people.

In *Prester John*, John Buchan has his narrator, nineteen-year old Davie Crawfurd, say of John Laputa, the would-be leader of the African nationalist uprising: "I said he was an educated man, but he is also a Kaffir. He can see the first stage of a thing, and maybe the second, but no more. That is the native mind" (102). In *King Solomon's Mines*, the actions of Haggard's British heroes belie some of the same racist attitudes which Crawfurd expresses. Quatermain, whom Ignosi calls "the wily old fox" (171), relies upon mental superiority to outsmart the Kukuana people who are portrayed as having "brains of mud" (98). After the war, Quatermain is quick to remind Ignosi that in return for helping him regain his kingship, he promised to guide the white men to the diamond mines. The "wily fox" persuades Ignosi to spare Gagool, who alone can lead them to the diamonds, and he coaxes the sorceress into taking them inside the mines to the treasure.

Once inside the treasure chamber, however, the tables are turned: although it costs her her life, Gagool deceives the white men and traps them inside the chamber behind five feet of solid rock. At this crucial point, the narrative takes on an instructive ambiguity. Gagool's earlier remark about the white man's greed for diamonds and material wealth begins to appear justified. Likewise, the White Dead—the past Kukuana royalty preserved in ice inside the mines—which the Englishmen discover after their entrance, seem to mock imperialist enterprise and ambition.

The reader begins to feel that the adventurous spirit of the English, which Haggard singles out for praise in all his adventure-empire novels, might here take the wily hunter and his friends to the same place that it takes Carnehan and Dravot in Kipling's "The Man Who Would Be King." Certainly, at this point in the narrative, the reader must wonder if Haggard's intention isn't the same as

Kipling's: a warning of what could happen if imperial greed were not governed by restraint. The instructive ambiguity of the closing scenes, however, is quickly dissipated. Several predictable events take place inside the treasure chamber that allow the white men to escape. First of all, Foulata, the native girl with whom Good falls in love, is conveniently killed. The dying Foulata professes her love for Good, but also her realization that their union is an impossible one: "I know that [Good] cannot cumber his life with such as me, for the sun cannot mate with the darkness, nor the white with the black" (227). A second fortuitous event is the Englishmen's discovery of a hidden passage which eventually leads them through a tunnel and a jackal-hole to safety out of the mines. Quatermain confides to the reader his Calvinistic belief in Providence: "some merciful Power must have guided our footsteps to the jackal hole at the termination of the tunnel" (239). Thirdly, before leaving the treasure chamber, Quatermain has made sure to fill his pockets with the choicest diamonds. Even though the twenty-eight hours they spend in the sealed chamber lead Quatermain to conclude that "wealth, which men spend all their lives in acquiring, is a valueless thing at the last" (231), his proprietary instincts make him reconsider leaving behind the diamonds.

It is revealing how so much early British colonial fiction ends positively: the stories of Haggard, Buchan, Henty, and Kipling concerning the Empire are rarely about failure. Their fictions, in which, as Patrick Taylor puts it, "the reality of anguished, historical struggle becomes lost in the harmonious closure of a mythical narrative structure" (179), comprise a chronicle of success, whether real or imagined. Providence plays a crucial role in *King Solomon's Mines*, as it does in Defoe's *Robinson Crusoe* (1719), a much earlier example of British colonial fiction. Like Crusoe, Quatermain and Curtis express their wonder and faith in a Providence which seems to take a special interest in them. Trapped inside the treasure chamber, Sir Henry tells his two companions, "I see nothing for it but to bow ourselves to the Almighty" (229). Once they discover the hidden passage, Quatermain, who has earlier told us he is not "a first-rate praying man, few hunters are" (63), gives the instructions: "Follow the stairs . . . and trust to Providence" (234). This belief in a providential destiny surely reflects the British view of themselves in southern Africa during the height of the Empire. Indeed, Providence has led the Englishmen to the treasure chamber, from which the earlier Portuguese explorer failed to escape, and similarly, the "Power who shapes the destinies of men" (63) leads them miraculously out again. Destiny leads Quatermain and company to this historic spot and helps them establish a British protectorate in Kukuanaland. Ignosi gratefully offers his British benefactors land and their pick of wives to remain in Kukuanaland, but just as marriage between Good and Foulata was a problem Haggard wanted to avoid, so the long-term residence of the three Englishmen in Kukuanaland was also something the author knew didn't belong in his narrative.

Haggard's portrayal of southern Africa as a wondrous land of adventure, preserved from civilization and the ravages of history, is reinforced by the novel's end. After the death of the ageless Gagool and the sealing off of the treasure chamber behind a thick wall of rock, verification of King Solomon's treasure and the existence of the ancient white civilization becomes virtually impossible. Like the Kukuana people, all traces of them are "lost" to history. Quatermain, Curtis, and Good are led out of Kukuanaland by Kukuana warriors and shown a secret route by which they can safely cross the desert and return to civilization. The Kukuana people thus remain as they were before the white men came: isolated, backward, cut off from civilization. As if the obstacles of the desert and the mountains were not enough to guarantee that isolation, Ignosi vows to wage war against any other white men who attempt to enter Kukuanaland. Haggard's fundamental ambiguity concerning "civilization" and "savagery" is clearly evident in the novel's close. The civilization represented by the white intruders is proven to be superior, and yet the possibility of their remaining in Kukuanaland would destroy Haggard's African romance. Haggard in effect uses the precincts of romance to show the superiority of English civilization, and then protects his African romance from the unromantic consequences of the civilizing process. Haggard's southern Africa thus remains a romantic adventureland to the end, simultaneously preserved and imprisoned beyond the penetration of civilization and the chroniclers of history.

Peter Abrahams' *Wild Conquest*

Peter Abrahams was born in Vrededorp, a slum of Johannesburg, in 1919.

His father, who traced his lineage to Ethiopia, died when Peter was still a baby. His mother, a Coloured woman originally from the Cape, was left alone to bring up Peter, his brother, and two sisters. In *Tell Freedom* (1954), Abrahams' autobiography, he recalls his youth with a sense of gratitude toward his mother, who "had performed a miracle in giving us a sense of family without the support of a husband" (278). As a Coloured in South Africa, Abrahams had to learn to live with certain restrictions. He did not begin school until he was eleven: free compulsory education was for whites only in South Africa. Due to financial difficulties, he was able to attend school for only three years; nevertheless, he progressed quickly. Abrahams found employment at the Bantu Men's Social Centre, a meeting place for the educated blacks of Johannesburg. It was at the Centre with its impressive library that Abrahams was introduced to the works of W. E. B. Du Bois, James Weldon Johnson, Countee Cullen, and other writers of the Harlem Renaissance who would later exercise a major influence on him as a writer. At this time, Abrahams also discovered Shakespeare and the English Romantic poets and began to nurture a desire to go to England.

> With Shakespeare and poetry, a new world was born. New dreams, new desires, a new self-consciousness, were born. . . . I lived in two worlds, the world of Vrededorp and the world of these books (*TF*, 155).

Because he was Coloured, Abrahams' educational opportunities in South Africa were severely limited. He had no chance of continuing his education at a white university. As a result of his work at the Bantu Men's Social Centre, he was able to enroll at Diocesan Training College, a teacher's college for blacks, in Pietersburg. In 1938, at the age of nineteen, Abrahams left the Transvaal for the Cape, having studied two years at the teacher's college. By this time, Abrahams had published some poetry and become interested in Marxism.

> I had tested the new creed called Marxism against the reality of my experience and the darkness of my land. And only by the Marxian theories of economics and imperialism had the racialism of the land made sense. Marxism had supplied an intelligent and reasonable explanation for the things that happened. Had it also the key to the solving of these problems? (*TF*, 244-245)

After a brief involvement in politics in Cape Town, he left for Natal in the hope of leaving South Africa and going abroad. In Durban, he signed on as a crew member of a ship eventually bound for England. It is at this turning point in his life that Abrahams ends his autobiography, *Tell Freedom*. He was twenty years old: "Perhaps life had a meaning that transcended race and colour. If it had, I could not find it in South Africa. Also there was the need to write, to tell freedom, and for this I needed to be personally free" (304).

After arriving in England in 1941, Abrahams married and settled down to write. During a fruitful period spanning the next ten years, he wrote a book of short stories, *Dark Testament* (1942); and four novels, *Mine Boy* (1946), *Wild Conquest* (1950), *A Wreath for Udomo* (1956), and *A Night of Their Own* (1965). Even though he chose to live in exile, Abrahams set all his early fiction in South Africa. In England, he continued his involvement with Marxism, finding employment with a book distributing agency of the Communist Party. He eventually, however, became disillusioned with politics. His writing at this time, beginning with *Wild Conquest*, also began to reflect a turning away from his earlier idealism concerning the problems of South Africa. Abrahams returned to South Africa in 1952 on assignment for the London *Observer* to report on conditions in his home country. A non-fictional work describing life in South Africa, *Return to Goli* (1953), was the result of Abrahams' return. In this work there is evidence of Abrahams' attempt to move beyond politics and race and to adopt a more humanistic approach:

> Painfully, I was slowly groping to a view of life that transcended my own personal problems as a member of one oppressed group of humanity. I felt that if I could see the whole scheme of things with the long eye of history I might be able to fit the problems of my own group into the general human scheme, and, in doing so, become a writer (*RG*, 17).

Abrahams' novel, *Wild Conquest* (1951), reflects his interest in history during the late 1940s and 1950s. In this work, Abrahams turns to the past to focus on the 1836 Great Trek of the Boers and their crucial confrontation with the Matabele whose land they invade and conquer.

In 1955, Abrahams moved with his wife and three children from England to Jamaica; since that time he has adopted the Caribbean not only as his new home, but also as a setting for two novels, *This Island, Now* (1966), a story of political unrest on a fictional Caribbean island ruled by a dynamic black president, and *The View from Coyaba* (1985), a work which, like *Wild Conquest*, re-creates history in a fictional context, tracing 150 years of historic developments from the slave trade to recent political events in Jamaica, Africa, and America. *The View from Coyaba* provides renewed evidence of Abrahams' novelistic interest in history as a heuristic tool—especially for readers from a post-colonial culture—and his ability to view controversial historic events in a balanced, dispassionate manner.

Abrahams' impartiality is one of the features that makes *Wild Conquest* a remarkable novel. In a striking departure from the one-sided narrative of *King Solomon's Mines*, Abrahams' omniscient narrator tells the story of the Great Trek from the viewpoint of both the Boers and the Matabele. The novel is divided into three sections. The first, "Bible and Rifle," focuses on a Boer family, the Jansens, who angrily respond to the British colonial government's emancipation of the slaves in the Cape by deciding to join with the other Boers on the Great Trek north in search of a homeland. The second section, "Bayete!", a Matabele term of salute, is about Mzilikazi's people in the city of Inzwinyani, the capital of the Matabele empire. In this section, we see South African history through the eyes of the Matabele and learn of their conflict with a neighboring tribe, the Barolong. Here, the Matabele also become aware of the threat posed by the sudden intrusion into their homeland by the *voortrekkers*. The final part of *Wild Conquest*, entitled "New Day," relates the inevitable conflict between the Boers and the Matabele. This confrontation, a pivotal turning point in the course of events in southern African history, augurs a new way of life for all the people of this region for years to come.

In her discussion of the African historical novel in *The Black Interpreters*, Nadine Gordimer writes, "The recreation of the past in imaginative writing is one of the ways by which a people may learn to recognise such phenomena in themselves" (15). *Wild Conquest* shares with two other historical novels by non-white South African writers, Thomas Mofolo's Sotho classic *Chaka* (1910) and Solomon Plaatje's *Mhudi* (1930), three important aspects: the recreation of an African past, the search for a link connecting this past with the present, and the search for an African hero. All three novels describe the life of an indigenous southern African people—the Zulu in *Chaka*, the Bechuana in *Mhudi*, and the Matabele in *Wild Conquest*—and all take as their point of departure a time just before the invasion of their territory by the white man. Mofolo's *Chaka* is set during a time in history previous to the other two novels; the arrival of the white man and the inevitable confrontation and change his arrival brings are not directly represented, but are clearly foreshadowed. Plaatje's *Mhudi*, after which Abrahams in part models his novel, tells the story of the Bechuana people of the town of Kunana, the destruction of their town by the Matabele, and their eventual joining of forces with the *voortrekkers* against the Matabele. Abrahams takes up Plaatje's story in *Wild Conquest*, but represents the clash of cultures more directly by examining the confrontation from the opposing viewpoints of the Boers and the Matabele. In these novels, history in the southern African context is depicted as a force which can sweep up an entire people like a whirlwind and change their life in unforeseen ways.

In a review of *Wild Conquest* in the London *Sunday Times* in 1951, C. P. Snow praised the novel, saying that "it may be the forerunner of an entire school of African literary art" (3). Abrahams' choice of a crucial turning point in southern African history as his fictional subject does indeed enable one to see *Wild Conquest* as a forerunner of later African anglophone novels, such as Chinua Achebe's *Things Fall Apart* (1959) and Ngugi wa Thiong'o's *A Grain of Wheat* (1967), which also fictionalize history. In an essay, "The Writer and His Past," Ngugi has recognized Abrahams as an important pioneer in African anglophone fiction who has "paved the way" for later writers (*Homecoming*, 43). Clearly in contrast with Rider Haggard's depiction of southern Africa as a romantic adventureland existing outside history, Abrahams attempts to restore southern Africa to history, and to give the indigenous people a sense of themselves as historic beings who have evolved through a process which has included triumph and tragedy. In other words, the people of southern Africa are not products of a "lost," backward civilization, as Rider Haggard would have the reader believe, but part of a historic process that is ever changing and still continues to change today. Although characters like Paul Van As, the Jansen family, Dabula, and Ntombi are fictional creations, many other characters in *Wild Conquest*, such as Hendrik Potgieter, Piet Retief, Mzilikazi, and Moshesh, are figures out of southern African history. By combining history with fiction, Abrahams attempts to give life to history and to show the indigenous southern African people (to borrow a phrase from Chinua Achebe) "where the rain began to beat them," that is, the point in history at which the descent to their present state began (*MYCD*, 58).

Abrahams takes his epigraph for *Wild Conquest* from Blake's *Songs of Innocence* and *Songs of Experience*, and the lines resonate throughout the narrative. The novel's progression is pessimistic: in almost every section of the narrative, we see the characters transformed from innocence to experience, and they become hardened, angry, and inhuman as a result. Blake's deceptively simple contrast of innocence and experience thus illuminates the tragic dimension of the fateful encounter between the Boers and Matabele:

For Mercy, Pity, Peace, and Love,
Is God, our father dear,
And Mercy, Pity, Peace, and Love,
Is Man, his child, and care.

For Mercy has a human heart,
Pity a human face,
And Love, the human form divine,
And Peace, the human dress.

*

Cruelty has a Human Heart,
And Jealousy a Human Face;
Terror the Human Form Divine,
And Secrecy the Human Dress.

The Human Dress is forged Iron,
The Human Form a fiery Forge,
The Human Face a Furnace seal'd,
The Human Heart its hungry Gorge. (9)

In the novel, the Blakean progress from innocence to experience reveals an ironic regression among the Boer and Matabele characters from humanity to bestiality. In resorting to violent means to resolve their conflict, both sides sacrifice their humanity, which has serious, and even tragic, consequences for future race relations in South Africa.

In Abrahams' balanced portrayal of the Boers and Matabele, a number of correspondences between the two seemingly disparate groups becomes apparent. First of all, both groups are enmeshed in a process of change and yet have only a vague sense of a future direction. As a result of their groping toward an uncertain destiny, both groups are wracked by tension, disunity, and conflict. Among the *voortrekkers*, the opposing views of two key members, Koos Jansen and Paul Van As, lead to disagreement and fighting. Likewise, among the Matabele, unity dissolves into factionalism as Tabata and Langa plan an unsuccessful coup against Mzilikazi and Gubuza. Among both groups, there is heightened suspicion towards any in the camp who do not fall into line with the rest, and who might be perceived as posing a threat to the group's internal security. For instance, Paul Van As is called "traitor" by the Boers, as is Gubuza by the Matabele, because both dare to advocate peaceful rather than forceful means of resolving disputes with other groups.

The instability of both the Boers and Matabele is further exacerbated by conflicts with neighbors: the Boers with the British and the Matabele with the Barolong. Later, of course, the two groups come into conflict with each other. Even though the movement from innocence to experience and from peace to conflict seems inevitable in the novel, there are several characters who advise a Gandhian course of non-violence and peaceful negotiation: Old Johannes, the freed slave who formerly belonged to the Jansens; Paul Van As, who expresses the minority view that the Boers must come to know the Matabele if they are going to live with them; and Moshesh, king of the Basuto, a Gandhi-like, enlightened leader who counsels the use of non-violence and cunning to deal with strong enemies like the Boers. But the wisdom these characters impart is unheeded, and in the rush to secure a safe homeland, both the Boers and Matabele resort to the old method of force rather than negotiation.

In *The Wretched of the Earth*, Frantz Fanon has said, "For a colonized people the most essential value, because the most concrete, is first and foremost the land: the land which will bring them bread and, above all, dignity" (44). In *Wild Conquest*, rather than a treasure-hunt or an adventure, the European-African confrontation is portrayed as a life-and-death struggle for the land. In the novel, the attachment of the Matabele to the land is profound and holy: from the mountaintop where the wise man Mkomozi goes to commune with the ancestral spirits, the narrator views the territory surrounding the capital city and tells us, "From the north, the way to Inzwinyani is a way of magic" (207). Or, as Gubuza, the Matabele general, succinctly puts it after hearing of the Boer intrusion into Matabeleland: "Land is the life of the people. For that, all men fight" (351). Similarly, it is clear why the Boers have come. Hendrik Potgieter, the Boer Commandant, tells his followers on the Great Trek:

> "Over there is the land. We have traveled far for it. We will take that land and build our homes and farms there. We will build a new State and a new people there . . . and no man will take it away from us again." (158)

The colonization of Matabele territory by the Europeans is a process already in motion at the outset of the novel. Although there are no characters representing the English in *Wild Conquest*, they are very much a part of the story. As Abrahams shows, the emancipation of the slaves in the Cape by the British colonial government precipitated the Boers' move northward in the first place, and the *voortrekkers* never forget the long arm of the British law close behind them. Martinus Van As tells the other Boers, "Mark my words, as soon as the Natal trekkers are settled, ships will sail in and hoist the English flag" (100). And he also assures the other Boers that the English will follow them to the Transvaal as well. In this situation, the Matabele are shown as victims of a process they can neither understand nor alter. Their eventual dispossession from their land and their subsequent colonization by the Europeans are only a matter of time. As the wise man, Mkomozi, tells the Matabele leaders when they first hear of the arrival of the Boers: "The matter is out of our hands. . . . This is the change that had to come" (351).

Early on in the novel we see how out of touch many Boers living in the interior of the Cape were from changes taking place in Cape Town: Koos Jansen returns on horseback from the Cape to the family farm with news of the emancipation nearly a year after the legislation was enacted. And yet during this time the Jansens have depended on their slaves, the family of Old Johannes and several other black families, to keep their farm going. At the same time, a freed slave who has also recently arrived from the Cape informs Old Johannes and the Jansens' other slaves of the emancipation. The atmosphere around the Jansens' farm is thus charged with a sudden awareness of the disturbing new concept of racial freedom. The narrator reinforces the meaning of the emancipation with a balanced presentation of both the Jansens' and the slaves' perspectives. Clearly, in the narrator's description of Koos Jansen, for instance, is the explicit idea that regardless of skin color all people are much the same:

> The visible parts of the man's body had been burnt to a reddish-brown. . . . The sun and air and rain and earth had transformed him into as near earth-colour as possible. Perhaps in a thousand years his children would be so transformed by sun and earth and air that they would have flat noses and full lips and kinky hair and dark, very dark copper-coloured skins. And perhaps his daughters of a thousand years hence would have the broad heavy hips and pointed breasts and round black eyes of the African women. Perhaps. (15)

The charged atmosphere leads to inevitable conflict. The former relationship of trust between Kasper Jansen and Old Johannes dissolves into mutual suspicion and hatred. This opening section leading up to the Jansens' decision to join the Great Trek is a foreshadowing of the later armed conflict between the Matabele and the *voortrekkers*. When Kasper and Koos confront the slaves and demand that they surrender their rifles, the latter refuse and a temporary stand-off ensues. Previously, Old Johannes, a man of peaceful negotiation, counseled his temperamental son, Paul, to employ patience and intelligence rather than resort to arms: "You are my son, but there is too much fire in your blood and not enough ice in your brain" (26). In the confrontation with Kasper and Koos, however, Paul suddenly reaches for a rifle, provoking Koos to kill him. At this point, Old Johannes, emboldened by the slaves' superiority in numbers, refuses to return the rifles, and, further, refuses to look down from his master's angry stare. As a result of Johannes's unprecedented act of defiance, the narrator tells us that a new "feeling was born in Kasper Jansen that minute" (44), a feeling of hatred toward all men with black skins. A short while later, for instance, when Kasper's son asks what the word "devil" means, his father answers, "A black and evil thing" (73).

After the confrontation with the slaves, Kasper's wife, Anna, also notices a change in her husband: "She had never seen him look so very much like Koos. . . . [There] was a strange, new, cold aloofness flowing from him now" (47). For Kasper, the dehumanization which afflicts so many other characters in the narrative has begun. Kasper's increasing resemblance to his brother, Koos, as a result of the fateful and sudden turn of events symbolizes one of the tragic occurences in the novel. Clearly, Abrahams intends Koos to be a negative character, a man of extremes whose moral certainties lead him to view life in terms of either/or: white is good, black is bad. As if in answer to Haggard's animalistic portrayal of the Kukuana in *King Solomon's Mines*, Abrahams' depiction of Koos as a violent "animal" suggests that all humans possess a bestial side, and that it becomes a matter of individual choice whether or not and to what extent to keep that side under restraint. Old Johannes, in contrast to both Koos and Kasper, is a man of compromise able to perceive the ambiguities lying between the irreconcilable dualities of white and black, good and evil. Just before the Jansens leave their farm and go to join the other Boers on the Great Trek, Kasper sets their house aflame to prevent his former slaves from living in it. On horseback, Kasper shakes a fist at Old Johannes and yells across the distance, "Black bastard!" (61). Johannes, seeing this, is struck by this expression of unyielding hate and can only wonder to himself:

> But I have been the slave. . . . It is I, not he, who have been deprived of freedom for so many years. The richest years of my life have been spent serving him and his, not me and mine. Why should his hate be stronger than mine? . . . And as he thought,

> the marvel grew in his mind till it was a huge unanswered question. (63)

Even though this is the last time the reader sees Johannes in the novel, his unanswered questioning echoes throughout the narrative, becoming an ironic commentary on the later encounter between the Boers and the Matabele.

In marked contrast to Haggard's portrayal of the Kukuana women as embodiments of evil in *King Solomon's Mines*, in Abrahams' novel women characters assume a vital role. Indeed, both the Boer and Matabele women characters serve as indicators of the level of humanity present in their respective peoples. Anna Jansen, for instance, is the character who most clearly perceives the high cost of the Great Trek to the humanity of the Boers. Anna's physical changes, and finally her death in childbirth, dramatically register that negative effect. As the primary consciousness in the Boer section, "Bible and Rifle," Anna is disturbed by the changes she sees taking place around her, especially the hardening of her husband, Kasper, in response to the sudden upheaval of their lives. She perceives the change in Kasper shortly after they decide they must leave the Cape and trek northward: "It flashed through her mind that here was a hard man, a man with steel in his heart. There was something knifelike about this hardness" (47). Anna feels that her relationship with Kasper has become distant, of secondary importance to the Great Trek. Although she perceives this subtle change in all the Boers as well as in her husband, she feels herself out of control, helpless to do anything about it: "She was a twig on a stream, carried by the waters, tossed and turned by them" (156).

Eventually, the Jansens meet up with several other Boer families and proceed northward with them on the Great Trek. The Boers are portrayed as suffering from internal conflict, one embodied in the disparate attitudes of Paul Van As and Koos Jansen. Whereas Van As believes the Boers must get to know the Africans "if we are going to live with them" (297), Jansen exclaims, "Never trust a Kaffir except a dead one" (102). Like Anna, Paul is concerned about the change taking place in his people as a result of the Great Trek: "My father says to win through we must harden our hearts. He says there is no other way. . . . But afterwards, would it be possible for hard hearts to turn soft again?" (155) Abrahams' impartiality in *Wild Conquest* is evident, for he presents both the worst and best sides of the Boers, and Paul is clearly among the most positive characters in the novel. Like Old Johannes, the Jansens' slave, and also like the Matabele wise man, Mkomozi, Paul is free from hate and prejudice. Abrahams places a high value on the qualities of racial tolerance and understanding in *Wild Conquest*. Paul is non-judgmental, and the only one among the Boers who perceives the Matabele as people who have their own right to live and their own historic claim to the land.

Like the Boers, the Matabele are wracked by disunity and internal dissension. Early on in the "Bayete!" section, Abrahams creates a situation in which the Matabele must choose between either show of force or peaceful negotiation. This situation arises as a result of the annual collection of tributes from weaker tribes in the empire as a show of loyalty to Mzilikazi. Since the Barolong town of Kunana lies within the Matabele empire, its inhabitants must pay this tribute in the form of sheep and cattle. In a moment of drunken impulsiveness, the Barolong king Tauana refuses to give up the livestock to the Matabele messengers, Bhoya and Bangela, and orders them killed. Shocked to hear of this turn of events, Mzilikazi responds by sending a batallion led by his son, Langa, to destroy Kunana in retaliation. Later, during a feast celebrating the Matabele defeat of the Barolong, Gubuza, the commander of the king's army who has been away, returns dismayed to hear of the use of force against the weaker Barolong. He interrupts the victory celebration to make a speech, injecting an unwelcome note of restraint into the joyous occasion: "Wise men of different tribes and nationalities are agreed that cheap successes are nearly always followed by the shadow of tragedy" (216). Here Gubuza unknowingly forecasts the coming tragic confrontation of the Matabele with the *voortrekkers*. Afterward, Mzilikazi speaks to the people, and expresses the importance of understanding a dispute from both sides, a precondition for peaceful negotiation: "[Man] has two ears to hear both sides of a dispute. He who listens to one side only, often finds himself wrong" (220). Mzilikazi's statement, like Gubuza's, echoes throughout the narrative: not only does the king's speech serve to enlighten the situation at hand, but also serves to justify Abrahams' narrative technique with its view of the Great Trek from both the Boer and the Matabele perspectives.

Abrahams' narrative contains several features prominent in *King Solomon's Mines*: a witch-hunt, a dispute concerning a king's rightful heir, and a portrayal of a tribe's first encounter with the white man as well as the conflict resulting from that encounter. Like *King Solomon's Mines*, *Wild Conquest* builds up to a climactic scene involving warfare. In parts of *Wild Conquest*, Abrahams comes close to parodying Haggard's portrayal of the Kukuana, as in the depiction of the false medicine man, Ntongolwane. Like Gagool in *King Solomon's Mines*, Ntongolwane is an agitator posing as a prophet or seer. Conspiring with Tabata and Langa to overthrow Mzilikazi, Ntongolwane instigates a witch-hunt and, after the king's reluctant agreement, forty-one people are put to death. The conspirators' plan is to take advantage of the temporary madness and excitement of the people during the witch-hunt to overpower Mzilikazi and stage a coup. The coup never materializes, however, for Mzilikazi's organization and protection prove invulnerable. Later, Ntongolwane attempts to cast a spell over a young Matabele woman whom he claims is a witch, but the spell is broken by Mkomozi who tells her, "The spell is only in your mind" (249). Unlike Ntongolwane, Mkomozi is thus shown to be more than a "witch-doctor": he is a man of medicine endowed with spiritual and psychological insight. In "The Writer and His Past," Ngugi wa Thiong'o comments on Abrahams' portrayal of Mkomozi and of African society in general:

> The traditional African society in *Wild Conquest* . . . is seen as a complex living organ: its doctors had a knowledge of psychology in the treatment of psychic disorders and disease. The Haggardian savage was thus turned into a modern psychiatrist. (*Homecoming*, 43)

In the witch-hunt scene, Abrahams shows us the power of the African medicine man and his importance in traditional society. Moreover, in Mzilikazi's ability to discourage the plot against him without having to resort to force, Abrahams not only shows us the military strength of the king, but also the cohesiveness of his political and social organization. At the same time, Abrahams shows that there is an ideological split among the Matabele: whereas some clearly approve of and enjoy the witch-hunt, others, including the king, are disgusted by the unnecessary slaughter. As Mzilikazi confesses to Mkomozi, "We are cursed by a bloodlust" (257). In this scene, Abrahams endows his Matabele characters with a level of sensitivity and self-awareness that Haggard never allows his Kukuana characters. In his answer, Mkomozi surprisingly places the responsibility for the Matabele "bloodlust" on the shoulders of the king himself. As architect of the invincible Matabele military machine, Mzilikazi has simply reaped what he has sown, and now he is at the mercy of his own creation. The army has given the Matabele empire an effective defense, but it has also led to internal conflict and a hunger for power. In building an empire based on military might, the Matabele have sacrificed the diplomatic skills which might have later proven more effective than force against the superior rifle-power of the Boers.

In *Wild Conquest*, we see a more vibrant, dynamic southern Africa than that represented in what Nadine Gordimer has called the "dream Africa; as Tarzan's Africa, paper jungle of the white man's adventure stories" (6). African spiritual life is not only portrayed as alive and vibrant, but the people are depicted as enmeshed in transformation prior to the arrival of the Europeans. Gubuza, for example, is represented as a forward-looking man who is the primary agent of change among the Matabele. Like Mzilikazi, Gubuza is a Zulu by birth who has broken away from Chaka, evolving from an early militaristic Zulu training to a sharing of the Basuto leader Moshesh's belief in the wisdom of peaceful negotiation. Although many Matabele are shown to resist change, Gubuza is such a strong figure and his reputation is so great that his ideas have a pronounced effect on the Matabele as a whole. We see this particularly in Gubuza's influence on Dabula, whose thoughts we share as a result of Abrahams' narrative technique. Gubuza is not a whole-hearted convert to Moshesh's doctrine of non-violence, however, as becomes clear when the Matabele under Gubuza's leadership decide to attack the Boers encroaching upon their territory.

In his essay, "The Conflict of Culture in Africa," Abrahams identifies the "most pressing problem in Africa today" as the "transition from the tribal past into the technological present" (387). Unlike many African writers, Abrahams portrays tribalism as negative: a burden which is holding Africa back from moving into the present. In his portrayal of the Matabele in *Wild Conquest*, for instance, Abrahams clearly favors the characters, like Gubuza, who press for change. Gubuza is like another Abrahams hero, Michael Udomo in *A Wreath for Udomo*, who sacrifices himself in order to bring about change for his people. The change Gubuza advocates for the Matabele is a "softening" process, and although some of the Matabele perceive it as a change which will ultimately weaken them as a nation, others, including Mzilikazi and the wise man Mkomozi, see the change as positive and necessary for the continued welfare of the people. Abrahams shows in his historical novel, however, that change takes time, sometimes even the passing of generations, to gain acceptance.

Abrahams' portrayal of the Matabele serves to humanize them as a people coming to grips with their particular position in southern African history. Taking place during "the days that measured the greatness of the Matabele" (208), *Wild Conquest* describes a nation going through growing pains, experiencing internal political conflict, and constantly changing and reshaping itself. Although Abrahams' Matabele have little knowledge of the European presence in southern Africa—Mkomozi alone has been to the Cape and seen "strange men with hair on their red faces" (228)—they are not, like the indigenous southern Africans represented in British colonial fiction, isolated and totally ignorant of the outside world. Abrahams' Matabele are portrayed as familiar with other tribes, such as the Barolong and the Basuto, whose ways of life are different from their own. Gubuza, especially, is well traveled, as he informs the people in his speech:

> "I have been to Swaziland, to Tongaland and to Basutoland. I know the northern forests, I know the western deserts, I know the eastern and the southern seas. I have made these journeys, not on a whim, but in search of wisdom." (216)

Dabula likewise gains insight through travel to other tribal lands. After the witch-hunt episode, for instance, the queen, Mnandi, flees to Basutoland for personal safety, and the king sends Dabula on a journey outside Matabeleland to search for her. The search ends successfully, but more important is the process of internal change Dabula goes through as a result of his travels.

Prior to his journey to Basutoland, Dabula is portrayed as an unhappy young man searching for answers he cannot find. He is shown caught between the old ways and the new. Even though he follows his foster father's example of breaking custom and taking only one wife, Dabula is internally resistant toward Gubuza as a model. When first shown, he is sitting with Gubuza and Mkomozi, but is spiritually apart, brooding, at odds with himself: "Rebellion stirred in him. Why should he do the bidding of Gubuza any more than any other warriors?" (190). Dabula sleeps with a woman from another village and this complicates his already guilty conscience. He then strikes a friend in a moment of impulsive anger and refusing to apologize, ends a long friendship. As a result of his journey, however, Dabula changes. His wife notices the transformation as soon as he returns, and remarks upon it to him, leaving him also to wonder: "How did she know? Mkomozi knew it too. But what was this change in him? If only he could understand" (365).

The reader already has a clue: while in Basutoland, Dabula has met the wise king Moshesh, the source of his foster father's new ideas. The Gandhi-like Moshesh, whose small physique and large head symbolize reliance upon wisdom instead of strength, informs Dabula of the coming "new day." He tells him not only of the Boers but also of the English and he sends a warning for Gubuza not to attempt to fight the Boers who invade Matabeleland but to negotiate with them. Moreover, Dabula has also met two Boers during his journey and has spoken with one, Paul Van As, who surprisingly knew his language. As a result of these experiences, Gubuza's ideas have begun to assume a reality for Dabula. He tells Mkomozi of the great changes he now realizes are inevitable: "Even if we win, it will never be the same" (365). We see Dabula's transformation unfold gradually in Abrahams' narrative: by the end of the novel, Dabula is a man with a new, broader vision of life and of the destiny of the Matabele people.

Michael Wade has pointed out that the Boers and Matabele in *Wild Conquest* are "historical analogues for white and black South Africans at the present time" (90). In *Wild Conquest*, Abrahams not only explores the southern African past in light of the cultural clash with the Boers, but also shows how certain historical events give an inevitable shape to the future, how the seeds of the future are sown in the past. The narrator makes this explicit in the novel's final section, "New Day": "An epoch has ended: an epoch has started. This is the point between yesterday and tomorrow. The old ends here: the new starts here" (379). When he hears how the Boer horsemen killed some Matabele men with rifles in an initial skirmish on the outskirts of Matabeleland, Gubuza concludes, "They come with new ways and new weapons but no new wisdom" (352). It is clear that the Boers adopt the approach of Koos rather than that of Paul: they come in war, not in peace. Abrahams' vision has proven to be prophetic, for the Boers' inflexibility and reliance upon force have engendered an escalating cycle of violence in South Africa that continues to the present day.

Even though Abrahams' narration of the "Bible and Rifle" and "Bayete!" sections of the novel are balanced and just to both the Boers and Matabele, in the concluding "New Day" section, the reader senses that the narrative favor has tipped toward the Matabele. Even so, the latter are portrayed, not so much as innocent victims, but as willing warriors who simply lack the means to overcome the superior fire-power of the Boers. Abrahams shows that history depends on chance and circumstance as much as anything else. Dabula returns from Basutoland with Moshesh's message of peaceful negotiation, but it is too late. Gubuza becomes the focal point of the "New Day" section: stirred to anger by the Boers' arrogant invasion of Matabeleland, he leads his forces to attack. Upon his return, Dabula meets Gubuza on a hill overlooking the battleground where the Matabele are being routed. From Gubuza, Dabula receives instructions not to take part in the fighting but to take care of Mzilikazi's son, Lobengula, the king's heir and thus the assurance of the people's continued welfare:

> "[Lobengula] will be king soon for his father is old and will soon die. You must be the guardian of the young boy. Teach him the

> wisdom you have learned from me. Teach him also the wisdom of Moshesh. Teach him not to fight white men but to intrigue with them and to make treaties with them. Teach him to be cunning in the ways of peace." (376-77)

In this episode and throughout the novel, Abrahams expresses the need for a new, Gandhian path of enlightened non-violence for the Matabele. Since history is a continuing process with one generation succeeding another, a new order must start with Dabula. Abrahams implies that the enlightenment of the Matabele must come, not in the form of force, but in the development of mental tactics and shrewdness. As a result of their defeat by the Boers and the loss of their land, the Matabele must also learn to adapt to a "new day" of their own, as Mzilikazi leads his defeated army out of Inzwinyani northward across the Limpopo River in search of a new homeland.

Although the Boers lay claim to their Promised Land and assume control of the future Transvaal, Abrahams also shows in *Wild Conquest* that they have paid a great price in their victory. As Paul Van As tells Anna, "We are losing ourselves to win" (155). The Boers win the land, but they sacrifice their humanity, or as Abrahams puts it, their "softness." We can see the continuation of this theme of the Boers' loss of humanity in the present-day South Africa portrayed in fiction by other non-white writers, such as Alex LaGuma in *A Walk in the Night* (1962), in which the Afrikaner policemen, Constable Raalt and his partner, are described in hard, inanimate terms: "these men who wore their guns like appendages of their bodies and whose faces had the hard metallic look, and whose hearts and guts were merely valves and wires which operated robots" (55). Abrahams' Matabele, on the other hand, suffer a defeat and lose their land, but they retain their humanity. As the survivors leave Inzwinyani, Mkomozi tells Mzilikazi: "That was your city, now it is nothing. For a city is made of its people" (382). Even though Mkomozi's words express defeat, they also suggest that the Matabele's strength lies in their recognition of themselves as a people whose cultural identity remains intact.

In *Return to Goli*, Abrahams states that "in the historical scheme of things it is only those peoples and institutions that have been flexible that have survived the changes of history. The inflexible have gone under and their institutions have perished" (198). Even though the story of the Matabele in *Wild Conquest* is one of defeat and tragedy, there is also a glimmer of hope for a better future for the indigenous people of southern Africa. Mzilikazi has learned something as a result of the defeat, and his decision to move his people to safer ground across the Limpopo reflects a new reliance upon strategy and cunning, as taught by Moshesh. Dabula, too, has adapted and gained strength in the face of adversity. The preservation of the social unity of the Matabele is symbolized in the final view of Dabula walking northward with his son on one arm, the king's son on the other, and Ntombi beside him carrying their baby. Thus, the loss of Inzwinyani is depicted as a temporary setback; the people must now face their "new day." *Wild Conquest* ends in a time of transition: we see the Matabele in the process of moving from the tribal past into the technological present. The Boers on their Great Trek are the harbingers of the new technology, symbolized by their rifles and their covered wagons. But, without any concern for human values, the new technology is an empty thing indeed.

In *Wild Conquest*, Abrahams implies that the South African future will be problematic for both whites and blacks. Although the Boers conquer the Matabele and take their land, Abrahams shows that the long-term effects of such "victories" are sometimes disastrous for the winners as well as the losers. The Matabele appear beaten, but Abrahams suggests that they are not yet defeated. Women will play a key role in the South African future, the author implies, for in *Wild Conquest*, women symbolize the human values which Abrahams sees as essential to a culture's preservation. Mzilikazi and his people are made whole again by the symbolic return of Mnandi, the queen. The Boers, by contrast, are left fragmented and emotionally crippled. The strained marriage of Kasper and Anna Jansen is never healed: Anna dies while giving birth to a son, symbolically perpetuating the hard, unfeeling male domination of the *voortrekkers*. Although it is not directly stated, Abrahams seems to suggest here that if there is to be a future based on equality and justice for South Africa, perhaps it will come as a result of the humanizing influence of the Africans upon the Afrikaners. In the pessimistic progression of Abrahams' narrative, however, the South African future is at best uncertain. Any hope for the future lies in the question of whether or not both sides can overcome the mutual hatred, suspicion, and intolerance which have grown out of their problematic and tumultuous history.

Chapter III
The Cultural Clash: Joyce Cary and Chinua Achebe

Joyce Cary's *Mister Johnson*

Joyce Cary came to Nigeria as a colonial official at the age of twenty-six. Besides a brief stint in the British Red Cross, his administrative position in the Nigerian Service was his first steady job. He was born in Londonderry, Ireland in 1888, the first of two sons of a prominent Anglo-Irish family. Cary's father, a consulting engineer who helped lay out the Indian Railway, came from an old land-owning family which was among those ruined by Gladstone's Irish Land Act of 1882. When Cary was still a young boy, his father moved the family to London, and thereafter England became their home. Early in his life, Cary showed an interest in painting. At the age of seventeen, he spent a year in Paris studying art, and the following year continued his studies at the School of Art in Edinburgh. Cary soon decided, however, that his talents lay in writing instead of painting. In 1909, he entered Oxford to study law as a preparation for a writing career, and graduated four years later, earning a disappointingly low Class Four. In 1913, after a brief period working for the British Red Cross in the Balkan War in Montenegro, Cary entered the Nigerian Service as an administrative officer.

Although indispensable for his later artistic development, Cary's six years in Nigeria were not particularly happy ones. He was posted in northern Nigeria, a predominantly Muslim, relatively rural, isolated part of the country. Shortly after reaching his post, World War I broke out and Cary was called upon to take part in the Cameroons Campaign against the Germans. He was wounded a year later and sent home. During his home leave, in 1916, Cary married Gertrude Ogilvie, and a year later, a baby son was born. After this point, his time in Nigeria became increasingly difficult due to the strain caused by the separation from his wife and child.

While in Nigeria, Cary constantly absorbed material he would later use in his four "African novels." One of Cary's duties as a District Officer, like that of Rudbeck in *Mister Johnson*, was making new roads; and, like his fictional character, he encountered numerous difficulties between the planning and building stages. He was called upon as well to serve as judge in the more important district judicial cases. At this time, Cary's assistant was a Nigerian named Musa, whom a fellow D.O. once described as an "old rogue, whom one couldn't trust but at the same time couldn't help liking" (Foster, 144). Later, Cary not only dedicated *Mister Johnson* to Musa, but also patterned his fictional clerk after him.

Cary's interest in Nigeria and Africa continued throughout his life. During his first ten years back in England, Cary was only able to publish a handful of stories, but after this point, he produced a steady succession of novels. Between 1932 and 1939, Cary wrote his four "African novels": *Aissa Saved* (1932), *An American Visitor* (1933), *The African Witch* (1936), and *Mister Johnson* (1939). With the publication of *Mister Johnson*, the last and best of his fiction set in Africa, he began to attract critical attention. After this point, Cary's continuing interest in Africa was expressed in numerous published articles, two works of non-fiction, and one film. In 1941, he wrote *The Case for African Freedom*, a non-fictional account of Britain's colonization of Africa, commissioned by the Liberal Book Club, and in 1942, he was commissioned by the Ministry of Information to write the script for a film on Africa.

Cary's work on this wartime film, which he entitled *Men of Two Worlds*, enabled him to return to Africa, and to get his first view of Nigeria after an absence of twenty years. During this trip, he also visited Sierra Leone (where he met Graham Greene), Uganda and Tanganyika. Cary enjoyed southern Nigeria, especially the chaotic street life of Lagos which he described as an example of "individual freedom getting its head loose and throwing out its front legs" (Mahood, *JCA*, 72). He was less impressed by what he saw in northern Nigeria where he had lived and worked over twenty years before:

> Of course, it has schools and hospitals, all very nice and clean and useful, but the real life of the people is still almost untouched. They jog along in the twelfth century, or thereabouts, an anachronism (Mahood, *JCA*, 72).

In 1946, Cary focused on West Africa and the history of Britain's involvement there in another non-fictional work, *Britain and West Africa*. Although he published over a dozen novels in a writing career which spanned twenty-five years, Cary today is probably most remembered for the Gulley Jimson trilogy, which includes *The Horse's Mouth* (1944), and the last of his "African novels," *Mister Johnson*. Cary died at his home in Oxford in 1957.

Cary's view of Nigeria in *Mister Johnson* is neither as affectionate as Kipling's view of India in *Kim* nor as romantic as Haggard's view of southern Africa in *King Solomon's Mines*. Perhaps the timing and nature of Cary's personal experience as a colonial officer in Nigeria from 1914 to 1920 is partly responsible for this difference in view. In *Kim*, Kim's wonder and joy in India represent Kipling's own childhood response to India and his early happiness and sense of magical security there. Similarly, the feelings of heroism, adventure, and escape Haggard experienced as a young man on the frontier of southern Africa are expressed in *King Solomon's Mines*. Cary, by contrast, came to Nigeria during a less romantic time, just before World War One, and in a position of authority, as a colonial administrator. His perception of a Nigeria in transition, under the guiding hand of an England experiencing grave problems of its own, is evident in *Mister Johnson* (1939). It is important to remember, too, that Cary's experience came much later than Kipling's or Haggard's. By the time *Mister Johnson* was published, India was less than a decade away from gaining its independence, and African countries would quickly follow suit. The uncertainty and self-questioning of the British imperialist endeavor are apparent in Cary's free criticism and undercutting of his British characters and in his portrayal of them as less than heroic. In many ways, however, Cary upheld the same paternalistic ideals and belief in the British Empire as Kipling; and though he might criticize his fictional colonial officers in the Nigerian Service, he also expressed faith in their good works and in their positive effect on Nigeria.

In Cary's writing, we get a more retrospective, less confident view of the Empire than in the writing of Kipling or Haggard. Due to developments in the colonies and the two world wars, national opinion in England about the Empire had gone through a great change. By 1946, many former officials in the Nigerian Service, such as Cary, looked back on the policy of indirect rule as largely ineffective, and they were put on the defensive about what tangible results their colonial management of Nigeria could show. Although Cary felt compelled by the times and the recent lessons of history to grant the Empire's imperfections, he also defended Britain's imperialism by recalling the old Kiplingesque values of responsibility and duty. In *Britain and West Africa*, Cary wrote:

> Talk of the white man's burden is now a joke. Probably it is good that it should be a joke, for it was too easily used to cover a mean complacence and to breed that hypocrisy which of all vices most quickly corrupts a nation. But the responsibility of Britain towards her dependents was not a joke to the Whigs who impeached Hastings; to the men who fought the slave trade; to the Church people who have always supported the missions; nor to a thousand humble officials in the British service whose duty, as they were taught, was to the African people (*CFAF*, 176)

In much of Cary's writing about Africa, we sense a defensiveness, which might be seen as a reaction to the growing nationalist movement and the demand for self-rule in the colonies at that time. In *The Case for African Freedom*, for instance, Cary draws an analogy between Gandhi and Hitler. Both men, he claimed, "think the world has gone backwards from a golden age in the past, when manners and morals were simpler, nobler, when Adam delved and Eve span" (37).

One of the strengths of *Mister Johnson* is Cary's use of the present tense to evoke the immediacy and non-stop fluidity of life. Indeed, as one critic has remarked, at times this narrative "sings" (Roby, 29). Cary describes Johnson in the novel's preface as a "poet," and he endows the clerk with a creative, artistic sensibility evident in his singing and dancing, his appreciation of beauty, and his capacity to revel in the immediacy of life. As the narrator tells us:

> To [Johnson], Africa is simply perpetual experience, exciting, amusing, alarming or delightful, which he soaks into himself through all his five senses at once, and produces again in the form of reflections, comments, songs, jokes, all in the pure Johnsonian form (112).

Clerk Johnson is also a comic character. Indeed, sometimes we must wonder whether we are laughing *with* Johnson or *at* him. Johnson's use of pidgin English, for instance, which contrasts humorously with the standard English of the narrator and the British characters, is an important component of his function as a comic character in this narrative.

We might say that *Mister Johnson* is about the rise and fall of an extraordinary man, for certainly Johnson is presented as extraordinary in the novel. *Mister Johnson* is like a *Bildungsroman* which becomes frustrated, for Johnson never actually learns anything about himself or his position in the colonial world which is represented in this narrative. Johnson, in fact, is like an innocent who never quite gains initiation into adulthood. Although he appears to be on the verge of learning an important lesson about life which would lead to self-realization, he meets his untimely end before he is able to put this lesson to practical use.

Mister Johnson is almost unique in British colonial fiction for the unusually large role given to a native character. Despite the novel's title, however, Johnson does not exclusively dominate the narrative: Rudbeck, the British District Officer, is actually more of a central consciousness than Johnson in Cary's third-person, omniscient narrative. We frequently share Rudbeck's thoughts, for instance, whereas we usually observe Johnson from the outside, as if, in fact, we were a member of the British administrative staff. The implication is that Johnson has no thoughts to share. Rudbeck thinks, Johnson performs. Johnson is a man of spontaneity who acts rather than reflects. And his unreflective nature is an important part of the novel's structure as a frustrated *Bildungsroman*. Johnson's carefree spontaneity and his stereotypic African reliance upon instinct eventually fail him when he finds himself caught between two powerful, merciless forces, the Emir and the British colonial government.

The action of the novel takes place around the 1920s, by which point the presence of the British has already had a considerable impact upon traditional Nigerian culture and society. The narrator informs us that the Fada district was the "scene of the desperate battle between the Emir's rearguard and the British forces in 1906" (15); and the early political struggles between the British and the Emir appear to have had a deleterious effect on the village itself. We see Fada in a time of transition, and its future stability and welfare seem to hang in the balance. The village is in a chaotic state, and appears to be going through a gradual process of falling apart. The quarters of the Waziri, the second most powerful man in the Emirate, for example, are "exactly like those of any poor laborer in Fada, a confusion of huts scattered without order, some new, some ruinous" (89). Johnson's compound is described as "three broken huts among a mass of scrub and weed. One has no roof; the second has lost a wall and . . . the third and largest has an immense hole in its rotten thatch" (9-10). The administrative office, where "the Fada typewriter is, as usual, out of order" (14), is in a similar state of disrepair. The office clock, an important indicator of efficiency in the colonial bureaucracy, "appears to have stopped some weeks ago—there is an ants' nest in the works" (136).

Although the colonial administration in Fada seems self-absorbed and out of touch with the villagers, the Emir's rule is certainly no better. The Emir himself never actually appears in the novel, but he is represented by the Waziri, a homosexual who is always accompanied by his favorite young boy, Saleh. Undoubtedly, the reader gets the impression that the Emir and Waziri, who are likened to "a corrupt swindler and petty tyrant" (184), are backward and oppressive, more interested in maintaining their rule than in the welfare of the village. The Emir and Waziri are opposed to the colonial government's project of building a district road, for instance, because it poses a threat to their authority. In a conversation between the Waziri and Johnson, we see two opposing views of the projected Fada Road:

> "I won't be surprised," Waziri says, "I know what your road will do—I've seen it before—everything turned upside down, and all for nothing."
>
> Johnson laughs at this pessimism. "You are not civilized, Waziri. You don't understand that people must have roads for motors."
>
> "Why, lord Johnson?"
>
> "Because it is civilized. Soon everyone will be civilized." (102)

Throughout the novel, these two views are in conflict, and to a certain extent, both views are vindicated. Johnson superficially advocates the building of the road in the name of "civilization," but in a real sense, Johnson is an individual caught between the corrupt traditional Emirate rule and the civilizing enterprise of the colonial government.

The villagers of Fada are portrayed as mired in inertia, a backward and ignorant people mindlessly willing to follow any leader, whether it is the oppressive Emir or the British colonial government, which longs to move the people forward into the twentieth century. Indeed, the narrator describes the backwardness of the Fada people in no uncertain terms:

> Fada is the ordinary native town of the Western Sudan. It has no beauty, convenience, or health. It is a dwelling-place at one stage from the rabbit warren or the badger burrow; and not so cleanly kept as the latter. . . . [The villagers] live like mice or rats in a palace floor; all the magnificence and variety of the arts, the ideas, the learning and the battles of civilization go on over their heads and they do not even imagine them. (121)

The people are seen here as animalistic and savage, like Haggard's Kukuana in *King Solomon's Mines*, but the possibility of change for the Fada villagers seems to exist. They are backward, but with the help of the British colonial government, they can move out from under the shadow of the Emir's stifling rule. Even though "poverty and ignorance, the absolute government of jealous savages . . . have kept [the villagers] at the first frontier of civilization" (121), they can still climb Cary's implicit ladder of human progress. Clearly, as Cary sets up the paradigm, the Emir's tribal rule is stagnant and boring, whereas the British colonial government holds out the possibility of change and progress. In *The Case for African Freedom*, Cary makes explicit his scorn for African "tribal life":

> It struck me that the tribal native is often extremely bored with tribal life. He finds the same attraction as Europeans in change and discovery; above all, in new freedom, even that small amount to be bought for a wage of sixpence a day. (38)

Johnson's rise and fall is bound up with Cary's portrayal of African society as backward and corrupt. Not only does the clerk's lack of "civilization" block him from gaining entrance into the colonial administration, but Johnson also becomes mired in the corruption which seems endemic in African society. Johnson is often described as "child-like," and as this description suggests, he is unable to exercise financial responsibility. As the narrator tells us, Johnson's financial difficulties are linked with his grandiose conception of his position as government clerk:

> [Johnson] gives parties every night and he seems to think that a man in his important position, a third-class government clerk, is obliged to entertain on the grandest scale, with drums and smuggled gin. (8)

Living beyond his means makes Johnson an easy mark for a bribe from the Waziri. The Waziri attempts to bribe Johnson twice, offering to pay off the clerk's mounting debts in return for access to Rudbeck's confidential staff reports. The first time, Johnson's idealization of the British Empire leads him to refuse the bribe, and he calls the Waziri a "damn rascal" (34). Later, however, he gladly accepts the bribe. As the clerk confides to Ajali, "I think I be damn rascal too" (80). By accepting the bribe, Johnson becomes a political pawn of the corrupt Waziri, but the naive clerk never seems to realize the serious implications of his act. He remains light-hearted and carefree.

Johnson's character is in large part conveyed through his relationship with Rudbeck, the District Officer who is his supervisor. The narrator describes their relationship in terms of a devotee worshipping an idol. "Like other devotees, [Johnson] cannot know too much, however trivial, about his idol" (63). Also, like that between devotee and idol, the relationship between Johnson and Rudbeck is completely one-sided: it is all in Johnson's mind. Whereas Johnson regards Rudbeck as his benefactor—the key to his entrance into the white ruling class—Rudbeck takes scarcely any notice at all of his clerk. Unlike Blore, Rudbeck's predecessor, who held a low opinion of Johnson and wanted to prosecute him for not paying off his many debts, Rudbeck is too absorbed in his pet project of building the Fada Road to worry about his clerk's petty debts, although as the narrative develops, Rudbeck pays increasing attention to Johnson.

Rudbeck's view of Johnson is affected by the influence of his British associates who take a negative view of the clerk. When Rudbeck arrives to take over administrative control of the Fada station, Blore, his predecessor, gives him a brief orientation, including a tip that the clerk is "the worst type—probably dangerous, too—a complete imbecile, but quite capable of robbing the safe" (18).

Rudbeck's wife, Celia, also influences her husband's opinion of Johnson. When Celia comes to Nigeria to join her husband, several months after his transfer to Fada, she imports the British tourist mentality along with her. As a matter of routine, Rudbeck asks Johnson to show her around Fada, and Celia reacts to everything Johnson shows her as if by formula—it's all either "nice" or "wonderful." For Johnson, Celia represents the "civilized lady" he would like his wife, Bamu, to become. Serving as Mrs. Rudbeck's guide on her tour of the village lifts the naive Johnson into a state of euphoria:

> Johnson, . . . full of pride and good nature, grins at every passer-by and shouts the warmest Hausa greetings, "Hail—God go with you." The more he swaggers the more he is charmed by all these nice people in this nice world; the nice trees and the nice sky, the nice sun. The very curl of his hat is a gesture of universal appreciation. He is full of gratitude to the whole world. (126)

Mrs. Rudbeck refers to Johnson as "Wog," at first privately, as part of a joke she shares with her husband, but later openly as well. Soon her husband also unconsciously uses the new name. When Johnson returns to Fada after his trip to the south, Rudbeck greets him with, "It's Wog—I mean Johnson" (186). Celia's effect on her husband is thus to remind him of the separation between the civilized world of England and the savage world of Africa. Clearly Celia represents the worst side of the Empire: the underlying contempt for the subject peoples. After Celia's joking references to Johnson, the unimaginative Rudbeck pays more attention to the clerk, "trying to see what deep truth about Johnson his clever wife has discovered and revealed . . . in the single word 'Wog'" (126).

It is only after Johnson rallies the road crew and spurs the surprising progress on the Fada Road that Rudbeck begins to see his clerk in a new light. Rudbeck does extensive paper-work in planning the Fada Road, but encounters obstacles when he attempts to put the plan into practice. Few villagers understand or share Rudbeck's enthusiasm for road-building, and thus the District Officer is unable to recruit a labor force. To make matters worse, it is the end of the harvest season, and most able males are occupied in annual celebrations. Johnson, however, is able to improvise a solution to Rudbeck's problem, as the narrator explains:

> Johnson has no special interest in roads, but he is as sharp as a sharp child to know what pleases Rudbeck. His enthusiasm throws out new ideas every second.
>
> "Oh, sah, we make it easy. You tell people new road make dem rich—dey do it for nutting."
>
> "Catch them—I've tried it."
>
> "Oh, sah, I tink perhaps if you make it like game for dem—get plenty drums, give dem plenty beer. Dis pagan people like game." (67)

Using this simple plan, Johnson quickly recruits an impressive road crew with the beat of drums and the promise of beer. Rudbeck, at this point, is sceptical about getting much done before the arrival of the seasonal rains, but the road crew makes surprising progress, spurred on by Johnson's singing:

> Bow down, you king of cotton trees;
> Put your green heads in the dust;
> Salute the road men of Rudbeck,
> Here come the motors, foot, foot, whang
> Full of beer and salt,
> Out of our way, this is the king road.
> Where he flies, the great trees fall
> The sun and moon are walking on our road.
> (188-89)

In the completion of the Fada Road, the narrative reaches a pinnacle. Johnson is shown to be completely absorbed in the act of creation, experiencing the "music, noise, the movement of the work, the approbation and nearness of Rudbeck and Rudbeck's triumph, which is his own" (p. 205). Not only does Johnson, driven by his devotion to Rudbeck, reach a personal high point in the narrative, but also the relationship between Johnson and Rudbeck attains an unprecedented level of mutual appreciation and understanding. When Bulteel, the

British Resident, comes to inspect the first fifty miles of work on the road and to congratulate Rudbeck, the latter nods toward Johnson: "Here's the chap who does it. . . . He's the man with the ideas" (189). Johnson can only laugh, and Rudbeck, too, is "surprised by his own remark":

> [Rudbeck] gazes at Johnson thoughtfully as if trying to get a new conception of him. Then he gives a snort of laughter, which means that the accepted idea will have to do for the present, and says, "He keeps us all merry and bright." (189)

Rudbeck here seems to acknowledge Johnson's humanity for the first time, and to appreciate the "power of Johnson's character" (257), as the narrator puts it. Ironically, Rudbeck's recognition of Johnson comes only after the clerk helps bring about the realization of the D.O.'s pet project. To gain perspective on this road-building episode, we might recall Fanon's assertion in *The Wretched of the Earth* that "hostile nature, obstinate and fundamentally rebellious, is . . . represented in the colonies by the bush, by mosquitoes, natives, and fever, and colonization is a success when all this indocile nature has finally been tamed" (250). Cary undoubtedly criticizes the British Empire here for its concentration on "tangible" progress to the exclusion of an appreciation for the humanity of the colonized people. Although Rudbeck would seem to be the representative impersonal colonizer in this case, he nevertheless demonstrates his humanity toward the end of the novel in his increasing concern for Johnson's welfare and in his disillusionment with the British imperial mission which he serves.

For the villagers, the road is portrayed as a breakthrough into a new world. As the narrator tells us, the villagers "have taken the first essential step out of the world of the tribe into the world of men" (203). A great change has been brought about, even though the African workmen have "no idea of its beginning or end":

> They are still like men brought up on a forgotten island far from ship routes, to whom the rest of the world is as much a mystery, a blank inhabited by monsters, as to their ancestors of the old Stone Age. They do not even imagine it. (207)

Johnson, too, seems to have little idea or concern about the significance of his achievement. Unlike Rudbeck who, following the realization of his dream of completing the Fada Road, "gives a sigh, taps his pipe with his thumb, and slowly makes his way toward a boring duty" (216), Johnson remains ever active. His inability to manage his limited finances and his penchant for giving parties leads him to charge an illegal fee of all those using the new road. Once Rudbeck finds this out, all his old doubts about Johnson, including Blore's early warning, return, as we see in his brief conversation with Celia:

> "It's just what Blore told me to expect—
> "Yes, I'm afraid poor Wog was always a bit of a bad egg—the only thing was, he looked so honest—"
> "Of course he did—he's been at it for years." (221)

Johnson, on the other hand, is confused and then angry at the injustice of Rudbeck who orders him to "clear out quick" (223). After this point, Johnson is transformed into an agent of destruction as he enters a downward spiral of frustration and desperation which ends only when he kills Sargy Gollup.

In a comment on the post-colonial poets of *negritude*, Frantz Fanon said:

> The unconditional affirmation of African culture has succeeded the unconditional affirmation of European culture. On the whole, the poets of *negritude* oppose the idea of an old Europe to a young Africa, tiresome reasoning to lyricism, oppressive logic to high-stepping nature, and on the one side stiffness, ceremony, etiquette, and scepticism while on the other, frankness, liveliness, liberty, and—why not?—luxuriance: but also irresponsibility. (212-213)

The duality Fanon describes here corresponds very closely to that created by Cary in *Mister Johnson*. In Johnson's singing and dancing and in his rallying of labor support from the villages with the beat of drums and the promise of beer, in his parties and elaborately embellished stories, we see African "lyricism," "high-stepping nature," and "liveliness," but in Johnson's inability to hold onto his job and in his perennial carefree indebtedness, we see the other side of the coin, African "irresponsibility." Similarly, the British in the novel are very much as Fanon suggests: Rudbeck's "tiresome reasoning" in planning his road and his "scepticism" that the plan can ever be enacted. In his role as D.O., however, Rudbeck demonstrates a reassuringly rational sense of responsibility and faith in the British work ethic. In *Mister Johnson*, Cary puts forth the two world theory in his colonialist view of Africa and Europe which, like Kipling's East and West, shall never meet. British civilization is held up as the model for the colonies, but, as the case of Mister Johnson shows us, the British model was not always an easy one to emulate.

The notion of Africa as a young, carefree, irresponsible culture and of England as an old, mature, responsible civilization is not a new one in British fiction set in West Africa. G. A. Henty's *Through Three Campaigns* (1903), part of which describes the Ashanti rebellion against the British in the so-called Golden Stool War of 1900-01, relates how the British troops had to teach the childish, unruly Ashanti a lesson so as to allow for civilization to make an inroad into the "dark continent." The notion of a young Africa and an old Europe is also clearly visible in *Mister Johnson* in the relationship of "dat fool chile" Johnson and the older, more mature Rudbeck. In *The Heart of the Matter* (1948), which is set in a fictitious West African country under British colonization, Graham Greene writes of an Africa where "human nature hasn't had time to disguise itself" (31), where one can openly witness "the injustices, the cruelties, the meanness that elsewhere people so cleverly hushed up" (31). Greene's main character, the colonial police chief Scobie, emerges as a sympathetic character despite his faults: a man who is responsible and mature, much like Cary's Rudbeck. Scobie is burdened by the "feeling of responsibility that I've always carried about like a sack of bricks. I'm not a policeman for nothing—responsible for order, for seeing justice is done" (305). Like Rudbeck, Scobie is guilt-ridden, but finally admirable in his willingness to accept responsibility for the dependent, child-like people of the colony.

The devoted but incompetent native servant is perhaps one of the most prevalent African stereotypes in British fiction set in West Africa. Not only do we usually see the African in British fiction in the lowly role of servant or underling, but often he is shown to be lazy, incompetent, and untrustworthy. Johnson is, of course, in part a perpetuation of this stereotype. Scobie's servant boy, Ali, in Greene's *The Heart of the Matter*, a novel more notable for the almost total absence of African characters than for their presence, is a similarly stereotypic figure. Although Ali appears honest and trustworthy early in the novel, Scobie later suspects his servant boy has betrayed him and he comes to believe in "the stale coast wisdom of the traders and the remittance man . . . 'Never trust a black. They'll let you down in the end'" (279). In a more recent novel, *A Good Man in Africa* (1981), by William Boyd, a British writer who was born in Ghana and has lived in Nigeria, most of the African characters are again cast in the role of servants. In this novel set in a fictitious West African country, Morgan Leafy carries out his duties for the British Embassy despite his African servants who are portrayed as constantly taking advantage of him. Leafy has no illusions about what Moses and Friday will do when he is not there to watch over them: "they'll just watch my television, eat my food and drink my booze" (41). The message about African servants in British colonial fiction—that they cannot be expected to carry out their job in a responsible manner—serves as an implicit justification of the British civilizing mission, even when, as in Cary's *Mister Johnson*, that mission is simultaneously questioned.

True to this stereotype, Johnson is untrustworthy and irresponsible. He continually throws parties and then steals from his master in order to pay for them. Johnson is portrayed as a creature of impulse. It is totally out of his character either to reflect on the past or to consider the future. Thus, Johnson is in a sense chained to the present, condemned continually to face the consequences of his actions for which he is unprepared. After Rudbeck fires him for collecting the illegal road fee, Johnson sees his illusion of being an "English gentleman" shattered. As he leaves Fada with his family, he angrily shouts in the direction of Rudbeck's bungalow: "I don' bless you, Mister Rudbeck. I don' say good-by and I don' bless you now. My heart is not kind to you now" (226). Here we might expect Johnson to have finally rebelled, like Toundi in Ferdinand Oyono's *Houseboy*, but such is not the case. As we see in the novel's ending, Johnson's idealization of Rudbeck and England remains strong, despite his temporary anger.

Losing his lowly clerical job in the colonial administration indeed spells disaster for Johnson: his entire life begins to fall apart. His wife, Bamu, senses trouble and leaves him. When he goes to the Waziri for help, the latter, who no longer needs Johnson now that he has lost his government job, refuses, ordering his men to give Johnson a physical beating. After this point, the impulsive clerk, turning desperate, reverts to throwing a continuous string of wild, drunken parties. When Benjamin, a fellow villager, asks Johnson how he will finance his extravagant parties, the clerk unthinkingly answers that he will steal money from Sargy Gollup's store. Benjamin, horrified, tries unsuccessfully to convince Johnson that stealing goes against the clerk's cherished idea of "civilization":

> "But, Johnson, if all people did so—there would be robbery on every hand—there would be nothing but bad trouble everywhere. There would be no civilization possible." (248)

This undoubtedly is Cary's point. Johnson desires to be a part of the colonial administration and to take part in what he calls "civilization," but he has only a superficial idea of what it means to be "civilized." Johnson—and by implication the other Nigerians as well—is simply not yet ready to accept the serious responsibility required in the administration of the country. Although a natural improviser, he remains incomplete, naive, irresponsible, too wild. Clearly, on one level, Cary admires Johnson for his creativity and spontaneity—qualities of the artist figure which Gulley Jimson also exhibits in *The Horse's Mouth*; ultimately, however, Johnson is little different from Haggard's Kukuana: a man of instinct who lacks the ability to think.

Cary once said of his real-life Nigerian clerk, Musa, who, like Johnson, also proved untrustworthy and accepted a bribe: "His feelings were shallow" (*CFAF*, 21). Indeed, we might say that shallowness is the root cause of many of Johnson's difficulties as well. Having failed to enter the colonial government, i.e. "civilization," Johnson "reverts to the primitive tribal pattern," as V. S. Pritchett has explained it (Cary, *MJ*, xv). Johnson has no choice but to steal money from Sargy Gollup, the retired British soldier, to pay for his parties, and when Gollup catches him, Johnson instinctively kills him with a knife. Just as the British Gollup, when drunk, comes "down" to the Africans' level—"he ceases to calculate and to reason, he wants to sing, to love, to talk, and to tell stories" (160)—so Johnson finally reverts to the stereotypic African reliance upon instinctive violence in order to survive. After murdering the Englishman, Johnson's final and most serious mistake, he is transformed into a hunted animal, a creature preyed upon by his former allies—the Waziri, the British colonial government, and his wife—who join forces against him.

In *The Wretched of the Earth*, Frantz Fanon writes:

> Because of a systematic negation of the other person and a furious determination to deny the other person all attributes of humanity, colonialism forces the people it dominates to ask themselves the question constantly: "In reality, who am I?" (250)

The answer to this question is the goal toward which a *Bildungsroman* moves. *Mister Johnson* never reaches that goal, however, because Johnson never questions who he is. Johnson is a powerless, impressionable African youth who has clearly been affected by the colonial presence in his country to the extent that he tries to deny his own identity by creating a glorious fantasy of himself as a member of the colonial elite. Early in the novel, we get a hint that Johnson might learn a lesson about himself. His wife leaves him, and Johnson goes to the Waziri and asks him to intercede. The Waziri helps Johnson regain Bamu, and then gives him a simple reminder, "You have to take care" (147). In the novel's ending, Johnson sits in jail, awaiting his execution at the hands of Rudbeck, and is suddenly shocked to find Saleh, the Waziri's former young boyfriend, beaten and tattered, also in jail. Saleh explains to Johnson how the Waziri found a new boy and had Saleh beaten and imprisoned on fabricated charges. Johnson, as if suddenly enlightened, remembers what the Waziri told him earlier. After Saleh leaves, Johnson turns to two Fulani prisoners, sitting nearby:

> "That boy was a most influential person—the Waziri's best friend—he had great power, and now, poor chap, well, you saw him. It makes you think, friends. . . . It makes you think that a chap has to look out for himself—yes, you've got to be careful." (260)

Johnson here seems to have finally learned one of life's rudimentary lessons: that the world can be a dangerous place, and that one must be careful. But Johnson's realization, and indeed his newfound ability to think and reflect upon his experience, comes too late to be of any use.

Johnson's main shortcoming is an inability to adapt in a changing society. To the native clerk, "civilization" is only an impressive-sounding word: he has no idea what the word means. Moreover, Johnson's instrumental role in completing the Fada Road comes as a result of his devotion to Rudbeck, not his conscious desire to bring about progress in Fada. Although Cary avoids an overly facile equating of progress with the new Fada Road, which is described as a "great raw cut extending through the forest as far as the eye can reach" (212), he clearly sees the road as a positive step for the isolated village. Actually, it is Johnson who makes the overly simplistic equation of the completion of the road with the gaining of "civilization." Rudbeck, in contrast, expresses worry about what effect the road will have on the village: "Could it be that dirty old savages like the Emir and Waziri were right in their detestation of motor roads; that roads upset things, brought confusion, revolution. And wasn't there confusion enough?" (212) And, later, in a surprising twist in the narrative, the road itself suddenly addresses the concerned Rudbeck:

> "I'm smashing up the old Fada—I shall change everything and everybody in it. . . . I destroy and I make new. What are you going to do about it? I am your idea. You made me, so I suppose you know." (215)

The road's question is never answered, as Cary mirrors the uncertainty and lack of conviction in the British imperialist cause during the 1920s and 30s. Rudbeck is filled with self-doubt, not only about the road but also about the execution of Johnson, but he emerges, paradoxically, as a more admirable character as a result of his self-questioning. In only a slight overstatement, JanMohamed has said that despite Cary's criticism of colonial society, the real heroes of his African novels are the district officers like Rudbeck, who appear "blameless, virtuous, good samaritans . . . pure and enlightened" (43). Cary implies that although the old, nineteenth-century certainties about human progress and civilization are now gone,

one must still make difficult decisions and accept responsibility for their out come; and this is exactly what Rudbeck does and what Johnson fails to do.

Cary is aware of the shortcomings of colonialism, and *Mister Johnson* offers a more retrospective view of that historical phenomenon, the British Empire, than the Indian fiction of Kipling, for instance. Nevertheless, Cary's attitude is quite similar to Kipling's in several ways. Like Kipling's India, Cary's Nigeria is a frequently bewildering, almost laughable chaos where little if anything constructive ever gets accomplished. In both *Kim* and *Mister Johnson*, we see the working out of the Western notion which Forster in *A Passage to India* calls "the celebrated Oriental confusion" (130). Neither Kipling nor Cary believed in the capacity of Third World people to bring about change on their own or to assume responsibility for themselves. Both believed that in order to progress in the onward march of civilization, Third World countries like India and Nigeria needed the help of European countries like England. Indeed, in *The Case for African Freedom*, Cary states unequivocally that "European conquest, with all its faults, has brought incomparably more good than harm to Africa" (19). Because of the moment in history in which he wrote, Cary was forced to see more of the imperfections of the Empire than Kipling, but he nevertheless finally saw the Empire very much as did Kipling: a positive, self-sacrificing venture which would ultimately bring light to the darkness of the Third World.

Chinua Achebe's *Things Fall Apart*

Chinua Achebe was born in 1930 in Ogidi in eastern Nigeria. The fifth of six children of devout Christian parents, Achebe was christened Albert Chinualomogo, but changed his name while a university student. Achebe has described his upbringing as being "at the crossroads of cultures," which gave him dual exposure to European education and traditional African culture (*MYOCD*, 98). His first language was Ibo, but by the age of eight he began to receive standard instruction in English at school, which he continued at Umuahia Government College and at the University College of Ibadan, where he originally intended to go into medicine but decided to study literature instead. Even though he was raised in the Christian church and received an education along English lines, Achebe felt a strong attraction toward indigenous African religion and customs. The distance his Christian parents imposed between Achebe and traditional Ibo life and ritual did not, he says, become a separation but a "bringing together like the necessary backward step which a judicious viewer may take in order to see a canvas steadily and fully" (*MYOCD*, 99).

As a university student in Ibadan, Achebe studied English literature, including the fiction of Conrad, Cary, and Greene dealing with Africa. At this time, Achebe began to write fiction, and he became fascinated by the history of his country and of his family. Achebe found himself especially interested in his father's maternal grandfather, who in his day had taken every title of the clan but one and had provided the village with a great feast still talked about in Achebe's day. The first missionaries in Ogidi were said to have come to see his great grandfather, and though he at first tolerated them, he later bade them leave. It seems likely that Achebe used his great grandfather as a model for the now well-known character Okonkwo in his first novel, *Things Fall Apart* (1958), begun while he was a student at Ibadan. Achebe has described *Things Fall Apart* as "an act of atonement with my past, the ritual return and homage of a prodigal son" (*MYOCD*, 102). His first novel was not only an outgrowth of Achebe's interest in African history, but also a product of his reading of the "African fiction" of British writers like Joyce Cary. This background gave rise to a desire to portray African culture and people from a sympathetic insider's perspective.

All of Achebe's fiction is informed by his upbringing at "the crossroads of cultures" and by the conflict between British colonialism and African traditional society, which played such an important role in Nigerian history. Following *Things Fall Apart*, Achebe wrote three novels in the next six years: *No Longer at Ease* (1960), which tells the story of Okonkwo's grandson Obi; *Arrow of God* (1964), which portrays British colonial rule in Nigeria and the tragedy of the priest Ezeulu; and *A Man of the People* (1966), about the post-independence difficulties many African countries experienced during the 1960s. In an essay, "The Novelist as Teacher," in the collection *Morning Yet On Creation Day* (1975), Achebe describes the role of the post-colonial writer as that of an educator and a leader who must not shy away from the political arena. According to Achebe, African writers must concern themselves with the problems of their people:

> The writer cannot be excused from the task of re-education and re-generation that must be done. In fact, he should march right in front. For he is after all . . . the sensitive point of his community (59).

While writing fiction, Achebe has continually involved himself in the ongoing political and social transformation of his country. In 1954, he began working for the Nigerian Broadcasting Corporation, and from 1960 to 1967, he was the Corporation's Director of External Broadcasting. During the Biafran War, Achebe served in the Biafran Ministry of Information, and journeyed to Europe and America to seek support for the Biafran cause. Since the war, he has been editor of *Okike*, a journal of new African writing. He has also traveled extensively in order to convey his stated interest in "universal human communication across racial and cultural boundaries as a means of fostering respect for all people" (Vinson, 15). In 1987, after a twenty-year period in which he wrote no novels, Achebe published his fifth novel, *Anthills of the Savannah*, a finalist for the Booker Prize. *Hopes and Impediments: Selected Essays* appeared in 1989. Throughout his career, Achebe has devoted himself to furthering the cause of his people and his nation. A mark of the positive effect of that career is the fact that today Achebe's novels, including *Things Fall Apart*, are standard reading for most schoolchildren throughout Africa.

Achebe has said in an essay, "The Role of the Writer in a New Nation":

> It is . . . dignity that many African people all but lost during the colonial period, and it is this that they must now regain. The worst thing that can happen to any people is the loss of their dignity and self-respect. The writer's duty is to help them regain it by showing them in human terms what happened to them, what they lost. There is a saying in Ibo that a man who can't tell where the rain began to beat him cannot know where he dried his body. The writer can tell the people where the rain began to beat them (Killam, 8).

Like a later West African writer, the Ghanaian Ayi Kwei Armah in *The Healers* (1979), Achebe in *Things Fall Apart* looks back to the pre-colonial history of his country to envision an intact African culture and to recover a sense of the communal traditions and customs of his people before they were altered by the coming of the white man. Not only is *Things Fall Apart* an act of homage toward Achebe's forefathers, it is also a heuristic experience for his fellow Africans. "I would be quite satisfied," Achebe writes in *Morning Yet On Creation Day*, "if my novels (especially the ones I set in the past) did no more than teach my readers that their past—with all its imperfections—was not one long night of savagery from which the first Europeans acting on God's behalf delivered them" (59).

Achebe has stated quite explicitly in essays and interviews that he first became interested in writing fiction as a result of reading British colonial fiction about Nigeria, in particular *Mister Johnson*. In *Morning Yet On Creation Day*, he states: "At the university I read some appalling novels about Africa (including Joyce Cary's much praised *Mister Johnson*) and decided that the story we had to tell could not be told for us by anyone else, no matter how gifted or well-intentioned" (102). Asked by Lewis Nkosi in a 1962 interview at what point in his career he first became interested in "writing as an art," Achebe returned to the same point:

> . . . around '51, '52, I was quite certain that I was going to try my hand at writing, and one of the things that set me thinking was Joyce Cary's novel set in Nigeria, *Mister Johnson*, which was praised so much, and it was clear to me that this was a most superficial picture of—not only of the country, but even of the Nigerian character and so I thought if this was famous, then perhaps someone ought to try and look at this from the inside. (Duerden and Pieterse, 4)

Achebe's first novel, *Things Fall Apart*, was thus originally conceptualized as a response to Cary: an insider's view of Nigeria to be juxtaposed with the outsider's appraisal in *Mister Johnson*. Achebe's strong reaction to *Mister Johnson* can be seen in his return to various elements in Cary's novel, not only in *Things Fall Apart*, but also in his later work, such as *Arrow of God*.

Things Fall Apart contains numerous parallels to *Mister Johnson*. Like Cary's novel, Achebe's work tells the story of the rise and fall of an extraordinary man, Okonkwo. The reader follows Okonkwo—as we follow Johnson in Cary's novel—from a point in his early manhood when he is in his teens, through his marriage and establishment in the community, to his untimely, tragic death when he is still a relatively young man. Thus, like *Mister Johnson*, *Things Fall Apart* is like a *Bildungsroman* that becomes frustrated. Okonkwo fails to realize the inevitable consequences of his increasingly problematic position between the traditional Ibo way of life and the new way represented by the missionaries and the British colonial government. Ultimately, Okonkwo, like Johnson, meets a tragic fate as a result of his contact with the white man: his inability to accept the consequences of the penetration of the British colonial government into his native

Ibo culture ultimately drives him to commit suicide.

Things Fall Apart is thus Achebe's rewriting of *Mister Johnson* in a way that more accurately reflects the Nigerian culture and national character. The many important parallels between Johnson and Okonkwo notwithstanding, there are also sharp, illuminating differences between the two characters. Cary's Johnson is an embodiment of the comic stereotype of the devoted but incompetent African servant, and his character is in large part portrayed through his inter-relations with the British A.D.O.'s, who are Johnson's superiors in the colonial administration. Johnson remains innocent and naive throughout Cary's narrative. He is an example of what Achebe calls "*simple natives*—houseboys, cooks, drivers, schoolchildren" who are often found in British colonial fiction set in Africa (*MYOCD*, 7). Although Okonkwo is similar to Johnson in that he fails to perceive his changing position in an evolving society, he is an independent, strong-willed man, fiercely determined to succeed in the traditional Ibo society, and is thus diametrically opposed to the happy-go-lucky, irresponsible Johnson. Okonkwo, like Johnson, has his shortcomings, but he is not innocent or naive in the "simple native" style. Okonkwo's main fault is a product of his chief virtue: his strong will and determination have made him stubborn and inflexible. As a result, Okonkwo is unable to adapt to the changes wrought by the British-Ibo cultural encounter.

The reader sees Okonkwo primarily through the eyes of his fellow villagers who function almost like the chorus in Greek tragedy. Achebe thus recreates Cary's basic story, but reverses the cultural perspective so that the reader sees the characters—both British and Nigerian—from the viewpoint of a Nigerian villager rather than a British colonial officer. Achebe's use of the Ibo communal pespective to comment upon the novel's action is significant in that it shows us a side of Nigerian society that we never see in *Mister Johnson*: the central role of the community as opposed to the individual in traditional Nigerian society. Achebe has said in an essay that a primary distinction of the African novel is "a consuming concern with community" which results, he believes, from "two things—the sense of a shared history and, even more important, of an assumed destiny" (*MYOCD*, 88). We can see a similar representation of communal mores and values in fiction by other West African writers, such as Amos Tutuola's *Palm Wine Drinkard* (1953), T. M. Aluko's *One Man, One Matchet* (1964), Wole Soyinka's *Season of Anomy* (1973), and Buchi Emecheta's *The Joys of Motherhood* (1979).

Achebe's third-person, omniscient narrative voice might easily be that of a village elder, familiar with the customs and beliefs of the Ibo people. The narrator takes a sympathetic insider's view of the tragic progress of Okonkwo and often conveys to the reader the communal perspective of the village "chorus" of elders. For instance, early in the novel, the narrator relates a village elder's view of Okonkwo's impressive rise to a position of esteem in the Ibo clan:

> "Looking at a king's mouth," said an old man, "one would think he never sucked at his mother's breast." He was talking about Okonkwo, who had risen so suddenly from great poverty and misfortune to be one of the lords of the clan. The old man bore no ill will towards Okonkwo. Indeed he respected him for his industry and success. But he was struck, as most people were, by Okonkwo's brusqueness in dealing with less successful men. (19)

Throughout *Things Fall Apart*, the Ibo elders comment on the novel's action and Okonkwo's character through proverbs. The elders' communal commentary thus enables the reader to understand Okonkwo's changing position within the clan.

In contrast to Western narratives, especially to *Mister Johnson* with its fast-paced, present-tense narrative, which one critic has described as "breathless," *Things Fall Apart* seems unhurried and drawn out, moving from the present to the past and back again (Innes, 31). In Part One, which spans half the novel, very little happens in terms of plot. Instead, Achebe uses Part One to acquaint the reader with Ibo society and to establish Okonkwo's important position in the clan. The narrator informs the reader that Okonkwo is "the greatest wrestler and warrior" (82) throughout the village and surrounding area, and thus it is not surprising that he would represent Umuofia in disputes with other villages. Early in the novel, Okonkwo travels to a neighboring village, Mbaino, to settle a dispute which arises when a woman of Umuofia is killed there. The dispute is settled peacefully and Okonkwo returns to Umuofia with a young boy, Ikemefuna, and a young virgin from Mbaino as compensation for the woman's death. In this episode, Okonkwo is not only the designated emissary of Umuofia, but he is also given the responsibility of raising the young boy as a member of his personal household. Okonkwo accepts this appointed role and brings up Ikemefuna as his own son. In Okonkwo's "adoption" of Ikemefuna, Achebe suggests the innate hospitality of the African extended family, its ability to absorb and care for new members, and its central role in African society. At the same time, Achebe also shows us a chief character trait of Okonkwo: his willing acceptance of familial and societal responsibility. Unlike Cary's Johnson, Okonkwo is shown to be an integral part of a meaningful social unit.

In *Things Fall Apart*, we see Okonkwo from inside the culture, as a family man and a lord of the clan, but we also see him from inside himself. Achebe goes further than simply giving us a sociological view of Okonkwo: we learn what motivates him and what makes him tick. Unlike the inscrutable, shadowy African characters we find in British colonial fiction, Okonkwo emerges in Achebe's novel as a complex human being, a man grappling with internal contradictions and anxieties, torn by conflicts never glimpsed from an outsider's view. Whereas Clerk Johnson is, in the words of C. L. Innes, "a man without roots, belonging to romance, rather than to historical narrative," Okonkwo is portrayed as the product of a coherent past and in the humanizing context of family (25).

Perhaps Okonkwo's most important personal relationship in the novel is with someone who has been dead for ten years: his father, Unoka. Through Achebe's relating of Okonkwo's problematic relationship with his father, we learn that, even though Okonkwo is a lord of the clan and appears to have a happy family life, all is not right with him. In fact, Okonkwo is insecure: he has a tough exterior, but a vulnerable, fearful interior. Ever since an incident in his childhood, when a playmate referred to Unoka as *agbala*, an Ibo term meaning woman or a man who has taken no titles, Okonkwo has been ashamed of his father. The narrator tells us that "Okonkwo did not have the start in life which many young men usually had. He did not inherit a barn from his father. There was no barn to inherit" (12). When Unoka died, he had not only taken no titles, but also left his family deep in debt. The narrator explains:

> In his day [Unoka] was lazy and improvident and was quite incapable of thinking about tomorrow. If any money came his way, and it seldom did, he immediately bought gourds of palm-wine, called round his neighbors and made merry. He always said that whenever he saw a dead man's mouth he saw the folly of not eating what one had in one's lifetime. (3)

Stories circulate in the village about Unoka, such as the time he went to the Oracle to discover why he failed as a farmer, and the priestess angrily sent him away, saying, "Go home and work like a man" (13). Furthermore, Unoka's death resulted from a particular type of stomach swelling which the Ibo consider an abomination to the earth goddess. Thus, he was never buried, but simply cast into the Evil Forest, a taboo area of the village inhabited by malevolent spirits.

The memory of "his father's contemptible life and shameful death" (13) serves as a powerful motivator for Okonkwo: he has a strong desire to succeed and to dissociate himself from Unoka. His effort to live down his father's infamous reputation, however, is also a constant source of anxiety for him: Okonkwo's fear of resembling his father comes to rule his entire life. The narrator tells us:

> [Okonkwo's] whole life was dominated by fear, the fear of failure and of weakness. . . . It was the fear of himself lest he should be found to resemble his father. (9-10)

Okonkwo is inarticulate and unable to express his pent-up feelings. The narrator tells us that Okonkwo "had a slight stammer and whenever he was angry and could not get his words out quickly enough, he would use his fists" (3). Okonkwo's fear thus results ironically in his tough exterior, his heavy-handed rule of his household, his occasional beating of his wives, and his often abrasive behavior toward fellow clansmen. This further sets Okonkwo apart from his fellow Ibo clansmen, among whom "the art of conversation is regarded very highly, and proverbs are the palm-oil with which words are eaten" (5).

Okonkwo attempts to master his insecurity and to keep it buried inside him. Eventually, however, we see that the fear becomes master of the man. The externalizing of Okonkwo's fear takes place during the sacrifice of Ikemefuna, which is decreed by the Oracle. Up to this point, things have gone well for Okonkwo and his family: Ikemefuna has fit smoothly into their household. Furthermore, as a result of Ikemefuna's influence, Okonkwo's son, Nwoye, has begun to develop into the man his father wants him to be. After the Oracle's decree, however, Okonkwo is torn between an allegiance to his family and an allegiance to the clan. The episode in which Okonkwo kills Ikemefuna is fraught with irony: he does not wish to sacrifice his adopted son much less to be the one to carry out that sacrifice, but his desire to prove his manhood forces him to act. As the elders lead the unsuspecting Ikemefuna in single file away from the village, Okonkwo looks away as one of the elders gets set to strike the appointed blow. The attempt somehow misses, however, and Ikemefuna runs toward Okonkwo crying, "My father, they have killed me!" (43) At this moment of crisis, Okonkwo's innermost fear emerges, and he makes a sudden, fatal decision. The narrator explains: "Dazed with fear, Okonkwo drew his machete and cut him down. He was afraid of being thought weak" (43).

Although it is not evident to the characters, the tragic disintegration of Okonkwo and his family begins with the slaying of Ikemefuna. Perhaps the main sign of the family's impending destruction is in the relationship between father and son. After Ikemefuna's death, Nwoye no longer goes to his father's *obi* in the evening, and he begins to shrink away from Okonkwo. Eventually, Nwoye leaves the clan entirely and becomes one of the earliest converts to the Christian church established by the British missionaries. Not long after Ikemefuna's sacrifice, there is an episode which may be seen as a corrective of Cary's portrayal of Johnson as instinctual and unreflective. Although the narrator describes him as "not a man of thought but of action" (48), Okonkwo possesses the ability to reflect upon his experience and to compare points of view with a discerning friend. In this scene, Okonkwo's friend, Obierika, visits him and the two men discuss the former's unfortunate, recent experience. Obierika's view of the sacrifice differs considerably from Okonkwo's. Okonkwo defends his decision to kill Ikemefuna by saying that if all men were afraid of blood, then the Oracle's decree would never be carried out. Obierika, however, perceives the complexity of the incident and thus offers a more moderate view, along with a dire forecast: "If I were you I would have stayed at home. What you have done will not please the Earth. It is the kind of action for which the goddess wipes out whole families" (46).

The discussion between Okonkwo and Obierika is indicative of Achebe's depiction of Ibo society in general. Clearly, the Ibo society in *Things Fall Apart* differs from the Emirate rule in northern Nigeria which Cary portrays in *Mister Johnson*. The Ibo have no kings or rulers. Unlike the hierarchical rule of the Emir and Waziri, Ibo society is based on equality and an internal system of checks and balances. Most of the clan's decisions are made by a democratic body of elders, known as the *egwugwu*, who represent the village ancestors. Throughout the novel, Achebe shows us various ceremonies and gatherings of the clan in which the Ibo cultural beliefs, assumptions, and perspective upon the strange appearance of the foreign colonizers are made clear. In one such gathering, Achebe portrays the Ibo view of the outside world and the villagers' obvious lack of preparation for the arrival of the strange British missionaries:

> "The world is large," said Okonkwo. "I have even heard that in some tribes a man's children belong to his wife and her family."
>
> "That cannot be," said Machi. "You might as well say that the woman lies on top of the man when they are making the children."
>
> "It is like the story of the white men who, they say, are white like this piece of chalk," said Obierika. He held up a piece of chalk, which every man kept in his obi and with which his guests drew lines on the floor before they ate kola nuts. "And these white men, they say, have no toes." (51-52)

Like other post-colonial writers, Achebe reverses the cultural perspective, and thus Western readers are made to see themselves through African eyes. In such a society as the Ibo, it is understandable how British colonialism, with its hierarchical system of "indirect rule," could encounter difficulties. It is also clear that a highly-motivated individual like Okonkwo would occupy an important position in this society: he is one of the nine *egwugwu* and a lord of the clan whom the other villagers regard highly.

In Part One, the reader sees Okonkwo as a complex man. He is capable of tenderness, such as his worry and concern for his daughter, Ezinma, during her illness. But he is also capable of brutality, such as his beating of his wife during the Week of Peace. As a result of Okonkwo's disadvantaged past and his struggle to become one of the lords of the clan, we sympathize with him. Throughout Part One, Achebe further draws upon our sympathy for his hero as he skillfully foreshadows Okonkwo's later tragic undermining. Okonkwo commits a series of transgressions against Ibo customs and thus jeopardizes his social position in the clan. Part of Okonkwo's difficulty seems to be his impatient and temperamental disposition, as when he almost shoots his second wife with his gun in a sudden fit of anger. Through Okonkwo's breaking of custom, Achebe illustrates the clan's rules of social conduct, and further, shows us that Okonkwo's position in the clan is a fragile one. In Okonkwo's later transgressions, he becomes increasingly vulnerable, a victim of circumstance, as if his life were spinning out of control.

Perhaps the main point to emphasize in regard to Part One is how deliberately and thoroughly Achebe responds to Cary's demeaning portrait of Nigerian culture as "primitive" and backward in *Mister Johnson* through his own description of the Ibo people and culture. In these first ten chapters, in which the plot barely moves, Achebe gives us a view of a colonial Nigeria which directly contrasts with Cary's Fada. In such seemingly offhand instances as the description of the positioning of huts in Okonkwo's compound, the Ibo calendar with its four-day market week, the requirements for the taking of titles, the intricate rituals used in greeting a visitor with chalk and kola nut, the marriage customs demonstrated during the wedding of Obierika's daughter, and the Ibo religious and justice systems shown through the *egwugwu* ceremony, Achebe provides detailed examples of the complexity and self-sufficiency of the Ibo social structure prior to the arrival of the missionaries. In later episodes that develop the plot, such as the funeral rites for Ezeudu, in which Okonkwo accidentally kills the son of the deceased, and the seven-year banishment of Okonkwo for involuntary manslaughter, Achebe again goes to great lengths to demonstrate the cohesiveness of Ibo—and by extension African—social rules and customs. Unlike Cary's dilapidated, helpless Fada, Achebe's Umuofia obviously has in place a clear, practical system for governing itself and dealing with any internal problems which arise.

It is more than halfway through the novel before the reader meets the British missionaries who are responsible for the changes in Ibo society. As a result of Achebe's organization of the novel, the reader perceives the missionaries as if through the eyes of Okonkwo and the other villagers. In the second year of Okonkwo's exile in his motherland, Obierika visits him and informs him of the arrival of the white missionaries and the destruction of the village of Abame. Obierika confides to Okonkwo that, in light of recent events, he fears what may happen:

> "We have heard stories about white men who made the powerful guns and the strong drinks and took slaves away across the seas, but no one thought the stories were true." (99)

Unlike Obierika, however, Okonkwo is not fearful. His reaction to Obierika's news reflects his lack of understanding of the recent changes and his stubborn reliance upon the old traditional ways of dealing with enemies:

> "[The men of Abame] were fools. . . . They had been warned that danger was ahead. They should have armed themselves with their guns and their machetes even when they went to market." (99)

Even though Achebe makes fun of the missionaries' initial attempts to reach the Ibo people—the missionaries' interpreter, due to poor pronunciation, refers to himself as "my buttocks" (102) and has difficulty explaining how the Christian god could have a son but no wife—his portrayal of them is not entirely negative. Unlike Joyce Cary's polarized portrayal of the responsible British administrators and the backward African villagers in *Mister Johnson*, Achebe breaks down stereotypic racial categories by portraying the British and the Africans as both good and bad. Achebe gives two of the British missionaries—Reverend Brown and Reverend Smith—fuller treatment than the other missionaries; and the two present an illuminating parallel to the two main Ibo characters, Okonkwo and Obierika. Like Okonkwo and Obierika, Brown and Smith serve as foils for each other: in both cases, a man of moderation is set beside a man of extremes. Whereas Okonkwo, for instance, is a man who "never does things by halves" (117), Obierika is "a man who thought about things" (87), who judges by degree rather than by absolutes. The contrast between Okonkwo and Obierika is visible throughout the novel, and Achebe's similar contrast between Brown and Smith shows that such differences in temperament and philosophical outlook transcend racial origin.

Much of the missionaries' initial success in establishing a church in Umuofia results from Reverend Brown's ability to compromise and to restrain his flock. Perhaps Brown's chief credit is his control over Enoch, a particularly fanatic convert whose zeal threatens to bring the church and clan into conflict:

> Mr. Brown preached against such excess of zeal. Everything was possible, he told his energetic flock, but everything was not expedient. And so Mr. Brown came to be respected even by the clan, because he trod softly on its faith. (126)

After a sudden decline in health, however, Brown leaves Umuofia and is replaced by Reverend Smith. An aggressive, uncompromising man, Smith leads the church into direct conflict with the clan. Unlike his predecessor, Smith's view of life is based on a self-righteous dualism:

> [Reverend Smith] condemned openly Mr. Brown's policy of compromise and accommodation. . . . He saw the world as a battlefield in which the children of light were locked in mortal conflict with the sons of darkness. He spoke in his sermons about sheep and goats and about wheat and tares. (130)

Clearly, Brown's "policy of compromise and accommodation" is more effective than Smith's absolutism, just as Obierika's ability to compromise and adapt is preferable to Okonkwo's reliance upon force to resolve disputes. Through these parallels, Achebe tries to show the falsity of a simplistic, good-evil, wheat-tares reading of colonial Nigeria, and instead portrays the complexity of the confrontation of two worlds and two ways of life.

The collision of cultures in *Things Fall Apart* is less violent and direct than that in Abrahams' *Wild Conquest* or in Armah's *The Healers*. No battles are fought or won. Rather, the disintegration of the Ibo culture is an internal process, gauged by the increasing number of converts won by the new religion and "the new dispensation" (126), which includes a school, a trading store, a court of law, and a government. Unlike Cary in *Mister Johnson*, Achebe describes the initial impact of the various colonial institutions on a Nigerian village and shows how these institutions were linked from the outset. As Achebe's narrator remarks, "From the very beginning religion and education went hand in hand" (128). Upon his return to his fatherland after seven years in Mbanta, Okonkwo finds that the "clan had undergone such profound change during his exile that it was barely recognizable" (129). Confused by his people's inability to expel the intruder, Okonkwo consults Obierika:

> "Perhaps I have been away too long. But I cannot understand these things you tell me. What is it that has happened to our people? Why have they lost the power to fight?" (124)

Obierika's answer shows an awareness of the internal fragmentation of Umuofia and might serve as a microcosm of the entire narrative:

> "How do you think we can fight when our brothers have turned against us? The white man is very clever. He came quietly and peacefully with his religion. We were amused at his foolishness and allowed him to stay. Now he has won our brothers, and our clan can no longer act like one. He has put a knife on the things that held us together and we have fallen apart." (124-125)

Like Abrahams' Gubuza, Okonkwo wants to remove by force an enemy who is stronger than he. Although unaware of the strength of the enemy, Okonkwo is willing to test it using his gun and machete. The reader therefore sees Okonkwo as head-strong and even foolish, perhaps, but also undaunted, ready to launch a counter-attack against a formidable enemy. In Okonkwo we can see the embodiment of an admirable African spirit of defiance and resurgence in the face of European colonialism. *Things Fall Apart* is thus a protest novel and a precursor of a group of important African protest novels, including Armah's *The Healers*, Ngugi wa Thiong'o's *Petals of Blood* (1977) and *A Grain of Wheat* (1967), and Kole Omotoso's *The Combat* (1972). The character of Okonkwo is the chief vehicle of Achebe's protest against colonialism, for indeed, in the tragedy of Okonkwo, we can see the microcosm of the larger tragedy of Nigeria. As a novel of protest, *Things Fall Apart* offers a much more sharply-pointed criticism of European colonialism in Africa than Abrahams' *Wild Conquest*. In *Things Fall Apart*, the European-African confrontation is not so much a struggle for the land as a psychological battle for hearts and minds.

In *The Serpent and the Rope*, Raja Rao, the Indian novelist, states: "The law is the death of truth" (393). An important point of divergence between British colonial writers and Third World post-colonial writers lies in the portrayal of colonial justice and the administration of law and order, which was such an important part of colonial rule. The law in British colonial fiction is a civilizing mechanism which serves to control the "natural chaos" of the Third World. Much British colonial fiction ends with the restoration of order, often achieved through the aid of the colonial judicial system. We might think of Forster's *A Passage to India*, Leonard Woolf's *The Village in the Jungle*, and Cary's *Mister Johnson* in this regard; and although *Kim* and *King Solomon's Mines* contain no judicial hearing, both novels nevertheless end with the restoration of order achieved through colonial intercession. In much post-colonial fiction, however, colonial justice is portrayed as an alien institution imposed on the indigenous people in order to legitimize the foreign rule of the outsider. In *Things Fall Apart*, for instance, Achebe provides an African's view of the British system of justice imposed on the Ibo people. Like *Mister Johnson*, *Things Fall Apart* ends with the restoration of order, but we see that "order" in an ironic light.

Okonkwo's answer to British colonialism is resistance by force: "We must fight these men and drive them from the land" (124), he tells his fellow clansmen of Umuofia. After Enoch, the overzealous convert, commits sacrilege against the clan by unmasking an *egwugwu*, the Ibo retaliate by destroying Reverend Smith's church. When the District Commissioner hears of the incident, he intercedes, inviting six leaders of the clan, including Okonkwo, to hold a palaver. The Commissioner's invitation is only a ploy, however, and the clansmen are seized and imprisoned. The Commissioner condescendingly explains the new colonial system of justice to the now powerless, humiliated prisoners: "We have a court of law where we judge cases and administer justice just as it is done in my own country under a great queen" (137). He then levies a fine of two hundred bags of cowries for the destruction of the church. Achebe, in an ironic twist, illustrates the corruption endemic in the imposition of this alien, colonial system of justice on Ibo society when a clever court messenger, who has already discovered an easy way to make a profit from the "new dispensation," suddenly increases the fine by fifty bags of cowries. Here Achebe makes his most telling point. The progress from a time when a man could work to become a great warrior and lord of the clan to a time when young men aspire to the rank of court messenger in an alien government reveals the ironic "civilizing" influence of British colonialism in Nigeria.

In the ending of *Things Fall Apart*, Achebe again responds to Cary. In *Mister Johnson*, Johnson submits to his death sentence, begging Rudbeck to shoot him because he fears being hanged. In contrast to Johnson, Okonkwo refuses to resign himself to colonial rule, choosing instead to end his life through an act of defiance—killing the Commissioner's messenger—and then hanging himself. Whereas Johnson is enslaved by his impossible desire to enter the white ruling class, Okonkwo, by killing himself, retains control of his life and escapes subjugation by the colonial government. In killing the haughty court messenger, who attempts to break up a meeting of the clan, Okonkwo finally perceives his untenable position between the traditional rule of the clan and the new rule of the colonial government. Finding himself alone in his call for force against the Europeans, Okonkwo realizes too late that "Umuofia would not go to war" (144).

In the last chapter, Achebe shifts to the British colonial point of view to achieve a final irony for his conclusion. This device, in which the reader suddenly perceives the action through the distant eyes of an outsider, is one used with similar striking effect by the Trinidadian Earl Lovelace in his novel *The Wine of Astonishment*. By relating the newspapers' superficial report of the death of the protagonist Bolo, a scene which the reader has just graphically witnessed "first-hand," Lovelace reveals how the villagers of Bonasse are routinely ignored and misrepresented by those in power in Trinidad (131-132). In Achebe's narrative, the outsider is the District Commissioner, who comes in search of Okonkwo, only to find that the latter has hanged himself. Learning that suicide is a shameful act for the Ibo, the Commissioner goes through a sudden change: no longer "the resolute administrator," he becomes "the student of primitive customs" (147) who is fascinated by the unique case of a native suicide. Ironically, in light of what the reader has already learned about Okonkwo in the course of the narrative, the Commissioner is able to distance himself from the tragic progress of events and to view Okonkwo's suicide objectively. Here, Achebe parodies Cary's District Officer, Rudbeck, and his gradual awareness of Johnson's humanity. The human tragedy the reader has witnessed in *Things Fall Apart* is transformed into "new material" for the Commissioner's planned book: an outsider's account of colonial Nigeria to be entitled *The Pacification of the Primitive Tribes of the Lower Niger*. In this brief, capsulized form, Achebe effectively captures the inevitable dehumanizing effect of European colonial rule in Africa.

In *Tell Me Africa*, James Olney perceives Okonkwo as a representative of his culture, finding "a virtual one-to-one relationship between Okonkwo as an individual and the Ibo as a people" (170). Surely, as Olney suggests, Achebe links Okonkwo to Ibo society as a whole and protests European colonialism through Okonkwo's downfall, but he does not elevate Okonkwo to an ideal. Okonkwo's absolutism, for example, goes against traditional Ibo beliefs, and thus the elders must admonish him on occasion.[1] Certainly, however, in Okonkwo we can see not only strengths, but also some weaknesses of the Ibo people as a whole. Among many of the Ibo elders, including Okonkwo, for instance, we see a nostalgic clannishness, an unwillingness to experience change. In this society, as in many, the elder generation looks down upon the youth as going astray or somehow failing to live up to their standards. We see this early in the novel when Okonkwo goes to the wealthy Nwakibie for help in getting started as a farmer. Okonkwo tells Nwakibie that "in these days when young men are afraid of hard work . . . I am not afraid." Nwakibie answers in kind, "It pleases me to see a young man like you these days when our youth has gone so soft" (16). Much later in the narrative, after Okonkwo has returned from his long exile, his nostalgia and idealization of the past grow into an obsession. He thinks back about the old days when Umuofia went to war with Isike and he reaches the facile conclusion: "Worthy men are no more" (141). Because of this backward-looking, reactionary attitude, many in the clan are unprepared to deal with the coming of the white missionaries and the cataclysmic changes their arrival brings about in the community of Umuofia.

Things Fall Apart is not only about the importance of community and tradition, it is also about the need for change and adaptability. It is part of the complexity of the novel that Achebe can express the seemingly contradictory need for both tradition and transformation, and thus define the mainsprings of the African concern for community as "the sense of a shared history, and even more important, of an assumed destiny." In an essay in *Morning Yet On Creation Day*, Achebe compares two different peoples of Kenya: the Masai, "who took one look at Western civilization and turned their backs on it," and the Wachagga, who "are always trying out new things." Achebe expresses his belief that "the future belongs to those who, like the Wachagga, are ready to take in new ideas," because "in the end, life will favor those who come to terms with it, not those who run away" (109). Even though Achebe's vision in *Things Fall Apart* is a tragic one, it also contains an implicit hope for a better future for Nigeria. Moreover, Achebe has stated that his aim in *Things Fall Apart* was to establish not "just a dialogue with the West, but also a dialogue with ourselves."[2] If the Nigerian people can learn "where the rain began to beat them," then they can set a positive course for the future. The title of Achebe's novel comes from Yeats' "The Second Coming," which is about resurrection and transformation. We might also think of another Yeats poem, "Easter 1916," about the Easter martyrs and the paradox that even in tragedy one may be "transformed utterly" so that a "terrible beauty is born." In *Things Fall Apart*, Achebe asserts that Africans must use the traditions of their past to meet boldly the demands of a new and terrible world.

Chapter IV
The Struggle for Independence: Elspeth Huxley and Ngugi wa Thiong'o

Elspeth Huxley's *A Thing to Love*

In her relationship to Kenya, Elspeth Huxley in many ways resembles Kipling with India, for her acquaintance with the country came during the early, impressionable years of her childhood. Elspeth Josceline Grant was born in London in 1907. When she was only six, her parents brought her with them to Kenya, where they hoped to start a coffee plantation. Life with her pioneering parents in colonial Kenya had a lasting effect on young Elspeth. Making their home initially in tents, the family lived off of the wild game they shot and the vegetables they grew. Elspeth later summed up this stage of the family's life: "Rough was the word" (*Observer*, 36). Her parents eventually managed to buy 500 acres of "virgin bush," which they had to clear in order to plant coffee, and also to build a simple dwelling in which to live. Life was rough, but young Elspeth apparently loved it. Forty-five years later, she captured her adolescent experiences in Kenya in two autobiographical works, *The Flame Trees of Thika* (1959) and *The Mottled Lizard* (1962), which were later made into a film. Much like India in *Kim*, the image of Kenya in these works is of a magical, exotic wonderland full of strange animals and people. Indeed, Huxley took the title and epigraph for *The Mottled Lizard* from a poem by Kipling.

After receiving her university education at Reading in England and Cornell in America, Elspeth married Gervas Huxley, a tea expert and cousin of Aldous and Julian, and began what has proven to be a long and prolific writing career. Huxley has written widely about Africa, both fiction and non-fiction. *White Man's*

Country: Lord Delamere and the Making of Kenya is a biography of and tribute to Delamere as well as a history of colonial Kenya from a British point of view. Of her numerous novels set in Africa, most of which deal with the clash of cultures between the British and Kenyans, perhaps *Red Strangers* (1939) and *A Thing to Love* (1954) have received the most critical attention. Ezekiel Mphahlele, for instance, in *The African Image*, found *Red Strangers* to contain stereotypes of Africans, but felt Huxley was more successful with her African characters in *A Thing to Love* (151). Huxley herself has said in the Foreword to *Red Strangers*: "I am well aware that no person of one race and culture can truly interpret events from the angle of individuals belonging to a totally different race and culture" (viii). Continuing her writing career into the eighties, Huxley has also written travel books, like *Four Guineas: A Journey Through West Africa* (1954); detective fiction set in Africa, such as *The Merry Hippo* (1963); commentaries on the African scene, like *The Challenge of Africa* (1971); biographies, including *Livingstone and His African Journeys* (1974); and reminiscences of pioneering days, such as *Pioneers' Scrapbook: Reminiscences of Kenya 1890 to 1968* (1980). *Out in the Midday Sun*, a book of personal observations on Kenya, appeared in 1985.

Huxley's writing on Kenya, like Kipling's on India, has drawn a mixed response. Although she has been praised for her "sympathy and imagination on behalf of the Africans" (Huxley and Perham, 24), she has also been called "the spokesman, or woman, of the [Kenya] settlers" (Petersen, 215) whose work represents "the best apologia for white settlement [of Kenya] that has been written" (Huxley and Perham, 24). Both Huxley's fiction and non-fiction are marked by a strong attachment to the ideals of the British Empire and a simultaneous awareness that, as a result of World Wars I and II and such events as the Mau Mau rebellion and the Emergency, those civilizing ideals have reached the point of diminishing returns. One of her comments in *White Man's Country* can perhaps suffice to illustrate this awareness on Huxley's part:

> Men like Sir Charles Eliot and Delamere worked for white settlement and for the foundation of a new British colony because they believed in it honestly as a proper ideal. Opinion cannot with justice condemn them for holding convictions which later events in Europe have shaken and perhaps destroyed (84).

Huxley adds that "the belief in the inherent excellence of civilisation was to a large extent destroyed between 1914 and 1918 and in the years that followed" (82).

Similar to Kipling in his relationship to India, Huxley often appears divided between an emotional, childhood attachment to colonial Kenya and an intellectual allegiance to the British Empire, which she sees as inevitably becoming a thing of the past. The title of *A Thing to Love* seems to reflect Huxley's emotional link to the country in which she grew up. Huxley's own conflict, moreover, is mirrored in the characters she creates in *A Thing to Love*: whereas she depicts the Foxleys' uneducated Gikuyu laborers, such as Raphaelo and Njombo, with sensitivity and affection, she clearly views the Mau Mau guerrillas, like Gitau, as ruthless and brutal savages who intend to destroy every vestige of white civilization in the country. We can see Huxley's ambivalent attitude toward Kenya also in the contrasting views of Patricia, who eventually accepts Kenya's changes, and of her conservative, reactionary father, who wants Kenya to remain a "white man's country."

From Kipling's *Kim* and Haggard's *King Solomon's Mines* to Cary's *Mister Johnson*, the historical transformation of ideas about the British Empire during the nineteenth century and early twentieth century is apparent. Kipling and Haggard capture the confidence and certainty of the British during the Empire's heyday; Cary mirrors the later deterioration of the colonizers' self-assurance in the aftermath of World War I. In Huxley's *A Thing to Love* (1954), set in colonial Kenya during the Emergency, still later developments in England's imperial destiny become visible. The ever-present fear of a "native uprising," expressed earlier in such British fiction as Henty's *Rujub the Juggler* and Buchan's *Prester John*, is realized as colonizer and colonized act out long-held hostilities. *A Thing to Love* portrays the puncturing of the settlers' notions of Kenya as a "white man's country," and thus an undercurrent of pessimism is generated in the novel—a painful awareness of the inevitable passing away of England's colonial era. Even though the novel ends on a positive note, *A Thing to Love* conveys a hopelessness and frustration, certainly in part due to World War II, which reflect the colonizers' realization that the Empire is being destroyed, ironically, by those it is supposed to help.

Throughout the nineteenth and into the twentieth century, the indigenous figure in British colonial fiction occupies an increasingly important role. In *Kim* and *King Solomon's Mines*, for example, the narratives focus almost exclusively on the main British characters—Kim and Quatermain. Several decades later, Joyce Cary gives Clerk Johnson a considerably larger role, although the central consciousness of *Mister Johnson* remains the British imperial representative,

District Officer Rudbeck. *A Thing to Love* continues this development. Huxley employs a multiple point of view, constantly moving back and forth between the two sides of the Mau Mau confrontation: the British settlers and the Gikuyu rebels. Although Patricia Foxley, a member of a British settler family, clearly dominates the narrative, Huxley's shifting point of view indicates the increasingly vital role played by the colonized, both in the British imagination and in reality. Furthermore, the educated Mau Mau leaders appear rational and intelligent—a striking departure from most earlier colonial fiction—but also, and perhaps not surprisingly, evil and bent on destruction. In Huxley's other category of Kenyans, the uneducated villagers, lies the implicit hope for the future, for these honest laborers accept the British as fellow countrymen and are willing to work in harmony with them for the benefit of the country as a whole.

Even though it deals with an actual historical occurrence, Huxley's novel, like so much British colonial fiction, makes little effort to re-create a specific historic event in accurate detail. Instead, Huxley utilizes history as a broad backdrop for the more personal drama she wishes to relate. There are no references, for example, to important historical figures, such as Jomo Kenyatta or Lord Delamere. *A Thing to Love* centers around Patricia Foxley's coming to awareness, not only of herself as an individual, but of her problematic position in colonial Kenya, the country in which she was born and raised and which she has learned to love. The Mau Mau revolt brings Pat's individual search for identity to a crisis. Unlike the first-person narrator in Huxley's autobiographical works, *The Flame Trees of Thika* and *The Mottled Lizard*, who views colonial Kenya through innocent, adolescent eyes, Patricia is a woman at the crossroads of her own life, facing difficult decisions regarding her future. Pat's inner turmoil is thus a reflection of the external world around her, which the narrator at one point describes as a "whole country turned upside down" (119). The outbreak of the Mau Mau trouble intensifies Pat's own internal conflict, which she is only able to reconcile at the close of the novel, when she makes the decision to remain in Kenya, a decision which affirms the purpose and necessity of British colonial rule in the country.

The novel's title and epigraph are taken from G. K. Chesterton:

> And death and hate and hell declare
> That men have found a thing to love.

After enduring the "death and hate and hell" of the Mau Mau rebellion, including the brutal murder of both her parents, Pat realizes a hard-earned love for Kenya.

Huxley implies in her title and her novel that such is the fate of the colonizer. As Kipling put it in his poem, "The White Man's Burden":

> Take up the White Man's burden—
> And reap his old reward:
> The blame of those ye better,
> The hatred of those ye guard—(Howe, 603)

Huxley's portrayal of Kenyan society in *A Thing to Love* focuses on the white settlers. Because the novel is only secondarily concerned with history, there is little indication that the British colonials have been present in Kenya only a relatively short time. The beautiful, spacious Rift Valley and the White Highlands indeed seem to be "white man's country." The only black Kenyans living in this exclusive area are the servants and laborers who work on the white settlers' farms. In *The Country and the City*, Raymond Williams asserts that British imperialism is "one of the last models of 'city and country'" (279):

> New rural societies entered the English imagination, under the shadow of political and economic control: the plantation worlds of Kipling and Maugham and early Orwell; the trading worlds of Conrad and Joyce Cary. (281)

Unlike the "trading world" of Cary's Nigeria, Huxley's Kenya is a "plantation world," a farming community, and thus conjures up for the English imagination memories of a simple, rural past.

Williams claims that the justification for the exploitation of this new colonial countryside is the traditional English emphasis upon the "improvement of the estate," an idea which reached the height of its expression in the eighteenth century. The idea of the improvement of the estate applies well to *A Thing to Love*. The novel makes clear that settler-farmers like Sam Gibson and Colonel Foxley have done much to develop the wilderness into truly productive farmland. Both farmers can thus justify their existence in colonial Kenya on the basis of improvement of the land. Sam Gibson, for instance, "hoped that his son would follow after on the land he was turning from rawness to fecundity" (15). Similarly, the narrator explains Colonel Foxley's transformation from a soldier to a settler:

> In early middle age he had fallen in love not with a woman but with a country and, giving up his career, had found scope for the singleness of purpose which the Army had increasingly frustrated. He had taken a stretch of bush and forest and turned it into a farm. (21-22)

The idea of the "improvement of the estate" implies an insufficiency in the status quo: things must not be left as they are; one must constantly alter and change in order to "improve." Like Cary's Hausa, who regard Rudbeck's passionate road-building with incomprehension, the Gikuyu laborers on the Foxleys' farm have little understanding of the settler family's commitment to change and improvement. In one episode, for instance, Mamie Foxley, the Colonel's wife, decides to replace the old wood-burning stove in the cook's quarters, but meets unexpected resistance from Karioki, the Gikuyu cook. Mamie "improves" the kitchen by removing the old smoky stove—"surely a provoker of ophthalmia and pneumonia" (69)—and installing a new, more efficient one. Karioki, however, prefers things as they were, and becomes "sulky and miserable" (69) as a result of the change. Eventually, Mamie must go against her own better judgment: she reinstates the old stove whose "smoke-bound fug [once] again produced smiling faces" (69). The implication in *A Thing to Love* is that the colonizers' self-appointed role in Kenya is far from over, and their beneficent effect on the native people must take time to show results.

Given Huxley's presentation of Kenya as a favorable contrast to industrialized England, her romanticization of the settler community farming the land, and her idealization of the simple Kenyan villager, it is not surprising that a strong anti-city theme runs throughout *A Thing to Love*:

> That was what cities could do to people, Pat thought . . . stifle the life within them, the spirit in the seed, so that they didn't grow but simply rotted inside. (61)

From Huxley's point of view, the deplorable Mau Mau revolt thus begins in the city, Nairobi, and is spread to the simple villagers living in the countryside. It is also not accidental that most of the members of the Council of Nine, the small group of urban Kenyans who mastermind the rebellion, are *been-to's* who have *been to* and have been educated in England, which in the context of this novel represents the Metropolis. Huxley portrays Mau Mau as a revolution which has no roots among the common people of the country. Far from a unified uprising, it grows out of the greed and envy of a small group of urban malcontents in Nairobi whose frustrated desire for power leads them to use violence and terrorism to seize control of the country from the white colonial minority. From their base in Nairobi, the Council of Nine attract a network of sympathizers who infiltrate the countryside and persuade the naive peasantry to turn against their colonial masters. The villagers, as Huxley portrays them, are victimized by the Nairobi conspirators, whose methods of persuasion include promises of the settlers' property as well as a mandatory oath-taking, which Huxley depicts as a grisly perversion of an ancient, sacred Gikuyu rite.

Gitau, one of the Mau Mau ring-leaders, is the central indigenous character in the novel. As *A Thing to Love* opens, we are presented with a contingency: a flight is about to leave London for Nairobi, and Patricia, Sam Gibson, and Gitau are all on board. Patricia and Gitau happen to sit next to each other, and we view them from the perspective of Sam, who sits in the seat behind. The coincidental meeting of the three on the plane is a foreshadowing of their later, more hostile confrontation during the Mau Mau revolt.

The characters' interaction during the flight illuminates the current problematic relations between colonizer and colonized in Kenya and the level of tension and misunderstanding which have created the climate for Mau Mau. When Sam asks Patricia about her "dark-skinned companion" (11), she reveals that he is a Kenyan who has been to England to attend a conference. This news seems to rankle Sam:

> "I wish someone would pay my return fare so that I could make a self-pitying speech saying I'm oppressed." (11)

Despite Sam's comment, Gitau is portrayed with a degree of sympathy in the first chapter. And even Sam sees him as a man "endowed with pathos because of . . . his belief that all the troubles, frustrations and evils of the world . . . would vanish like smoke if only he and his tribesmen could have their country to themselves" (16). Gitau, however, becomes increasingly less sympathetic as the narrative progresses. In part this happens because the reader becomes acquainted with the families of Patricia and Sam, learning the intimate details of their backgrounds. Huxley, by contrast, presents Gitau as an isolated specimen with no humanizing ties to family, and thus seemingly beyond the pale of humanity. *A Thing to Love* centers upon the Foxleys as a family; but none of the indigenous, non-white characters in *A Thing to Love* are portrayed in this humanizing context. In this way, Huxley's Kenyans seem similar to those in Isak Dinesen's *Out of Africa* and *Shadows on the Grass*—menials without any understandable family ties. The relationships between the Gikuyu laborers on the Foxleys' farm, for example, are portrayed as barely comprehensible: "almost everyone on the farm was related in some way" (68).

The reader observes Gitau attend clandestine meetings of the Council of Nine in back rooms of out-of-the-way shops in Nairobi, concealed by the darkness of the night. Gitau takes his orders from a shadowy, sinister figure called the

Spokesman who is never identified but who is intended perhaps to resemble Jomo Kenyatta. The turning-point in Huxley's portrayal of Gitau comes when police raid a meeting of the Council of Nine. Gitau and a fellow Mau Mau conspirator, Josiah, flee into a nearby Indian shop and implore the shop assistant, a young Gikuyu boy, to help them escape by exchanging clothes with Gitau. The young boy refuses, fearing the shop-owner will know something is wrong, and Gitau instinctively reacts by strangling him. The narrator describes the bizarre after-effect of the event upon Gitau: "He had never strangled anyone before and was surprised to find that it was so easy, and so pleasureable; the feel of the boy sagging under his hands was a most delightful sensation" (114). This portrayal of Gitau's savage murder of the boy has its roots in other portraits of Africans in British fiction. In spite of Gitau's education and veneer of civilization, he is shown to be, at base, as irrational, lawless, and inherently brutal as Haggard's Kukuana. Gitau's action, moreover, sets the tone for the later massacre of the unsuspecting, innocent British settlers by the black conspirators, a massacre that unleashes the terror and chaos of Mau Mau.

Just as Gitau casts off restraint and succumbs to savage impulses when he kills the boy, so the Mau Mau revolt appears an abandonment of civilization to the dark, chaotic instincts of savagery and butchery. Like Chief Dinamaula in Nicholas Monsarrat's *The Tribe That Lost Its Head*, a novel set in the fictitious African island of Pharamaul in which there is a native uprising—the "Pharamaul version of Mau Mau" (126)—and also like Buchan's Reverend John Laputa in *Prester John* and Cary's Aladai in *The African Witch*, Huxley's Mau Mau conspirators quickly shed their European education and revert to what she portrays as primitive African savagery. The foundations of the revolt, such as the Spokesman's powerful influence on the other members of the Council and the hypnotic effect of the oath upon the rural Gikuyu peasantry, appear irrational and superstitious—a quasi-religious impulse rather than a political one. George Rutinu, a European-educated member of the Council, for instance, is clearly under the spell of the Spokesman's irrational appeal:

> He knew that if the Spokesman told him to do this or that, he would do it without argument, even if the order was to kill his wife, or brand a son or cut off his own hand. He did not know why this should be, and nothing he had read helped him to understand it. (50)

Thus even the educated and presumably reflective Africans in Huxley's novel are quickly reduced to the level of unthinking, barbarous instinct.

The view of Africa that Huxley offers, however, is clearly meant to be seen not as reactionary but rather as progressive. In *Something of Value* (1955), Robert Ruark's treatment of the Mau Mau revolt, one of the British settlers remarks: "Colonies, my dear boy, just ain't fashionable any more" (94). Huxley's British characters seem to operate under a similar realization in *A Thing to Love*. The historic transformation of the British Empire is obvious, for instance, in the generation gap between Patricia and her parents. In contrast to Patricia's efforts to find a constructive role for herself in a Kenya nearing independence, Colonel Foxley resists change, preferring instead to view Kenya through outdated colonial assumptions. Although clearly emotionally attached to her father, Patricia recognizes the Colonel's "improvement of the estate" approach to his farm. She has to "stifle a twinge of irritation" (24) at his typical desire to transform Kenya into a "white man's country," made obvious in his effort to transplant daffodils in unsuitable African soil. Colonel Foxley's outdated views are also visible in his frequent criticism of what he calls the "younger generation" (28) of Kenyans, whom he considers to be troublemakers and loafers. Pat's decision to teach African schoolchildren in the Mission School, moreover, further reveals her parents' backward-looking attitudes: "And then, after all these hopes and ambitions, and in spite of all argument, to see her turn into a missionary! A teacher in a mission school, drumming a lot of nonsense into those black wooly heads. . . . It was deeply distressing" (26).

For many British colonial writers, the cataclysmic changes in the British Empire following World War II rendered their early fictional appraisals of the colonies all but obsolete. For example, in 1932, Evelyn Waugh satirized the laughably chaotic state of affairs in Ethiopia in his novel, *Black Mischief*. When the novel was reissued in 1962, however, Waugh decided to add a preface to the novel in order to "update" its portrayal of an African country:

> Thirty years ago it seemed an anachronism that any part of Africa should be independent of European administration. History has not followed what then seemed its natural course. (9)

In *A Thing to Love*, Huxley perhaps inadvertently captures the changes taking place in almost every British colony by the mid-twentieth century. The characterization of Colonel Foxley, for instance, is a measure of the significant changes in the colony. His lack of awareness of the Mau Mau revolt, in which his own laborers are deeply involved, reflects how out of date he is. When a fellow settler asks the Colonel if any of the laborers on the Foxley farm can be trusted, he answers: "I'd bet my last cent that Raphaelo's absolutely trustworthy" (90). Colonel Foxley's confidence proves fatally misplaced, for Raphaelo, the Foxleys' headman, eventually deceives the Colonel by allowing a group of terrorists to break inside the Foxleys' house to murder the Colonel and his wife.

Raphaelo is one of Huxley's simple, honest Gikuyu peasants led astray by the false promises and mass hysteria of Mau Mau. Prior to the uprising, Raphaelo was the ideal native from the British standpoint, having completely accepted and adapted to the ways of the Europeans. As a result of his employment by the Foxleys, Raphaelo rejects his own religion and is baptised a Roman Catholic. He also learns "the art of writing" (61) and works his way up to the position of headman. His success on the farm enables him to accumulate some private savings and to enroll his sons at the Mission School where Patricia teaches. And Patricia feels an almost familial bond with Raphaelo: she has known him since she was a baby and can talk to him about anything. Puzzled by the mysterious maiming of settlers' livestock—the first signs of Mau Mau terror—Patricia goes to Raphaelo and asks if the crippling of the cattle has "got anything to do with Mau Mau?" (63). Although Raphaelo feigns ignorance, Patricia notices his involuntary reaction to the term "Mau Mau," and thus perceives that the stirrings of revolt have indeed reached the Foxley farm. The realization that Raphaelo is probably involved disturbs Patricia, because she has come to identify with him and to see him, a Christian, as an understandable part of her world:

> [The Kikuyu] were a clever, tenacious, unforgetting people who could nourish feuds and hatreds as relentlessly as any Sicilian. They didn't easily give up. She had a lot of sympathy with the Kikuyu. . . . But a conspiracy founded on hatred by seekers after power, and built up by intimidation, couldn't be the answer. And Raphaelo, of all people—a trusted man, a Christian—to be frightened by it! (64)

Raphaelo's superficial understanding of Mau Mau is almost comic and illustrates how totally the conspiracy is the invention of a small group of Nairobi agitators. With his small savings, Raphaelo has hopes of buying a farm and livestock of his own. He is thus vulnerable when the Mau Mau leaders tell him "that if he paid his money to the conspiracy, he would get the whole of Colonel Foxley's farm, with the house and all the buildings on it" (79). This promise is clearly a ploy, but Raphaelo is taken in, exemplifying the manipulation of the simple villager by the educated, sophisticated representative of New Kenya, the recently emergent figure whom Colonel Foxley, Sam Gibson, and even Patricia find disturbing. The narrator makes clear Raphaelo's naive lack of understanding of Mau Mau and its tragic consequences:

> Raphaelo bore no personal grudge against the Colonel, in fact he liked him as much as he liked any European. . . . He did not suppose it would be necessary to kill all the Europeans, and, for himself, he had no wish to kill any. He expected that men would come from Nairobi for that. (82)

Raphaelo's innocent desire for the Foxleys' estate might be seen, not as an integral part of the Gikuyu love and worship of the land, but, ironically, as an example of the extent to which Raphaelo has adopted Western ideas, especially the notions of personal wealth and private ownership of property. Despite his involvement in Mau Mau, however, Raphaelo remains an innocent, ignorant villager who has been manipulated for the evil purposes of the Mau Mau leaders.

Huxley endows the Mau Mau leaders with a high level of intelligence unusual in British colonial fiction, but she shows that their intelligence only makes them greedy and power-hungry. The maiming of the settlers' cattle, for example—the brainchild of Gitau—is a carefully thought-out attempt to demoralize the settlers, by forcing them not only to watch their cattle die but also to take an active hand in the killing. The individual greed underlying the "conspiracy" is apparent in the Council's lack of unity and the distrust and dishonesty among its members. Gitau, for instance, is jealous of the power exercised by the Spokesman, and feels "he himself could do almost as well—perhaps even better, as his experience grew" (53). The maiming of the cattle, in fact, is an example of Gitau's taking matters into his own hands without prior consultation with the Spokesman.

Some weaknesses in the conspiracy have to do with Huxley's overall portrayal of African society as corrupt and lawless. Solomon, the Council treasurer, for instance, whose "front" is a job in the Mission hospital, must constantly deal with the problem of bribing askaris, the corrupt and incompetent African policemen, as well as other African officials in order to insure their complicity. There is at best a shaky alliance between the educated elite who run the conspiracy and the rank and file peasantry who are pressured into participating. In a conversation between two Council members, Josiah and Solomon, the contempt the leaders feel for their less educated followers is apparent: "What fools these country bumpkins are! They expect everything to be done in a few days" (189). The villagers are similarly distrustful of their leaders. Raphaelo, for instance, begins to feel like a fool for handing over all his money to the conspiracy and getting nothing in return, and he is also deeply disturbed by the rebels' murder of Chief Kimani, a highly respected tribal leader among the rural villagers:

> Would the spirits of the ancestors be satisfied at the shedding of Kimani's blood? Raphaelo doubted it, and sometimes he wished that the conspiracy had never started, so that everyone could go back to things as they were before the Spokesman had come to Tetu. So he went to Solomon and said: When is the land to be mine for which I have paid two thousand shillings? And Solomon had not been able to reply. (190-91)

Commentators on colonialism, such as Gandhi and Fanon, have expressed the crucial importance of the involvement of the rural peasantry in any successful struggle to throw off colonial rule.[1] In *A Thing to Love*, Huxley portrays Mau Mau as lacking the support of the masses in the countryside. She returns several times to Raphaelo as the representative uneducated villager and shows how the more intense his involvement in the conspiracy becomes, the more he is haunted by misgivings and regret. The conspiracy has seemingly gone much further than the innocent villagers ever intended. Raphaelo, like many villagers, is caught in the middle: he regrets his early agreement to become an oath-giver, and feels he was deceived by the Mau Mau leaders. At the same time, he must now practice that very deception on others in order to administer the oath. Raphaelo's self-doubt comes to a head when he deceives Njombo, the Foxleys' loyal houseboy who refuses to take the oath, by sending Njombo's daughter to lure him into a trap. Njombo's outburst of anger and steadfast refusal to take the oath represent an indictment of the entire Mau Mau conspiracy:

> "Raphaelo, I will not join with men who make daughters deceive their fathers, and separate husbands from wives, and steal money by false promises, and you can kill me if you like, but I will not eat this oath." (195)

In this scene, Huxley suggests that the Mau Mau determination to overthrow the British colonizers not only leads to great bloodshed, but also undermines the integral Kenyan social unit of the family, eventually proving destructive for the whole country.

Even though the British colonial forces appear on the defensive and face an up-hill battle, moral right is clearly on their side. *A Thing to Love* is in part a revenge fantasy, founded on what Abdul JanMohamed has called "the ahistorical abstractness of wish fulfillment" (Gates, 100), and as such it represents the intense level of anger and frustration experienced by the British during the Emergency. Huxley focuses the colonizers' desire for vengeance upon Gitau, the embodiment of Mau Mau evil. Gitau is clearly motivated by personal vanity rather than by a desire to help his people. Gitau's vanity is gratified, for example, when he learns that the police offer a lucrative bounty for his capture. In a related episode, he notices a wanted poster bearing his likeness in the Tetu post office and feels annoyed by the unflattering representation. Gitau's unfettered egotism and moral bankruptcy are further underscored when he commits adultery with his cousin, Martha, the wife of Chief Kimani's son, Matthew.

By the time contingency brings them together again, Sam Gibson, the avenging angel of Huxley's reprisal fantasy, and Gitau, the diabolical instigator of Mau Mau, appear in a markedly different light. Although Sam's frankly stated colonialist assumptions appear initially as a sign of his being out of touch with change in Kenya, he is shown to the reader in an increasingly positive light—as Gitau's antithesis. To a Gitau who is secretive, conniving, and evil is juxtaposed Sam as sincere, frank, and good-hearted. Sam expresses his views of colonial Kenya to Gitau with disarming openness and candor:

> "[Colonialism] isn't always such a disadvantage as one thinks. [England] was filled up by wave after wave of conquests and it did us good, on the whole. De-barbarized us, anyway. We got so used to the Romans that we implored them not to take their legions away. . . . I'm not a policeman. But turning on each other won't get us anywhere. Africa's defeated everyone so far and it'll go on doing so if you drive away the irritating but essential outsiders." (101-106)

As the novel progresses, Sam's pronouncements appear increasingly to fall into line with those of the narrator and, by extension, Huxley herself. In Huxley's characterization of Sam as a hero out of a boy's adventure story—simple, brave, and true to the colonialist cause—we can see her in part as a throwback to Kipling, in perpetual conflict between her emotional attachment to her idyllic childhood home and her intellectual awareness that Britain's colonial control of Kenya is on the wane.

The ending of *A Thing to Love*, in which Sam tracks Gitau through a dense forest and finally kills him, illustrates Huxley's conflict between the old, colonial and the new, soon-to-be independent Kenya. Sam is aided in his man-hunt by an appealing group of African Home Guards, for whom Huxley feels an obvious affection. This group of "weedy Kikuyu who lived on starches" (246) show an amazing stamina as they progress effortlessly through the dense forest. Sam is impressed by the "unvoiced, almost instinctive action of the group will" which reminds him of "the sudden wheeling of a flock of birds" (249). Like Haggard's instinctual Kukuana, Huxley's Home Guards live on a pure, uncomplicated level. Moreover, similar to the uneducated laborers on the Foxley farm, they fit into Huxley's stereotype of the simple, industrious, happy villager whom she valorizes, since they clearly represent less of a threat to British control than the educated, aspiring city-dwellers, like Gitau. The eclipse of the simple villager by the educated Kenyan represents the beginning of Kenya as an independent nation, and this is a change which Huxley, with her emotional attachment to her childhood home, finds difficult to accept.

In the novel's ending, Huxley implies that there is still a place in Kenya for the British to work in cooperation with the Kenyans to build a better, more secure future for the country. Sam joins forces with the leader of the Home Guards, called the Tracker, who has personal "motives of revenge" (238) for joining the man-hunt: Gitau is responsible for the murder of the Tracker's son and the son's family. Sam and the Tracker work in smooth harmony. Like Robinson Crusoe and Friday, Kim and the lama, or Quatermain and Umbopa, Sam and the Tracker seem to embody a classic British view of the ideal working relationship between colonizer and colonized: the Tracker calls Sam "bwana" and respectfully follows his every order. This episode ends with a face-off between Sam and Gitau: the latter's gun providentially jams, enabling Sam to shoot him through the head, and thus bring the story to its unified end. The Mau Mau revolt may be far from put down, but the central target of revenge, Gitau, is dead.

As the novel concludes, Huxley's persona, Pat, faces a choice between two different roles for herself in Kenya's already anticipated independent future: she can follow in her parents' footsteps and take up a settler's life as Sam's wife, or she can continue her life of sacrifice and service as a missionary and teacher. Pat realizes that she and Sam belong "to different worlds" (254) and that their reasons for wishing to remain in Kenya "were too much at variance" (254). Huxley frustrates the reader's expectations by having Patricia reject Sam and choose to remain at the Mission, thus concluding the novel on a seeming note of resignation. To the violent revolution, which Gitau represents, Huxley obviously prefers a peaceful evolution for Kenya, which Pat embodies.

Pat's decision reflects her awareness throughout the novel of the fundamental difference between herself and Sam. The implications of Mau Mau are clear to

Pat, if not to Sam. Whereas Sam wishes to relive the past, Pat, in her difficult decision, attempts to face squarely the problematic future. It is in the ending of *A Thing to Love* and the depiction of Pat's hard choice that Huxley effectively captures the nature of a colonial Kenya enmeshed in change. More than her contemporaries, Ruark and Monsarrat, Huxley reflects the complex, difficult position of the British settler in the wake of Mau Mau, a time which, as Sam expresses it to Gitau, is "a bit like walking across a bog in the dark for both of us" (106).

Like Cary's *Mister Johnson*, *A Thing to Love* gives us a later view of the great changes brought about in the British Empire since its glorious heyday, captured so clearly in the fiction of Kipling and Haggard. Whereas Sam Gibson is an extension of such colonial heroes as Kim, Allan Quatermain, and Sir Henry Curtis—figures in what Huxley calls at one point "the far-fetched melodrama of a boy's adventure story" (64)—Patricia is an extension of the later, guilt-ridden, uncertain colonial administrators of Cary, Greene, and William Boyd. As Patricia faces the African children she presumes to educate at the Mission, she is filled with doubt and self-recrimination: "Was it, then, she, and not they, who stood in need of help and enlightenment? Had their eyes seen truths denied to hers? Was it a question of the blind trying to lead the clear-sighted?" (134). Pat's anxieties reflect the larger pessimism of the British concerning the Empire during the beginning of decolonization, when Kenya in the throes of Mau Mau seemed like "an empty, hostile and utterly remorseless world" (207). Huxley is also similar to Cary in that even though she can reflect the inevitable passing of imperial England, she is also strongly attracted to the ideals of the Empire and remains loyal to those ideals to the end. In *A Thing to Love*, we can see at once Huxley's nostalgia for the old days when colonial life was simpler and less fraught with tension and her realization that change was bound to come, and that, furthermore, the British must now be realistic in discovering an effective role for themselves in a newly independent Kenya.

Ngugi wa Thiong'o's *A Grain of Wheat*

James Thiong'o Ngugi was born in Limuru, a small village near Nairobi, in 1938. His father had four wives, in keeping with Gikuyu tradition, and twenty-eight children. Ngugi has recalled the hardships of his family during his upbringing:

> My father with his four wives had no land. They lived as tenants-at-will on somebody else's land. Harvests were often poor. Sweetened tea with milk at any time of day was a luxury. We had one meal a day—late in the evening. (*Homecoming*, 48)

Ngugi received his early education at a mission school, and his B.A. degree at Makerere University in Kampala, Uganda, where he served as editor of a student literary journal, *Penpoint*. While a student at Makerere, Ngugi began his writing career, completing two novels, *Weep Not, Child* (1964), the first novel in English by an East African, and *The River Between* (1965). After graduation from Makerere, Ngugi completed a year of post-graduate study at the University of Leeds in Yorkshire, England. Although originally intending to write a thesis on Conrad, Ngugi utilized his time in England to finish his third novel, *A Grain of Wheat* (1967), which recaptures the Mau Mau rebellion and the Emergency in Kenya from the point of view of a native Kenyan.

After returning from England, Ngugi taught for a time in East African schools before his appointment in 1967 as special lecturer at Nairobi's University College. A year later, he served as Lecturer in African literature at Northwestern University (Evanston, Illinois), in the United States. Back in Kenya, Ngugi served from 1972 to 1977 as Senior Lecturer and Chairman of the Department of Literature at the University of Nairobi. During these years, he also continued his writing career under the name of Ngugi wa Thiong'o. *Homecoming*, a collection of essays on African and Caribbean literature, appeared in 1972, and *Petals of Blood*, an indictment of neo-colonialism in independent Kenya and Ngugi's last novel in English, came out in 1977. Giving up English as his literary medium, Ngugi began writing in the Kikuyu language. After a performance of his play, *Ngahika Ndeenda* (trans. *I Will Marry When I Want*) in 1977, he fell into trouble with the Kenyan Government, and was imprisoned for a year without trial under the Public Securities Act.

Following his detention, Ngugi has lived with his wife and five children in exile from Kenya, and continued writing in Kikuyu. *Caitani Mutharabani* (trans. *Devil on the Cross*), a novel, appeared in 1980. Another novel, *Matigari*, in which Ngugi further developed the satirical style first used in *Petals of Blood* and *Devil on the Cross*, was published in 1987. Continually active in the struggle of his people "to seize back their creative initiative in history" (*Decolonising*, 4), Ngugi has also published two works of non-fiction since his detention: a personal account of his imprisonment, *Detained: A Writer's Prison Diary* (1981), and an analysis of the political element in African literature, *Decolonising the Mind: The Politics of Language in African Literature* (1986).

The greatest literary influence on Ngugi is perhaps Achebe. In "Chinua Achebe: a Man of the People," an essay in *Homecoming*, Ngugi praises Achebe for his commitment to the people of Africa. Moreover, Ngugi's creative output bears striking parallels to that of Achebe. Like Achebe's first three works, Ngugi's initial three novels offer a revision of an African country's history by replacing the traditional Eurocentric view with an African point of view. *The River Between* takes place during the 1927-29 Female Circumcision Crisis and foreshadows the British colonial takeover of Kenya. *Weep Not, Child* reconstructs the years before and during the Mau Mau rebellion of the early 1950s. *A Grain of Wheat*, set on the eve of the country's independence, offers a retrospective of the Kenyan people's historic struggle for independence against British colonial domination. Furthermore, Ngugi's fourth novel, *Petals of Blood*, like Achebe's *A Man of the People*, turns to the present problems of post-colonial Kenya beset by divisions between the "only two tribes left . . . the 'haves' and the 'have nots'" (*Homecoming*, xvii). Echoing the general model established by Achebe, the major West African novelist, Ngugi has secured his position as the leading voice among East African writers.

Like Achebe, Ngugi conceives the novelist's role as an educator whose duty, to quote Achebe, is "to help [African] society regain its belief in itself and put away the complexes of the years of denigration and self-denigration" (*MYOCD*, 51). Ngugi has perhaps gone further than Achebe, however, in charting a viable course for the African future. Implicit throughout *A Grain of Wheat*, for instance, is Ngugi's call for a new future direction for African society which reflects its unique heritage and institutions. Here, Ngugi is in complete agreement with Frantz Fanon, whose *The Wretched of the Earth* has been an important influence on much of Ngugi's work. In *The Wretched of the Earth*, Fanon writes:

> The Third World ought not to be content to define itself in the terms of values which have preceded it. On the contrary, the underdeveloped countries ought to do their utmost to find their own particular values and methods and a style which shall be peculiar to them. (99)

Along with advocating a return to past traditions, Ngugi calls for a unification of the divisions that beset independent Africa and the building of a new political and economic base with the "traditional African concept of the community" at its center (*Homecoming*, 25). Ngugi's vision of a new "African socialism," made explicit in *Petals of Blood*, is also clearly foreshadowed in *A Grain of Wheat*.

A Grain of Wheat might be meaningfully juxtaposed not only to Elspeth Huxley but more largely to British colonial fiction set in Africa, characterized by Ngugi as "Crusoe's naive view of Friday" which is "blind to the possibility that Friday could be a complex being with a complex culture" (*Homecoming*, 51). In his essay, "The Writer and His Past," Ngugi specifically refers to Huxley as "a liberal apologist for Kenya settlers" (43), and criticizes her simplistic representation of the African as "a child at the mercy of irrational forces" (*Homecoming*, 42-43). It is the lack of complexity in Huxley's portrayal of Africans that Ngugi finds especially disturbing: "their will to act melts away even without the kind of inner conflict which we would normally expect in any human being confronted with alien forces he cannot comprehend" (*Homecoming*, 43). Ngugi again criticizes Huxley in *Decolonising the Mind* for codifying Africans into two types: the good African who "co-operated with the European coloniser" and the bad one "who offered resistance to the foreign conquest and occupation of his country" (92).[2] In *A Grain of Wheat*, Ngugi provides us with a view of Mau Mau in direct opposition to that of Huxley. Unlike Huxley's monolithic portrait of Mau Mau, *A Grain of Wheat* renders this controversial historic period, which Ngugi has called "the one historical trauma that has left an indelible mark on the quality of life and literature in Kenya," with complexity and with an innate understanding of Kenya's colonized people (*Homecoming*, 70).

In "The Writer and His Past," Ngugi defines one of the primary objectives of the African writer: "What the African novelist has attempted to do is restore the African character to his history" (*Homecoming*, 43). Like so much post-colonial fiction, including Rushdie's *Midnight's Children*, Abrahams' *Wild Conquest*, and Achebe's *Things Fall Apart*, *A Grain of Wheat* takes history as its subject. Although most of the principal characters are fictional, there are frequent references to important figures in Kenya's colonial history. Actual historical events dictate the novel's progress. The reader learns, for instance, about the legendary warrior-leader, Waiyaka, one of the first to resist the white man's domination of Kenya. Later, Harry Thuku, a Kenyan resistance leader who "denounced the whiteman and cursed the benevolence and protection which denied people land and freedom," emerged to lead the resistance (16). After the death of Waiyaka and the imprisonment of Thuku, another great figure, Jomo Kenyatta, emerged as the Gikuyu spokesman. Following Kenyatta's arrest in 1952, a state of Emergency was declared and a storm of protest arose among indigenous Kenyans. And it is this period that Ngugi covers in his novel.

At one point in *A Grain of Wheat*, the people gather for the Uhuru celebrations on Independence Day, to sing songs and to hear speeches.

> Again they recreated history, giving it life through the words and voices: Land alienation, Waiyaka, Harry Thuku, taxation, conscription of labour into the whiteman's land, the break with the missions, and, oh, the terrible thirst and hunger for education. They sang of Jomo (he came, like a fiery spear among us), his stay in England (Moses sojourned in the land of Pharoah) and his return (he came riding on a cloud of fire and smoke) to save his children. (248)

In *A Grain of Wheat*, Ngugi recreates history much as the people recreate it in their singing. Ngugi orchestrates his novel in such a way that Mau Mau and the Emergency are seen in retrospect through the memories of those who lived through this period. *A Grain of Wheat* thus takes us beyond the time of *A Thing to Love* to the aftermath of the Emergency, when only a few days remain before the country attains its independence on December 12, 1963. The characters reflect upon the traumatic events of the past and call up painful memories as if to ready themselves for a new and difficult future. Ngugi implies in the novel that to move forward into the future, people must first come to terms with their past, for, he has explained, "what has been . . . is intimately bound up with what might be: our vision of the future, of diverse possibilities of life and human potential, has roots in our experience of the past" (*Homecoming*, 39).

Along with an awareness of the past and history, Ngugi also underscores the connection to the soil as a crucial aspect of a people's cultural and national identity. The attitude toward the land among the Kenyans in *A Grain of Wheat* presents an illuminating contrast to the "improvement of the estate" ethic of Huxley's settlers in *A Thing to Love*. All the Gikuyu beliefs, as Ngugi makes clear, are linked to the land and the mountains of Kenya: the people worship the god Ngai, who is said to live high atop Mount Kenya. Ngugi has explained the sacred connection the Gikuyu people feel toward the land:

> In the traditional Gikuyu setting, land was always more than a piece of earth for economic purposes: it was a religious inheritance, the people's very life. (Mugo Githae, 53)

Huxley's emphasis is on private economic development of the land in *A Thing to Love*, but Ngugi portrays the Kenyan landscape as the embodiment of the indigenous people's identity. It is in terms of the land and the soil, in fact, that Ngugi describes the birth of the people's organized resistance to colonialism:

> Then nobody noticed it; but looking back we can see that Waiyaka's blood contained within it a seed, a grain, which gave birth to a political party whose main strength thereafter sprang from a bond with the soil. (15)

Thus whereas Huxley posits Mau Mau as a rebellion exported by Nairobi agitators, Ngugi depicts Mau Mau as a grass-roots movement that found its unity in the people's traditional relationship to the land.

The title and epigraph of *A Grain of Wheat* are taken from 1 Corinthians 15:36:

> Thou fool, that which thou sowest is not quickened, except it die. And that which thou sowest, thou sowest not that body that shall be, but bare grain, it may chance of wheat, or of some other grain. (1)

Ngugi implies that in this crucial moment of Kenya's history, the people must put aside personal considerations and sacrifice themselves to the national cause. Mugo, the central character, is much like Njoroge, the protagonist of Ngugi's earlier novel, *Weep Not, Child*, in that he is too absorbed in his own personal problems to be effective in his country's drive for independence. Unable to act decisively, Mugo fears involvement and is condemned to a private nightmare of guilt, uncertainty, and self-recrimination.

A Grain of Wheat is in part a mystery novel which revolves around Mugo's strange spiritual malaise. The reader learns, only toward the novel's end, about the clouded past events which have led to Mugo's state of silent suffering. As the novel opens, Mugo awakens from a disturbing dream—a reference to Kenya's colonial history—and proceeds toward his shamba (or plot of farming land) to carry out the mechanical routine of his day. Mugo's efforts to work the soil are dispirited, as if all his physical energy had been mysteriously sapped—as if his nightmare and waking reality had become one and the same. He "raised the jembe, let it fall into the soil; lifted it and again brought it down," before he stops to wonder "where was the fascination he used to find in the soil before the emergency?" (9) Mugo appears cut off from his fellow villagers as well as from himself and the soil. Walking to and from his shamba, he attempts to avoid any contact with his countrymen. One persistent villager named Githua, however, manages to stop Mugo momentarily, and after exchanging greetings, this crippled veteran of the Emergency perhaps best sums up the burden of history weighing down the people when he suddenly and inadvertently blurts out, "The Emergency destroyed us" (6) and then hurries away.

The implication in *A Grain of Wheat* is that the Emergency indeed "destroyed" the people, but that they also did considerable damage to themselves through what Salman Rushdie in *Midnight's Children* calls the "optimism disease" (39). Based on their unity in opposition to the British during the Emergency, the people have high expectations for their independent future. They find themselves, however, with only a few days remaining before the independence celebrations, paradoxically disillusioned as they reflect on the price they have paid to get where they are. In *African Literature and Society*, Peter Nazareth reveals that before writing *A Grain of Wheat*, Ngugi read Frantz Fanon's *The Wretched of the Earth* (128). *A Grain of Wheat* often puts the reader in mind of Fanon's third chapter, "The Pitfalls of National Consciousness," in which the author asserts that nationalism is not enough to sustain the people's revolutionary unity once independence is achieved (159-160). The dominant tone of *A Grain of Wheat*, in keeping with this chapter of *The Wretched of the Earth*, is disillusionment and irony, and the central story of Mugo, cast by the people of his village into the false role of Mau Mau hero and liberator of his people, sets the overall ironic tone. Momentarily suspended between the painful past and an unexpectedly problematic future, the Kenyan people desperately seek a leader to unify and guide them. Ngugi implies, however, that the task of unification will not be easy. He echoes other post-colonial African writers, such as Achebe in *A Man of the People*, Armah in *The Beautyful Ones Are Not Yet Born*, Aluko in *One Man, One Matchet*, and Soyinka in *Season of Anomy*, by suggesting that a true man of the people is difficult to find in this post-independence time of need.

In V. S. Naipaul's *Guerrillas*, the black revolutionary, Jimmy Ahmed, writes, "When everybody wants to fight, there's nothing to fight for. Everybody wants to fight his own little war, everybody is a guerrilla" (7). Ahmed's conclusion also applies to *A Grain of Wheat*. Ngugi suggests that national unity is a difficult ideal to attain, for the people are too easily swayed by self-interest and individual pursuits. Mugo, for instance, wants simply to be left alone, untouched by the turbulence of his times. Gikonyo, the carpenter, longs to return home to his family after years of detention. He tells Mugo that "a time came when I did not care about Uhuru for the country any more. I just wanted to come home. And I would have sold Kenya to the whiteman to buy my own freedom" (79). Furthermore, General R. reveals that the crippled Githua, who pretends to be a victim of the nationalist struggle, actually injured his leg in a lorry accident: "to die fighting for freedom sounds more heroic than to die by accident" (172). These and other revelations take away from the people's jubilant celebration of their long-awaited freedom. Only Kihika, the leader of the forest fighters in the Thabai region, is genuinely willing to sacrifice himself to Kenya's independent future. The narrator tells us that "Kihika lived the words of sacrifice he had spoken to the multitude" (19) in his many speeches, and indeed it costs him his life.

Kihika is Ngugi's answer to the colonial writers' portrayal of the Mau Mau leader as a bloodthirsty criminal, as, for instance, Huxley's Gitau and Ruark's Kimani. Unlike the stereotype of the "been-to" who reverts to primitive African savagery, Kihika emerges as an admirable figure who has a clear realization of his own motives and ultimate aims. Furthermore, unlike Huxley's Gitau, Kihika is portrayed in the understandable, humanizing context of family. The reader is introduced to his father, Mbugua, "a well-known elder in the ridge" (87); his mother, Wanjiku; his brother, Kariuki; and particularly to his sister, Mumbi, who also plays an important role in the novel. The reader is also taken back into Kihika's past, which serves further to humanize him. The reader learns, for instance, that an early experience in mission school shaped the course of Kihika's life. After challenging the teacher's interpretation of a Biblical verse, Kihika is ordered to come forward to receive punishment. He decides, however, to escape out of the nearest window, climbing "out of the church to freedom" (101). Thereafter, Kihika taught himself to read and write, and began to attend political gatherings, from which he acquired "a new vision" (101). Like Peter Abrahams' Josiah in *This Island, Now* and Udomo in *A Wreath for Udomo* or like the sympathetic portraits of Gandhi in R. K. Narayan's *Waiting for the Mahatma* and Mulk Raj Anand's *Untouchable*, Kihika emerges as a hero of his country's nationalist revolution: a true man of the people.

Unlike Huxley's Gitau, who tries to subvert his cousin's Christian faith and carries on an adulterous relationship with his wife, Kihika is portrayed as a religious man: one village elder refers to him as a "high priest of freedom" (28). The sources of his inspiration are the Bible and the example of Gandhi. Indeed Kihika perceives a link between Christ and Gandhi in the latter's crusade against British colonial rule in India, which he explains in a speech:

> "No struggle for [independence] can succeed without such a man [as Christ]. Take the case of India, Mahatma Gandhi won freedom for people and paid for it with his own blood." (109)

Kihika interprets the scripture to fit the situation of the colonized people in Kenya: "But a few shall die that the many shall live. That's what crucifixion means today. Else we deserve to be slaves" (217).

Ngugi has stated that "the failure in imaginative comprehension of the African character in European fiction lies in the fact that the African is not seen in an active causal-effect relationship with a significant past" (*Homecoming*, 43). Indeed, it is Ngugi's delineation of his characters within the context of "a significant past" that makes them believable and fully human creations. Unlike Huxley's flat portrait of Gitau as an allegorical figure representing Mau Mau Evil, Kihika emerges as a rounded, plausible character shaped by history. Like the other Kenyans in *A Grain of Wheat*, Kihika is affected in complex ways by the Emergency. Although he takes a leadership role and is regarded as a hero, Kihika's single-minded devotion to the nationalist cause also makes him insensitive to people as individuals. He is perceived by some as too coldly political: the narrator, for example, describes him at one point as "a man following an idea" (112). After once hearing a speech by Kihika, Mugo becomes almost physically sick, feeling that "Kihika had spoken of blood as easily as if he was talking of drawing water in a river" (19).

Ngugi portrays Kihika as a man whom British colonial rule forces into an uncompromising and violent position. Gandhi claimed that the strength of a resistance movement is based not on the number of participants involved, but on the depth of the participants' commitment (Fischer, 36). Kihika's willingness to sacrifice his life for Kenya's independence is a measure of his commitment. When Kihika talks of Kenya's need for its people's sacrifice, his sister Mumbi comments, "I would hate to see a train run over my mother or father, or brothers. . . . I would faint at the sight of blood" (103). But Kihika does not advocate violence for the sake of violence, nor does he enjoy committing violent acts. General R. remarks, for instance, that Kihika "was never the same person after the day he shot D. O. Robson" (27). Rather, Kihika's awareness that violence is necessary to overthrow British colonial rule and to liberate Kenya parallels Fanon's similar realization in *The Wretched of the Earth*. Fanon defines colonialism as "not a thinking machine, nor a body endowed with reasoning faculties. It is violence in its natural state, and it will only yield when confronted with greater violence" (61). Ngugi's portrayal of colonialism as a form of aggression is thus similar to Abrahams' in *Wild Conquest*, in which the Boers forcefully invade Matabeleland, and Achebe's in *Things Fall Apart*, in which the British destruction of the village of Abame is meant to serve as an example to the people of Umuofia.

Contrasting with Kihika's violence of liberation, the British colonial officers, Thompson and Robson, perpetrate violence in order to secure their position of authority and power over the Kenyans. Kihika, for example, makes an explicit comparison between himself and Robson in his discussion with Mugo, in whose hut he seeks shelter after raiding Mahee prison camp and shooting Robson:

> "We don't kill just anybody. . . . We are not murderers. We are not hangmen—like Robson—killing men and women without cause or purpose. . . . We only hit back. You are struck on the left cheek. You turn the right cheek. One, two, three—sixty years. Then suddenly, it is always sudden, you say: I am not turning the other cheek any more." (216)

Thus, for Kihika, the Mau Mau revolt is a direct way of meeting the colonizers on their own terms: using force against force. It is also a means of unifying the people by introducing them, in Fanon's words, to "ideas of a common cause, of a national destiny, and of a collective history" (*WE*, 93). Even though both Thompson and Robson believe in the British civilizing mission in Kenya, the Mau Mau crisis reveals that the colonizers' position of authority actually depends solely on the superiority of British military force.

Ngugi's portrayal of John Thompson illustrates the corrupting influence of power, in this case the power the colonizer naturally assumes over the colonized. Even though on one level Thompson represents colonial domination of Kenya, Ngugi portrays him with complexity as an individual with ideals who is eventually corrupted by the colonial mission he serves. The reader learns that Thompson originally came to Kenya with noble intentions: after a brief stint in the Madagascar Campaign in World War II and the completion of his studies at Oxford, Thompson decided to return to East Africa, inspired by a conviction that "the British Empire was the development of a great moral idea . . . embracing peoples of all colours and creeds, based on the just proposition that all men were created equal" (62). During the Emergency, Thompson puts aside the "great moral idea" of Empire and uses his position of authority to mete out punishment to the detainees. Ngugi satirizes Thompson's conception of Empire, made clear in the latter's notes for his work-in-progress, *Prospero in Africa*:

> Dr. Albert Schweitzer says, "The Negro is a child, and with children, nothing can be done without the use of authority." I've now worked in Nyeri, Kisumu, Ngong. I agree. (64)

Furthermore, Thompson's complacent attitude regarding the achievements of the British Empire in Kenya are based on a stereotypic view of the subject people:

> Where was the irrationality, inconsistency and superstition so characteristic of the African and Oriental races? They had been replaced by the three principles basic to the Western mind: i. e. the principle of Reason, of Order, of Measure. (62)

In his portrait of Thompson as a man of high ideals who succumbs to brutality, Ngugi shows how extremes meet: as with Conrad's Kurtz, there is a short leap from an idealization of Empire to a brutalization of African prisoners. In a related episode, just before he dies, Thompson's predecessor, Tom Robson, repeatedly intones his last word, "brutes" (212), which recalls Kurtz's phrase in *Heart of Darkness*: "Exterminate all the brutes!" (51). In *A Grain of Wheat*, Ngugi answers Huxley's depiction of Mau Mau as an African atavistic return to primitive savagery by showing the brutality and savagery to which the British colonizers succumb. Ngugi utilizes his narrative voice, switching from that of novelist to that of historian, to remind the reader of actual atrocities committed in the detention camps during the Emergency, and to support his indictment of colonial officials like Thompson and Robson:

> Why . . . did the incident at Rira Camp capture the imagination of the world. . . . The men were rounded up and locked in their cells. The now famous beating went on night and day. Eleven men died. (149, 152)

Ngugi here reinforces an important distinction: whereas Mau Mau violence serves a noble purpose—national liberation—the British colonizers succumb to brutality in order to keep Kenya in a subjugated position. During the Emergency, Ngugi suggests, the true nature of colonialism was revealed for the world to see.

Despite British colonial rule and the chaos and violence of the Emergency, the "traditional African concept of the community," to which Ngugi obviously attaches great importance, still shows signs of life (*Homecoming*, 25). One of the central concerns of *A Grain of Wheat*, in fact, is the welfare of the Thabai community. Like Achebe's Umuofia, Thabai becomes the equivalent of a primary character in the novel. The narrator frequently speaks in the first person plural, as if representing the collective voice of the community speaking to an acquaintance from a nearby village:

> Most of us from Thabai first saw him at the New Rung'ei Market the day the heavy rain fell. You remember the Wednesday, just before Independence? (202)

Furthermore, the importance of the community and its traditions are underlined by Ngugi's positive portrayal of the elders, such as Warui and Wambui, who embody the history and traditions of the village. Gikonyo's mother, Wanjiku, and Karanja's mother, Wairimu, are also portrayed as strong, stable pillars of the community. Wairimu, for instance, gives Karanja good advice which the latter does not heed: "Don't go against the people. A man who ignores the voice of the people comes to no good end" (256). One might say that whereas Kihika listens to the voice of the people, Karanja, Mugo, and Gikonyo alienate themselves from the community because they ignore that voice.

In *A Thing to Love*, Huxley shows sympathy toward the simple villagers, like Raphaelo, who are manipulated by the urban Mau Mau leaders into turning against the British. Ngugi, on the other hand, criticizes the Kenyans who failed to take part in the national liberation movement. We might say that Huxley's emphasis on individualism is evident in her implication that to join the group or mob is wrong. Ngugi's emphasis on community is similarly evident in his argument that to refuse to identify with the popular cause amounts to a betrayal of Kenya. Ngugi, nevertheless, obviously sympathizes with the Kenyans who fail to join in the Mau Mau effort more than he does with the colonial representatives, Thompson and Robson. Of the three characters—Karanja, Mugo, and Gikonyo—who withdraw from the community and nation during this time of need, however, Ngugi feels the least compassion for Karanja. For the latter's renunciation of the oath and his cooperation with the British against his fellow countrymen is tantamount to a total, unqualified betrayal of his nation.

We might think of Karanja as the logical extension of Achebe's court messenger who serves the colonial authorities in *Things Fall Apart*: he is the white man's lackey. His joining the British colonial government, where he serves as Thompson's messenger, exemplifies the placing of his own personal welfare before the good of his country. Through his position in the colonial government, Karanja is able to share vicariously in the colonizer's power over the colonized:

> At Githima, people believed that a complaint from him was enough to make a man lose his job. Karanja knew their fears. Often when men came into his office, he would suddenly cast them a cold eye, drop hints, or simply growl at them; in this way, he increased their fears and insecurity. (43)

In part, Karanja's betrayal of the national cause represents a logical choice: he clearly believes that the Mau Mau revolt is in vain and that the British are in Kenya to stay. The advantage in linking his fate with the colonial authorities seems obvious to him. But Karanja also joins the British, paradoxically, out of an unrequited love for Mumbi. The ultimate destructiveness in Karanja's aims is thus made clear in their intended result: breaking apart the unity of the Gikuyu people, symbolized by the Mumbi-Gikonyo relationship.

Karanja, who eventually becomes Chief officer, uses his position of power in the colonial government to grant Mumbi special favors denied to others—giving her food, providing official clearance for her brother, Kariuki, to attend secondary school—in order to win her affection. It is in this way that Mumbi finally succumbs to Karanja's advances and eventually bears his child. Karanja's cynicism during this time is evident in the way he justifies his actions to Mumbi:

> "Take this maize-flour and bread, or else you will die. I did not betray Kihika, I did not. As for carrying a gun for the whiteman, well, a time will come when you too will know that every man in the world is alone, and fights alone, to live." (166)

Karanja's inividualistic outlook is also visible in his competition against Gikonyo in the foot race during the Uhuru celebrations, and in his jealousy of Kihika. Eventually, however, Karanja's mistaken conviction that the British colonizers will never leave Kenya transforms him into an alienated man, scorned by those he once controlled. General R. perhaps best sums up the villagers' attitude toward Karanja when he says that "in betraying Kihika to the whiteman Karanja had really betrayed the black people everywhere on the earth" (174). The irony that Mugo and not Karanja actually betrayed Kihika notwithstanding, General R.'s remark remains true because Karanja consciously puts his own welfare before that of his people.

Ngugi obviously feels more sympathy for Mugo than for Karanja, for Mugo's alienation from the community is due more to circumstance than choice. As an orphan raised by an alcoholic aunt who despises him, Mugo is in a sense born outside the community. And it is Mugo's painful awareness of this separation that makes the reader sympathize with his plight:

> He wanted somebody, anybody, who would use the claims of kinship to do him ill or good. Either one or the other as long as he was not left alone, an outsider. (11)

Moreover, Mugo's outsider status has much to do with his own jealousy of Kihika as a revolutionary leader. Mugo sees Kihika's loving family—"people who would mourn his end, who would name their children after him" (221)—as an example of the revolutionary leader's good fortune in life. Because of Kihika's secure position within a family and a community, he can afford to "play with death" (221). Mugo, on the other hand, feels that he has everything to lose and nothing to gain by joining the forest fighters and openly opposing British colonial rule. Mugo, the self-made man, thus comes to share Karanja's outlook on the Emergency; and like the latter, he places his personal welfare before that of his village or country.

Clearly, Ngugi strikes a balance between sympathy and criticism in his authorial attitude toward Mugo. In the novel, the fate of each of the indigenous characters is marked by his or her response to British colonial rule. Kihika opposes colonialism, and he dies fighting it. Karanja joins the colonial government, and after its end, he is banished from the community. Mugo, on the other hand, attempts to walk a tight-rope between the two sides of the Mau Mau conflict. Perhaps unconsciously, however, Mugo adopts a colonial mentality to a greater degree than he realizes. His individualistic emphasis on getting ahead, for instance, would seem to represent a British colonial influence on his character. Mugo clearly sees himself in competition with his fellows: one of his reasons for avoiding participation in the conflict is because it might harm his chances of personal advancement. The narrator tells us that "all his life [Mugo] had avoided conflicts: at home, or at school, he rarely joined the company of other boys for fear of being involved in brawls that might ruin his chances of a better future" (221). Mugo's personal code is a simple one: "if you leave people alone, then they ought to leave you alone" (221). Thus it is that Mugo sees Mau Mau as having nothing to do with him: "this was a drama in a world not his own" (212-13). Alienated from the community by choice as well as circumstance, Mugo retreats into an internal dream world in which he envisions himself as the messianic savior of Kenya. Like Mumbi, who enjoys frequent day-dreams in which she assumes an identity based on Esther in the Old Testament, Mugo spends much time "revelling in the dreams he loved" (212), in which he casts himself in the role of Moses:

> Mugo lay on his back under the shade . . . [and] he let the gentle voice lure him to distant lands in the past. Moses too was alone keeping the flock of Jethro his father-in-law. . . . And God called out to him in a thin voice, Moses, Moses. And Mugo cried, Here am I, Lord. (143)

Later, Mugo thinks to himself that he, "an only son, was born to save" (153). Mugo's dreamy identification with Moses is not only a mark of his being cut off from reality, but also an indication of the strong effect the British colonial missionaries have had on him as well as on Gikuyu society in general. Mugo's distorted view of himself, moreover, mirrors the villagers' illusions concerning his detention, his relationship with Kihika, and his role as a Mau Mau hero.

Mugo's withdrawal from the community and the Mau Mau conflict into a private realm of dreams amounts to an abdication of responsibility. Because of the disastrous effect Mau Mau has on his personal fortunes, Mugo comes to see his life governed by forces he is powerless to control. He therefore decides to accept his fate passively and makes no effort to change the course of his life:

> Things had been fated to happen at different moments. One had no choice in anything as surely as one had no choice on one's birth. He did not, then, tire his mind by trying to connect what went before with what came after. Numbed, he ran without thinking of the road, its origin or its end. (195)

Mugo's failure to perceive a connection between action and consequence, past and future, is belied, however, by the narrator's version of Kenya's history, in which resistance to colonial rule has borne the fruit of national independence, and also in the constant narrative shift from past to present, establishing a causal link between the two. Mugo's colonial indoctrination and lack of responsibility are evident, moreover, in his betrayal of Kihika. Mugo arrives at colonial headquarters as if he were sleep-walking: his "tumult of thoughts . . . acquired the concrete logic of a dream" (223). As he unburdens his thoughts to Thompson, Mugo feels secure and grateful, likening himself to Isaac narrowly escaping Abraham's knife. Throughout the novel, we see that Mugo's understanding of Christianity is directly opposite to that of Kihika. Whereas Kihika gives the Bible an activist, revolutionary interpretation—"Everybody who takes the Oath of Unity to change things in Kenya is a Christ" (110)—Mugo's understanding of the scripture leads him to passivity and an abdication of personal responsibility.

In *A Thing to Love*, Gitau, the evil representative of Mau Mau, is unable to transform himself. Similarly, Raphaelo, unwittingly caught up in the rebellion, cannot alter his increasingly ominous circumstances. In *A Grain of Wheat*, however, Ngugi has, in his own words, "given back to the African character the will to act and change the scheme of things" (*Homecoming*, 43). Mugo, for example, undergoes a transformation, deciding to atone for his betrayal of Kihika by making a public confession at the Uhuru celebrations. After a long talk with Mumbi, which "cracked open his dulled inside and released imprisoned thoughts and feelings" (195), Mugo gains "a glimpse of a new earth" (266). Mugo's revelation to Mumbi that he betrayed her brother, Kihika, enables him to perceive the effect of his actions on others and the connection between past and present. The thread of continuity and meaning Mugo seeks finally becomes apparent to him as he stands before the village gathering:

> He was conscious of himself, of every step he made, of the images that rushed and whirled through his mind with only one constant thread: so he was responsible for whatever he had done in the past, for whatever he would do in the future. (267)

By confessing, Mugo sacrifices himself for the symbolic purification of the community. Furthermore, Mugo's action has an important salutary effect on Gikonyo, who also must undergo a transformation in order to become a vital, effective member of his symbolic family, the Gikuyu people.

Gikonyo's metamorphosis is an important structural aspect of *A Grain of Wheat*. The happy union between Gikonyo and Mumbi early in the novel represents the order and stability of pre-colonial Kenya. When the Emergency is declared, however, Gikonyo is torn between the plight of his country and the threat to his own personal welfare. After spending five years in detention camps, Gikonyo longs to return home, confident that his "reunion with Mumbi would see the birth of a new Kenya" (121). Gikonyo's subsequent discovery of Mumbi's unfaithfulness mirrors the general disillusionment of the Gikuyu people during this historic time. As a result, Gikonyo becomes embittered and alienated from the community, adopting an individualistic outlook much like Karanja's and Mugo's:

> One lived alone. . . . Gikonyo greedily sucked sour pleasure from this reflection which he saw as a terrible revelation. To live and die alone was the ultimate truth. (135)

Gikonyo's continued disillusionment through the transference of power from the colonial government to independent Kenya symbolizes the post-independent realizations of the majority of Kenyans. After his request for a loan from the new M. P. is turned down, Gikonyo realizes that those who actually fought for independence have been disenfranchised, and that opportunistic, power-hungry

Kenyans have simply taken over the colonial rulers' positions:

> "Whom do we see riding in long cars and changing them daily as if motor cars were clothes? It is those who did not take part in the movement. . . . At political meetings you hear them shout: Uhuru, Uhuru, we fought for. Fought where?" (80)

In the last section of the novel, entitled "Harambee," a slogan meaning togetherness initiated by Jomo Kenyatta, Gikonyo shows signs of renewal. He asks himself what "difference was there between him and Karanja or Mugo or those who had openly betrayed people and worked with the whiteman to save themselves?" (278). His decision to resume his carpentry work and to begin by making a stool for Mumbi in an effort to revitalize their marriage, symbolizes Kenya's effort to make a new start following the years of British colonial domination and the Emergency. In the final scene, Gikonyo appears optimistic as he chooses a design for the stool that will embody his new-found hope: "a woman big—big with child" (280). The child in this case represents Kenya's future, but Mumbi realizes that the child also demands the need for responsiblity, and she therefore sounds a more cautious note in response to Gikonyo:

> "Things are not so easy. What has passed between us is too much to be passed over in a sentence. We need to talk, to open our hearts to one another, examine them, and then together plan the future we want. But now, I must go, for the child is ill." (280)

Ngugi suggests that the child, or Kenya, is "ill," but that it will survive. The country must first heal the wounds of the past before a fresh, hopeful course for the future can be set. In this closing, Ngugi also underscores the need for a return to traditional African values, centered in the family and based on an open dialogue between all members of the community.

On the simplest level, Ngugi answers Huxley's indictment of the Mau Mau "conspiracy" by charging the British colonizers with brutality and savagery in their determination to subjugate Kenya. On another level, however, Ngugi's response takes the form of an explanation of the mainsprings of Gikuyu society and the people's sacred relationship to the land. In *A Thing to Love*, Huxley gives us a material view of Kenya as a piece of property, which reflects the British emphasis on development and productivity in their colonial rule. The British ethic of "improvement of the estate" can be seen as a justification of their colonial occupation of Kenya. According to Huxley and the British view, the Kenyan people's demand for the return of the land came only after the British had made it rich and productive. Because of Huxley's material view of Kenya and this emphasis on development, she sees the Mau Mau revolt as deplorable, for it destroys everything the British have built up. Thus Huxley's title aptly sums up the British attitude toward Kenya: the colonizers have come to love the country as a result of giving something of themselves to it, and this is what they see ruined by Mau Mau.

In *A Grain of Wheat*, on the other hand, Ngugi gives us a spiritual view of Kenya, reflecting the sacred relationship the Kenyan people feel for their soil. From this perspective, the British colonial seizure of the land amounts to a severing of the Kenyan people from the source of their identity and strength as a people. By focusing on history, Ngugi also reflects the Kenyan peoples' view of their own independence movement, which began with the British colonial arrival and steadily gained momentum through Mau Mau and the Emergency until Uhuru was finally attained in 1963. Rather than a lust for material property based on envy, the Kenyans' demand for the return of their land was a spiritual longing which found its expression in resistance to colonial rule. Clearly, from Ngugi's perspective, the Mau Mau revolt is a positive liberation movement; he has, in fact, called it "the first modern anti-colonial guerrilla movement in Africa" (*Kunapipi*, 139). If the Mau Mau uprising failed ultimately to bring about the independent, united Kenya for which many hoped, the movement nevertheless represented a crucial step in the direction toward the future attainment of that goal.

Chapter V
The Demise of Empire: Alec Waugh and George Lamming

Alec Waugh's *Island in the Sun*

Alec Waugh's *Island in the Sun* (1956) is perhaps the most thorough and sustained treatment of the West Indies in modern British fiction. In much British fiction, the West Indies have been depicted as a conveniently exotic setting for the portrayal of moral and spiritual decay. In *Jane Eyre* (1848), for instance, Rochester's "dissipated youth" was spent in the West Indies. In *Wide Sargasso Sea* (1966), Jean Rhys's re-telling of Bronte's story, there is a similar depiction of the West Indies as a breeding ground for moral degeneration, and in Graham Greene's *The Comedians* (1966), Haiti represents an earthly Hell. Other British novels set in the West Indies, such as Richard Hughes's *A High Wind in Jamaica* (1929) and Patrick Leigh Fermor's *The Violins of Saint-Jacques* (1953), also emphasize the exoticism and sensuality of the islands. Although Waugh's *Island in the Sun* evokes similarly salient aspects of the West Indies, his novel also provides an expansive, panoramic view of the region caught up in the turmoil of decolonization. In addition, Waugh gives the reader an exciting account of the waning power of the British Empire in the West Indies in the aftermath of the two world wars.

Alec Waugh was born in London in 1898, the son of publisher Arthur Waugh, and older brother of the well-known writer Evelyn Waugh. It was only in his later life, following his participation in the two world wars, that Waugh made frequent trips to the West Indies and became fascinated with life in the tropics. Alec's early life was marked by controversy. He was expelled from

Sherborne School in Dorset and later attended a military academy. At the age of 17, Waugh began to write "the story, term by term of my four years at Sherborne" (*EYAW*, 39). This story became his first novel, *The Loom of Youth*, a candid treatment of life at a boys' public school, including accounts of homosexuality, that created a scandal among the English reading public. Unlike many British colonial writers, Waugh felt alienated by the Empire, which was in decline by this time. Later in his life, Waugh was to identify the public school as one of the "main pillars" supporting the British Empire, Kipling as the Empire's "uncrowned laureate," and the plucky, young hero in Kipling's short story, "The Brushwood Boy," as the public school model of behavior:

> To criticize Kipling was to impeach the crown, and 'The Brushwood Boy' was accepted as the ideal type which the perfect educational system was endeavoring to produce. I knew that the average public school boy was not in the least like 'The Brushwood Boy'. (*EYAW*, 49)

Waugh had the ill fortune of being old enough to fight in World War I and yet still young enough to serve in World War II. In *Abroad: British Literary Traveling Between the Wars*, Paul Fussell relates that *The Loom of Youth* was popular reading among the soldiers in the trenches during World War I (*Abroad*, 5). Although he was wounded and later taken as a prisoner-of-war, Waugh looked on the war as a positive experience for two reasons, both of which had to do with his chosen career as a writer. In his autobiography, Waugh claims that World War I gave him the "experience of commanding men in battle, than which there is no more important masculine experience" (*BWL*, 137). He would later draw on that experience in several of his novels. Moreover, the time he spent in a prison camp in Mainz allowed Waugh the chance to read Somerset Maugham's fiction set in the South Seas, which was also popular among the soldiers during World War I. Maugham's work became an important influence on Waugh's writing and on his life.

Having settled in London after the war, Waugh felt a "niggling persistent sense of everything's ultimate unimportance. There seemed no point to anything" (*EYAW*, 213). His reading of Maugham led him to wonder if life among the Polynesians might not be more fulfilling. He bought a ticket for an around-the-world ocean cruise. After a brief stopover in Tahiti midway through the trip, Waugh decided to remain behind and the ship sailed on without him. In his autobiography, *The Early Years*, he gives a frank account of a love affair with a

Tahitian woman whom he saw as an "antidote to the capricious tyranny of the ex-debutantes of Mayfair" (215). Waugh's desire to escape post-war England and western civilization, in general, more largely reflected the longing of an entire British generation, as Fussell shows in *Abroad*.[1] Waugh expresses the general post-war feelings of his generation in *The Early Years*:

> The Kipling legend was in disrepute. My generation was impatient with the narrow, uncompromising attitude of the retired pukka Sahib. Was not that talk about the White Man's Burden in part responsible for the war? Had not our Empire inflamed Germany's jealousy? What right had we in India anyhow? (223)

Tahiti provided a brief antidote to the insanity of war, but did little for Waugh as a writer. Waugh discovered that the South Sea islands were Maugham's exclusive province, and that he would have to "plough some other field" (*EYAW*, 231).

Although Waugh continued to write both novels and travel books, he failed to attract the early readership he had gained with *The Loom of Youth*. In 1928, after a five and a half month trip to the West Indies, Waugh wrote *Hot Countries*, a book chronicling his travels in the tropics. In 1940, he wrote a novel, *No Truce With Time*, which in the author's own words was about "adultery in the West Indies," but it fared poorly (*BWL*, 150). After World War II, in which he served in military intelligence in the Middle East, Waugh began to make annual trips to the West Indies, in search of both solace after a broken marriage and material for a novel. Recalling that Kipling had once told Maugham that "the West Indies were full of stories," Waugh began an active search for the makings of a bold, new enterprise (*BWL*, 263). The fruit of that search was *Island in the Sun*, which became an instant best-seller. Waugh later wrote that *Island in the Sun* "came out exactly at the right time, when the aeroplane had brought the West Indies within range of tourism, and in Britain's Colonial Empire 'The Wind of Change' was bringing demands of independence" (*BWL*, 174). Not only was the novel rushed through a first printing of 10,000 copies and serialization in several popular magazines, but it was also later made into a highly successful motion picture.

Although Waugh's pronouncements on "the Kipling legend" make him seem at odds with the Empire, he nevertheless felt a strong allegiance to England and its colonial mission. If he had not become a novelist, he once asserted, he would have joined the civil service in the colonies. Perhaps as a result of his intelligence work in World War II, Waugh developed a strong identification with England.

One can see some of this identification in Waugh's positive portrayal of Governor-General Templeton in *Island in the Sun*. After the publication of *Island in the Sun*, Waugh continued to travel in the West Indies and to retain a great love of the tropics. In Evelyn Waugh's *A Little Learning*, the author refers to his brother as "indefatigably nomadic," and adds that Alec carried into "his sixties a zest for life" (25-26). In *The Early Years*, Alec also describes himself as "a restless, perchless traveller, avid of change and of the sun, searching for his plots and characters between Capricorn and Cancer" (*EYAW*, xiii). He died in Tampa Bay, Florida in 1981.

The Caribbean of *Island in the Sun* is, on the surface, a carefree, sunny land of warmth, relaxation, and sexual indulgence. Waugh's description of Barbados in *Hot Countries* anticipates the exotic setting of *Island in the Sun*: "The sun shines. Every one is carefree, happy, at ease. Time does not exist" (*HC*, 185). The description in *Island in the Sun* of Santa Marta as a primitive and colonial scenic backdrop for adventure links Waugh with other British colonial writers, from Haggard to Huxley, who likewise describe British characters' romantic adventures in exotic, faraway, and often tropical places. Waugh's Caribbean setting, moreover, recalls the geographic/sexual nexus found in the Jamaica of Patrick Leigh Fermor's *The Violins of Saint-Jacques*, and the Dominica of Jean Rhys's *Wide Sargasso Sea*. Such novels are continuing testimony that far from a solely economic venture, the British Empire provided an important psychological outlet for the English, for these works suggest the Empire as a possibility for adventure and escape into sexual license, and not merely as a setting for the self-imposed duty to "civilize" alien peoples.

One common aspect of the British colonial novels examined thus far is the image of the colony as a huge playground, which represents a return in space and time to a primordial form of life. It is revealing that so many of these novels involve an initiation into manhood. In Kipling, Haggard, Cary, and Huxley as well as in Waugh, the colonies offer the ideal environment for male (and female, in Huxley's novel) maturation based on an experience unavailable in an increasingly industrialized, restrictive England. In *When the Going Was Good*, Evelyn Waugh reflects on his generation of English writers traveling abroad and writing about exotic lands:

> We turned our backs on civilisation [and] . . . set off on our various stern roads; I to the Tropics . . . with the belief that barbarism was a dodo to be stalked with a pinch of salt. . . . At that time it seemed an ordeal, an initiation to manhood. (xi)

This aspect of empire is pointedly evoked in Thomas Pynchon's *Gravity's Rainbow* when the narrator rebukes Marx's narrow definition of colonialism as "nothing but Cheap Labor and Overseas Markets":

> Oh, no. Colonies are much, much more. Colonies are the outhouses of the European soul. . . . Out and down in the colonies, life can be indulged, life and sensuality in all its forms, with no harm done to the Metropolis, nothing to soil those cathedrals, white marble, noble thoughts. . . . No word ever gets back. (368-369)

There is ample support for Pynchon's definition of colonialism in *Island in the Sun*. Where else but "out and down in the colonies" would the Governor-General announce after dinner at Government House that the "lavatories are at the end of the passage, or there's the garden" (414) and several guests choose the latter? Where else but in the colonies could one drink rum punches at any time of day without fear of social stigma? In one revealing scene, for instance, Maxwell Fleury "limits" himself to two rum punches before giving an important political speech. Where but in the colonies could a government official such as the ADC Denis Archer have a private apartment in which, on break from his duties, he could carry on an affair with his coloured secretary without his superior ever finding out?

Like other British colonial novels, *Island in the Sun* also provides us with a valuable account of British colonial rule. Waugh describes the dissolution of Empire in a Caribbean island as perceived by the rulers. As such, Waugh's novel continues developments in the British colonial novel that we have traced thus far. In line with the preceding colonial writers, who take an increasingly disillusioned view of the Empire, Waugh expresses a pessimistic attitude, as if by his time the imperial breakup is a foregone conclusion and there is nothing to be done about it. Furthermore, Waugh, like Huxley in *A Thing to Love*, utilizes a number of different narrative consciousnesses and shifts constantly from one to another, rather than seeing all the action from a single narrative viewpoint. This tactic would seem to suggest that the views of the colonized are as important as those of the colonizers and, further, that to understand the complex colonial situation, both sides of the conflict have to be understood.

The underlying pessimism of *Island in the Sun* reflects the British attitude toward actual historical developments at the time, in particular the passing of Britain's colonial era. The British colonial administrators and planters in Waugh's fictional Santa Marta come to realize that there is no longer a future in the West Indies for the white man and that they now face an uncertainty which contrasts with earlier colonial attitudes of assurance and confidence. Julian Fleury, an established Santa Marta plantation owner, for instance, worries about the future of his family:

> In a day when every Englishman of a certain class had been brought up to an assurance of security through the mere fact of having been born an Englishman, his duty had been clearly marked: duty to his family, his school, his country, "the white man's burden" . . . but nowadays in a changing world that was not enough. (52)

Many of the British characters in the novel are old and at the end of their careers. Fleury, like Governor Templeton, whom he has known since their days together at Eton, appears aged and in the twilight of his career. Another British planter, Colonel Carson, a former colonial officer in India and military officer at the Malta siege and in the Western desert at Alamein, personifies recent British historical experience. Following his recuperation from a wound received at Alamein, Carson learns that his wife has divorced him. He comes to feel adrift in the present, left cynical and bitter, "brooding about the past. . . . But how could he help living in the past when it was much more alive?" (124). Although the Caribbean continues to be a paradise for some of the characters in the novel, it is not for Colonel Carson, who considers it an injustice that after a brilliant military career, "he would finish up like this, alone, in a two-penny-ha'penny West Indian island" (124).

Of the many characters in *Island in the Sun*, Governor Templeton perhaps emerges as the most positive. Although Waugh celebrates the exotic appeal of the Caribbean—the warm, sunny climate and the beautiful women—it is significant that he would also have a high regard for the British administrator who runs the colony. Like other British colonial writers, Waugh is clearly pulled in opposite directions about his colonial setting: he feels an attraction for the carefree life the island has to offer, on the one hand, and a high regard for the order and duty required of the people who are responsible for the colony's welfare, on the other. Waugh seems to invest some of himself in Governor Templeton: like the author, Templeton has a background in military intelligence, which he uses to his advantage in governing the island. Also like Waugh, Templeton is a survivor of the World War I trenches of Passchendaele. In the novel, Templeton is more than the Empire's administrator; he is its symbol. The narrator gives a surface description of him as "a typical Englishman who . . . never questions, never needs to question, the essential foundations of his faith. . . . duty and responsibility." The narrator also reveals, however, that "beneath his impersonal military manner [Templeton] was constantly harassed by uncertainty" (11). One can see in this description that Waugh's attitude toward the Empire is far from simple. Although he portrays Templeton as a man of high moral standard and as a fair and able administrator, Waugh also implies that Templeton is caught in a system that has lost its moral and political capacity for command. In short, Waugh suggests that Templeton is the right man for the job, but that the Empire which he serves is out of order.

In *Hot Countries*, Waugh says, "To wander today through the Antilles is rather like reading the last chapter of a Galsworthy novel. . . . An era is passing" (205). Change and the British colonizers' inability to adapt are the central themes of *Island in the Sun*. The British administrators seem well-intentioned, but their system of colonial rule is outmoded, an empty relic of a bygone era. Although once prosperous, Santa Marta is portrayed as economically troubled. Moreover, the trade union movement, led by the arrogant Socialist firebrand, David Boyeur, poses distinct problems for the island's planters and its colonial administration. Julian Fleury goes so far as to tell a visiting American journalist that the colonizers are "sitting on a keg of dynamite" (32), and the journalist adopts the image for the reports that he sends back to his newspaper, the Baltimore *Sun*. The Governor also feels the pressures of the times and he responds by calling for a new constitution which will bring about universal suffrage and give the island's non-white population control of the powerful Executive Council. Although these reforms are clearly necessary, the island's planters see them as dangerous because they will allow "these people [to] have their heads too soon" (31). The planters' concerns are echoed in the reports the American journalist, Bradshaw, writes for the Baltimore *Sun*, in which he asks: "What will happen when the demagogues of an undisciplined proletariat are in control?" (31). Throughout *Island in the Sun*, in fact, change is seen, not in terms of its effect on the Barbadian people, but rather as a British and even an American problem.

At one point in the novel Waugh refers to an Osbert Sitwell story, "The Machine Runs Down," and indeed Waugh might have taken Sitwell's title as his own, for constantly in the background of *Island in the Sun* is the suggestion of a breakdown in the imperial machine. When the journalist Bradshaw comes to Government House to dine, for instance, he gives the reader a revealing, outsider's view of the British colonizers:

> It was the first time that Bradshaw had dined at Government House in a British colony. He was impressed. These Englishmen had something. They had lost their empire, their coinage was debased, their mines were obsolete, their navy was minute, yet they still behaved as though they owned the universe. (108)

Island in the Sun shows the English in the habit of rule, but without the reality of inalienable power. Waugh depicts the colonizers with obvious sympathy as men in the unenviable position of having inherited the rulership of an ineffectual, crumbling Empire. British administrators, such as Templeton, Archer, and Carson, would undoubtedly be effective in an earlier time, but now they have no system to support their abilities. The post-World War II realities which Waugh's novel reflect clearly complicate the colonizers' already difficult job. Governor Templeton, for instance, must not only try to influence Bradshaw to give the island favorable press coverage, but also pacify the edgy Westminster colonial officials who already have their hands full with the wave of nationalism in Kenya and Malaya. In addition, Governor Templeton's top priority, of course, is to maintain order in Santa Marta, which requires him to deal with such sensitive issues as the "colour line."

Waugh's fictional island of Santa Marta, like Barbados, has a sizable African population and strong sensitivity about the "colour line" between black and white. In *Hot Countries*, Waugh asserts that in Barbados, "the oldest and most English colony . . . the colour line has been retained," and the same can clearly be said of the fictional Santa Marta (204). When the journalist Bradshaw asks about "the issue" (117) in Santa Marta, the Anglican Archdeacon quickly responds, "Colour, my dear fellow, colour" (118). The color issue seems, if anything, to have become more sensitive with time. The Archdeacon explains to Bradshaw how the derogatory phrase "touch of the tarbrush" has been replaced by "passes for white," although every family tries "to pretend that, as far as itself is concerned, those two words 'passes for' do not exist" (118). The Archdeacon acquaints the reader as well as Bradshaw with this central West Indian issue. "When I first came out," he explains to Bradshaw, "I was astonished to realize how much that trace of colour meant, how many social barriers it creates" (118).

Frantz Fanon describes the colonial world as "compartmentalized," and surely the imposition of colonial barriers applies to the sensitive issue of the "colour line" in Santa Marta (*WE*, 37). In fact, barriers excluding the colonized from places frequented by the colonizers exist throughout the island. When Governor Templeton arranges a welcoming party for his son, Euan, who is on leave from his military duties in the Middle East, the invitation list becomes one sign among many of the colonial barriers in Santa Marta society. An invitation from Government House is equivalent to a badge of prestige for a non-white Santa Martan. Ironically, the Governor takes considerable pains to include as many non-white guests as possible, because he wants to create a favorable image of the island for the visiting American journalist. The Governor gives strict instructions to his ADC Denis Archer: "The party must not . . . be allowed to form itself into separate groups of white, near white, brown, and black" (11). Despite such careful planning, however, the party quickly divides itself into precisely those racial groupings. After the party, Grainger Morris is reminded of how slowly change occurs in the West Indies and "how rigid still . . . the barrier between black and white" (45). Here Waugh indicates that the changes which the white planters regard as dangerously rapid are perceived by the non-whites as frustratingly slow.

The colonizers' exclusive existence is reflected in the novel's primary settings: Government House, the Belfontaine plantation, and the Club. In *Hot Countries*, Waugh writes: "The English carry their own lives with them. They make no attempt to assimilate into the character of the countries that they occupy. . . . In the same spirit have the English colonised India, the Antilles, and the Far East" (197-198). A large portion of *Island in the Sun* takes place inside the claustrophobic atmosphere of the Country Club. Here the reader is undoubtedly reminded of similar portraits of the Club in such colonial fiction as Kipling's story, "Without Benefit of Clergy," Forster's *A Passage to India*, Orwell's *Burmese Days*, and Cary's *The African Witch*. Seen from the inside, the Club represents the maintenance of British identity and values, but from the outside, it represents a boundary, a mark of exclusion. In *Island in the Sun*, these colonial barriers seem desperately artificial, as if at this late point in history they are all that remain of the once-proud Empire. Only inside the Club can the colonizers pretend that life outside is not changing. The existence of clubs, for non-whites as well as for whites, also clearly reveals the color awareness among West Indians and, further, differentiates the members from the plantation laborers and peasants who cannot gain membership to any club and whom this novel treats only in passing. Late in the novel, the reader gets a rare view of the peasant and laborer class—"naked and half-naked children tumbling in the dust before their huts"—and learns that for these children's parents, "the liquor store was [the] club" (450).

The narrator of *Island in the Sun* reflects the color awareness by describing almost every Barbadian character according to race. Waugh's narrative voice resembles that of a seasoned colonial officer who views the island from the privileged position of Government House. From the omniscient narrator's subtle hints, the reader learns some of the island's secrets: that the Kellaways who pass for white have some African ancestry, and that the mother of the Governor's close friend, Julian Fleury, is a coloured woman from Jamaica. Fleury's mother died in childbirth, and he has thus been able to keep the details of his birth a secret. David Boyeur, clearly the most threatening character in the novel, is also the most noticably African: "he had little if any white blood in his veins. His lips were thick, his teeth very white and even, his nose broad at its base" (20). Boyeur's penchant for ostentatious clothing also follows the racial stereotype that his character represents. Margot Seaton, the ADC Denis Archer's girlfriend, is similarly described in racial terms, but because she appears less African than Boyeur, she is portrayed in a more positive, acceptable way: "There was no sign of African blood in her appearance; she seemed a mixture of Indian and Spanish" (20). The Barbadians are thus judged on a scale devised by Government House. Governor Templeton's perception of Boyeur as dangerous, for instance, obviously shapes the reader's view of the latter, just as the Governor's cultivation of Grainger Morris as his future Attorney General makes Morris not only acceptable but admirable.

Much like a smooth, diplomatic colonial officer, moreover, Waugh's narrator attempts to side-step any signs of overt racism. The planters who show an obvious racist outlook, for instance, are portrayed in a negative light. In Waugh's portrait of the racist planter, Maxwell Fleury, in fact, the author comes as close as any British writer to making a white colonizer a villain. Maxwell represents David Boyeur's white counterpart: like Boyeur, he is loud and boastful, attempting to conceal an inner insecurity and inferiority complex by demeaning others. Maxwell's attempt to make his wife Sylvia sexually subservient to him mirrors Boyeur's earlier effort to master Margot Seaton sexually. In the first half of the novel, Maxwell appears virulently racist, spewing racial epithets, and berating the black laborers on his family plantation: "Lazy sods, what you need is an overseer with a whip! That's the only way you can be got to work. Come along now, on with it" (75). In the second half of the novel, however, Maxwell Fleury undergoes a self-redemptive change, and this represents an important difference between him and David Boyeur.

Maxwell's transformation as a result of his discovery of his family's African ancestry reveals a perhaps inevitable bias on the part of Waugh. Maxwell can transform and redeem himself, but David Boyeur is incapable of such a transformation. Boyeur remains static: the dark Other whom Fanon describes in *Black Skin, White Masks* (154). Waugh, like other British colonial writers, is finally unable to see a white colonial character as totally reprehensible. Such characters are too close to the writer's own experience. We might think of other "negative" white colonials in British fiction—Forster's Adela Quested in *A Passage to India*, Evelyn Waugh's Basil Seal in *Black Mischief*, Cary's Rackham in *The African Witch*, and Conrad's Kurtz in *Heart of Darkness*—and in each case we see that the character finally shows some redeeming feature or quality. By contrast, indigenous characters in British colonial fiction, such as Kipling's Blind Mullah in "Head of the District," Haggard's Gagool in *King Solomon's Mines*, and Huxley's Gitau in *A Thing to Love* are, like Boyeur, beyond redemption because they remain forever on the other side of the colonial boundary. As Fanon shows, in the We/Them colonial world, such characters represent the Other: a mysterious, untrustworthy alien.

In *The Colonizer and the Colonized*, Albert Memmi asks: "Who can completely rid himself of bigotry in a country where everyone is tainted by it, including its victims?" (23). Maxwell Fleury would seem to provide a case in point. Fleury represents the dark underside of the Empire: like Rhys's Antoinette in *Wide Sargasso Sea* and Conrad's Kurtz in *Heart of Darkness*, he is a product of the fear and distrust which underlie the colonial world. As a result of Maxwell's discovery of his African ancestry, his outlook seems to change entirely: he begins to show genuine affection for his wife and to treat his laborers humanely. After his impulsive murder of Colonel Carson, however, whom he suspects has carried on an adulterous affair with his wife, Maxwell is able to rationalize his fit of jealous rage as the savage effect of his newly discovered African blood:

> If he had been white, would that blind fury have taken control of him when his hands had fastened upon Carson's throat? . . . At certain moments he was a beast, not a man. It was in his blood to be. A thin, thin trickle, but it had forced this desperate remedy upon him. (475)

In this episode, Waugh comments ironically on racist notions about the effect of "blood," or race, on character. In earlier British colonial fiction, such as Kipling's story, "His Chance in Life," a fraction of British blood was considered to be enough to make a native character act heroically, and, conversely, Maxwell can explain his savage act as the result of his West Indian blood. Rather than accept responsibility for his act, Maxwell seeks to place blame on something over which he has no control. Waugh seems to satirize Maxwell's attempt to evade responsibility, but Waugh's intention, nevertheless, is far from clear, especially in light of Maxwell's continuing transformation into an increasingly sympathetic character.

Island in the Sun is in some ways an uneasy mixture. Waugh's portrayal of the Oxonian, Grainger Morris, as a positive character, for instance, might be seen as a corrective of earlier negative portraits of the educated native in British colonial fiction. Moreover, Waugh does not conveniently end the romance between the white ADC Denis Archer and the coloured Margot Seaton, as Kipling and Haggard undoubtedly would have, but instead portrays them returning to England to marry, thus creating the possibility of a long-term love relationship between colonizer and colonized. At the same time, however, Waugh counters such effects by reflecting a disturbingly conventional colonialist attitude. Archer, for instance, who, like Governor Templeton, is portrayed in positive terms throughout the novel, can remark that "all [coloured West Indians] looked alike" (13). Waugh also uses Grainger Morris as a convenient medium through which to disparage the West Indian peasants and laborers. Although Waugh is pessimistic about the Empire, the exhausted system of British control, he seems certain, nevertheless, that the British ought to control. Men like Templeton, Julian Fleury, and Carson have the experience and the ethical authority to rule, and therefore should be the ones to administer the colony. Even as questionable a character as Maxwell Fleury demonstrates that he can improve morally, and thus like the other British, he too seems to deserve a share of the political and ethical control of the island.

Although the reader rarely sees the typical West Indian laborer or villager in *Island in the Sun*, the fact that the laborers' leader, David Boyeur, is described as dangerous and threatening does not reflect well on those he leads. Throughout the novel, Santa Marta is described in explosive images—a "keg of dynamite" or a "volcano"—and the plantation laborers, who are said to follow a "herd instinct" (31), contribute to the island's instability. The Archdeacon describes the Santa Marta people as having "no roots; they are featherdown in the wind, and the winds blow strongly" (114). Like the colonized peasantry in most colonial fiction, the Santa Martans are portrayed as mindless sheep easily led into a violent frenzy by the inflammatory rhetoric of demagogues like Boyeur. Certainly, the portrayals of

Lame Foot Sam in *A High Wind in Jamaica*, of Daniel Cosway in *Wide Sargasso Sea*, and of the Macushi Indians in *A Handful of Dust* do nothing to dispel this stereotype of the mindless, latently violent West Indian peasant. The difference between the British colonizers and the Caribbean colonized is thus one between order and chaos. The West Indians are "featherdown in the wind," with no history and no tradition to give them the necessary foundation for stability and continuity.

To the English-educated West Indian lawyer, Grainger Morris, *superimposed* is a keyword for understanding West Indian life:

> He had seen in England the confidence and security that the English derived from their long past. On every side of them, they had reassurances of survival. And at the apex of the social pyramid was the Crown, the symbol of continuity. . . . The English because of their past were confident in their future . . . How could a West Indian with his untraced roots in Africa feel like that? (312)

Although Grainger obviously understands and sympathizes with the plight of his people, he also judges them harshly. He sees the annual Carnival celebrations in Santa Marta as exemplary of the chaos and irrationality of the West Indians. He tells Mavis Norman, with whom he observes the throngs dancing and parading through the streets, that the dynamics of the historic slave risings and the Carnival celebrations are the same: "There's an inflammable situation [and] the first spark touches it off. You know how these people are. How excitable, how quickly worked up they are" (180). Through the character of Grainger, Waugh shows a degree of sympathy for the West Indians, but the author's primary focus remains the colonized people's rootlessness and helplessness, rather than the historic causes of their predicament.

Waugh makes clear that the Empire brings a sense of order to Santa Marta, and that the laborers' strike threatens this order. The laborers appear little more than pawns for Boyeur to manipulate. The narrator describes one of Boyeur's speeches to the laborers:

> [Boyeur] was like a bandmaster, with arms outstretched . . . conducting the outbursts . . . now calming them, now exacerbating them. The crowd had become a single person, obedient, mesmerized, his to do what he chose with. (471)

Waugh here attempts to answer the question Bradshaw posed earlier: "What will happen when the demagogues of an undisciplined proletariat are in control?" (31). Boyeur is just such a demagogue: an irresponsible agitator driven by his own inordinate vanity. Furthermore, like the other West Indians in the novel, he is said to be superstitious, which obviously adds to his unpredictability. Boyeur builds up the laborers' expectations, telling them that their power lies in their ability to strike: "We may be hungry for a little, but [the planters] will be ruined and the land will become ours" (472). But, the reader is made to wonder, what will happen after the laborers gain the land? Waugh suggests that such an outcome would likely cripple an already weak economy, ruin Santa Marta's prospects for the tourist trade, and inevitably lead to an eruption of violence and chaos.

Waugh's pessimism is evident throughout the novel in his implicit notion that major political events often result from the cross purposes of individuals selfishly pursuing personal ends. In one of his newspaper articles, for instance, Bradshaw expresses this implicit view of Waugh's: "High affairs of state are as often as not determined by the personal equation" (479). In this way, Waugh reminds the reader that the strike which jeopardizes the welfare of the entire island is the result of a petty dispute between two selfish egotists, Maxwell Fleury and David Boyeur, who are willing to sacrifice the island in order to gain personal ends. The dispute between Fleury and Boyeur, which results from a misunderstanding, grows increasingly acrimonious until it eventually leads to Boyeur's impulsive call for the laborers' strike.

The strike proves not only to be the death of Maxwell Fleury, but also the end of the political careers of Boyeur and of Governor Templeton, who is recalled by the Colonial Minister in London because it is feared that a military man like Templeton might react too forcefully and create an "equivalent situation [to] Amritzar" (421). The strike is the making, however, of the career of Bradshaw, the American journalist, whose pieces in the Western press have enjoyed immense success. Bradshaw, like the Western journalists who journey to Ishmaelia in Evelyn Waugh's *Scoop*, helps to instigate the stories he sells, and thus bears responsibility for the resultant violence in the colony. Like Boyeur and Maxwell Fleury, Bradshaw is shown to pursue personal ends with little or no concern for the ultimate effect of his reports on the island's welfare. In Westminster, too, where Waugh intermittently conveys the reader, the "personal equation" takes precedence over the welfare of the colonies. In the viewpoint of the Colonial Minister who recalls Templeton, for instance, the "wretched little West Indian islands were like mosquitoes, trivial and maddening" (421).

Waugh clearly believes in the old Kiplingesque values of duty, responsibility, and self-sacrifice which long supported the Empire, but those values appear hopelessly out-of-date. The administrators' half-hearted efforts to carry out their duties and their retreat to colonial refuges, such as the Club, mirrors the crumbling of the imperial ideals, which this novel chronicles. Waugh shows that once the guiding principles of imperial rule break down, nothing remains. The Empire becomes not only directionless, but also a hollow sham, and the British administrators are left with no higher calling than personal aggrandizement.

Island in the Sun functions in part as an allegory of Empire: Governor Templeton's administration might be seen as a microcosm of Britain's entire colonial experience in the West Indies. Even though Waugh implies that another Governor-General will come to replace Templeton, the finality of the novel's ending seems to represent something larger: the end of an era. By the novel's close, practically every British character prepares to pull up stakes and return to England. Only a handful of planters and Grainger Morris remain; and they seem desolate at the prospect, as if stranded against their will. In *Island in the Sun*, we find a theme, also common in the fiction of Evelyn Waugh, of the transformation of an Edenic "lush place" into a self-imposed prison (Heath, 5). In Evelyn Waugh's *A Handful of Dust*, for example, Tony Last leaves London in search of the City of God and ends stranded in the jungles of British Guiana. *Island in the Sun* finally achieves a similar effect of disillusionment and decline.

British colonial fiction, whether intentionally or not, often served to provide the English reading public, usually assumed to be misinformed and naive, with an account of the nation's colonial rule. Kipling's *Kim* and Haggard's *King Solomon's Mines*, for instance, paint an exciting picture of adventure as well as duty and sacrifice on the part of the builders of Empire. Conrad's *Heart of Darkness*, written about the same time as *Kim*, gives a more disturbing account of the colonies, but the English public could safely assume that Conrad's setting is a Belgian, not a British, colony. By the time Cary published *Mister Johnson*, great changes in the British public's attitude had occurred, as a result of such national nightmares as the Boer War and World War I. Cary treats Britain's colonial administration more ironically than his predecessors, and yet he also asserts that the British altruistic colonial mission is an important one. With Huxley's *A Thing to Love*, new historical developments are evident: the colonized are in revolt, and thus the author's role is not to celebrate the Empire, but rather to defend its increasingly precarious position in the world. In *Island in the Sun*, Waugh brings the British colonial novel to an apparent end. Waugh analyzes the malfunction of

Empire and confirms the British public's view that the imperial machine has simply run down.

George Lamming's *In the Castle of My Skin*

George Lamming was born in a small town known as Carrington's village two or three miles outside of Bridgetown, Barbados, in 1927. An only child raised by his mother, Lamming has summarized his childhood with a memorable phrase: "It was my mother who fathered me" (Herdeck, 115). As a youth, Lamming left the working class environment of his hometown to attend a secondary school for middle-class Barbadian boys. His attendance at Combermere High School introduced him to Frank Collymore, the editor of *BIM*, an important West Indian literary journal, in which some of Lamming's early poetry was published. Collymore was also instrumental, later, in arranging a teaching position for Lamming in Trinidad and, perhaps more importantly, in nurturing the young man's talent as a writer. Lamming later dedicated his first novel, *In the Castle of My Skin*, to his mother and to Collymore, "whose love and help," he wrote, "deserve a better book" (v). In 1950, Lamming emigrated to England, and he has since that time established his home in exile in London and Canada.

In London, Lamming initially supported himself by working in a factory, and later, by hosting a book review program for the West Indian Service of the BBC. Several years later, after the publication of *In the Castle of My Skin*, Lamming made his first trip to the United States on a Guggenheim Fellowship. Since that time, he has given lecture tours in India and Australia, and served as a visiting professor in Europe, America, Africa, and Australia. Between lecture tours and professorships, Lamming has continued to write. Since *In the Castle of My Skin*, he has written five novels, including *The Emigrants* (1954), *Of Age and Innocence* (1958), *Season of Adventure* (1960), *Water With Berries* (1971), and *Natives of My Person* (1972), as well as a non-fictional study of colonial dynamics, *The Pleasures of Exile* (1960). He has also returned periodically to the West

Indies, where he has continued to play an active social role. In 1974, Lamming helped to open the Barbados Labour College, the first school of its kind on the island.

Much of Lamming's writing is informed by an awareness of the portrayal of the West Indies in British literature. In *The Pleasures of Exile*, Lamming indicates that his reading of Shakespeare's *The Tempest* had an important influence on him as a writer. Throughout his fiction and non-fiction, Lamming has returned continually to the relationship of Prospero and Caliban, which he sees as symbolic of the colonizer-colonized relationship. In *The Pleasures of Exile*, for instance, he writes:

> Caliban had got hold of Prospero's weapons and decided that he would never again seek his master's permission. That is my theme: a theme which embraces both literature and politics in our time. (63)

Thus like other post-colonial writers as well as other Caribbean writers, such as Edward Braithwaite and Derek Walcott, Lamming conceives his fiction as in part an answer to the earlier portrayal of the West Indies in British colonial literature.

To witness the influence of *The Tempest* on Lamming's thinking one need only turn to *The Pleasures of Exile*, which might be described as a sustained meditation on the significance of the Prospero-Caliban relationship. In Lamming's view, Caliban is more than a fictional character; Caliban more largely represents a condition of life for all colonized or formerly-colonized people. Elements of Shakespeare's play can also be seen, if implicitly, in much of Lamming's fictional work as well. One of his more recent novels, *Water With Berries*, takes its title from Caliban's famous complaint to Prospero:

> This island's mine by Sycorax my mother,
> Which thou tak'st from me. When thou cam'st first,
> Thou strok'st me and made much of me; would'st give me
> Water with berries in't; and teach me how
> To name the bigger light, and how the less,
> That burn by day and night; and then I loved thee
> And showed thee all the qualities o' th'isle,
> The fresh springs, brine-pits, barren place and fertile.
> Cursed be I that did so! All the charms
> Of Sycorax—toads, beetles, bats, light on you!
> For I am all the subjects that you have,
> Which first was mine own king; and here you sty me
> In this hard rock, whiles you do keep from me
> The rest o' th'island. (Harbage, 1377-1378)

For Lamming and other West Indian writers, early British colonial works, such as *The Tempest* and Defoe's *Robinson Crusoe*, have achieved a mythic status in their delineation of the colonizer-colonized relationship, a relationship that continues to remain pertinent to the contemporary West Indian faced with a complex history of colonial subjugation.

The archetypal figures of Prospero and Caliban re-appear continually not only in fiction by West Indians, but also in British colonial writing, such as Alec Waugh's *Island in the Sun*. One might see Waugh's perpetuation of Shakespeare's portrayal of the colonial myth in characters such as Governor-General Templeton as a modern-day Prospero and the militant labor leader, David Boyeur, as an updated Caliban. Thus, in a comparison of *Island in the Sun* and *In the Castle of My Skin*, it is possible to see not only how differently a British and a post-colonial writer portray the West Indies on the verge of decolonization, but also how the dichotomy between colonizer and colonized is evident in their differing portrayals of an old, but continually relevant myth.

Published three years before *Island in the Sun*, *In the Castle of My Skin* is clearly not a response to Waugh's novel in the same way that *Things Fall Apart* forms a direct answer to *Mister Johnson*. Lamming's novel, nonetheless, represents an insider's view of the West Indies that stands in opposition to the outsider's appraisal presented in *Island in the Sun*. Perhaps because the two novels were written at almost the same time, they bear remarkable similarities to one another. Both novels are about a British-ruled West Indian island on the verge of decolonization, and in both a destabilizing labor strike figures prominently in the plot. Furthermore, both novels describe a West Indian island society divided by a "colour line," although in Lamming's *Bildungsroman*, the perspective is altered. In Waugh, the reader sees island life from a white perspective. In Lamming, the reader views the West Indian world from the opposite, the non-white, perspective. *In the Castle of My Skin* takes the reader outside the environs of Government House in the capital city, in which Waugh's novel takes place, to the small community of Creighton's Village and the insulated life of a young boy who gains an increased awareness of himself, his race, and the political situation in his native island.

The West Indian critic Michael Gilkes has written that "the crisis of identity is a peculiarly Caribbean theme, amounting, at times, almost to an obsession" (x). The situation in the West Indies, with its history of imported African slaves and indentured Asian laborers, might represent a miniature of the dynamics of colonialism across the globe. Gilkes's focus upon the Caribbean crisis of identity also calls to mind Fanon's assertion in *The Wretched of the Earth* that colonialism "forces the people it dominates to ask the question constantly: 'In reality, who am I?'" (250). Because of this concern with identity, the *Bildungsroman* has proven to be a useful form for West Indian writers. In addition to *In the Castle of My Skin*, other notable examples are V. S. Reid's *New Day*, Michael Anthony's *The Year in San Fernando*, Merle Hodge's *Crick Crack, Monkey*, Jamaica Kincaid's *Annie John*, Austin Clarke's *Amongst Thistles and Thorns*, and several of V. S. Naipaul's novels, including *Miguel Street* and *A House for Mr. Biswas*. Furthermore, the West Indian writers' search for personal and national identity links them in important ways to other post-colonial writers: to Rushdie's fashioning of a representative Indian persona in *Midnight's Children*, Abrahams' re-creation of an indigenous southern African past in *Wild Conquest*, Achebe's exploration of his ancestral roots in *Things Fall Apart*, and Ngugi's elevation of the Mau Mau conflict to a near mythic national struggle for freedom in *A Grain of Wheat*. Clearly, these post-colonial writers are all involved in a search for an identity lost or severed during the colonial interval in their nations' history.

Lamming's *In the Castle of My Skin* and V. S. Reid's *New Day* are especially important in the emerging tradition of the West Indian novel because they represent the earliest attempts to portray West Indian people as having a tradition and culture of their own. That tradition and culture, the authors assert, reflect the cultural mix and the colonial heritage which make up the uniquely-blended West Indian identity. Both *New Day* and *In the Castle of My Skin* focus on an indigenous West Indian family, and both attempt to show how West Indian identity and culture have grown out of the region's fragmented history. At first glance, *In the Castle of My Skin* seems to have a much narrower field of historical reference than Reid's saga, which spans four generations of a West Indian family and covers approximately 80 years (1870-1950). Seen as an allegory of Empire, however, as readers such as Sandra Paquet and Ngugi suggest, *In the Castle of My Skin*, like *Island in the Sun*, might be said to span symbolically the entire colonial history of a West Indian island through decolonization and independence.[2]

Lamming's *Bildungsroman* operates almost continually on both the literal and figurative levels. Lamming, for instance, uses the image of the castle to represent different, and even antithetical, realms of West Indian experience. Early in the novel, the castle symbolizes the British colonial presence in Barbados: the idea of "the Great, which the landlord and the large brick house on the hill represented" (28-29). Lamming's Barbadian village is demarcated by a distinct boundary separating white Belleville from the non-white sector. The looming presence of the landlord Creighton's house reinforces the colonial compartmentalization of the village. It looks down on Creighton's Village with "a quality of benevolent protection. It was a castle around which the land like a shabby back garden stretched" (29). Later, however, the castle comes to represent G.'s emergent identity: "the you that's hidden somewhere in the castle of your skin" (261). These two images of the castle form two poles between which the narrative moves: the colonial domination, from which the people only slowly emerge, and the sacred mystery of identity which G. comes to discover. Lamming has said, in fact, that in *In the Castle of My Skin*, the title of which comes from a Derek Walcott poem—"You in the castle of your skin, I among the swineherd"—he attempted to "restore the castle where it belonged" (*PE*, 228).

Like Waugh's *Island in the Sun*, *In the Castle of My Skin* is about change. The novel opens with G.'s ninth birthday—"my ninth celebration of the consistent lack of an occasion for celebration" (9)—and ends with the protagonist as an eighteen-year old about to leave Barbados to become a teacher in Trinidad. During the course of the narrative, Creighton's Village also takes on a new complexion, which is marked by a transference of land ownership from the colonial landlord, Creighton, to a local politician, Mr. Slime, whose metamorphosis throughout the narrative has an ominous meaning for the well-being of the village. Slime rises to power after he begins the institutions of the Penny Bank and the Friendly Society, which supposedly will enable the villagers to buy and own their own land. Using this scheme to bilk the villagers of their small financial resources, Slime acquires the land himself, sells to the highest bidder and then dispossesses the naive peasantry of their homes and property.

Fredric Jameson has employed the term *national allegory* to define much if not all Third World literature: as Jameson puts it, "the story of the private individual destiny is always an allegory of the embattled situation of the public third-world culture and society" (69). Jameson's theory surely applies to Lamming's text. Slime's rise symbolizes the post-independence difficulties of many colonial societies, in which an indigenous leader abuses the people's trust for his own personal benefit. Rushdie's *Midnight's Children*, Achebe's *A Man of the People*, and Naipaul's *The Mimic Men* also chronicle this all-too-familiar post-colonial phase. The changes that occur in this West Indian village, moreover, are made clear in their effect on particular characters. Charles Larson has pointed out in *The Novel in the Third World* that the old indigenous couple, Ma and Pa, represent the past traditions which are undone as a result of the changes brought about by Creighton and Slime (90-91). The collective village stands for the present, slowly gaining awareness of its increasingly ominous situation. And G. represents the future—the West Indies to come that will perhaps be less vulnerable to duplicity and corruption.

Although G.'s coming of age is an important part of the novel, *In the Castle of My Skin* is more largely concerned with the life of an entire Barbadian shanty-town community. Like Waugh's *Island in the Sun*, Lamming's narrative focus moves back and forth among a variety of characters rather than remaining with a single central consciousness. Lamming's reason for adopting a multiple point of view, however, is different from Waugh's. Whereas Waugh uses a shifting narrative focus to examine the hierarchical imperial machine and the way it affects and is affected by a large number of people, Lamming employs a multiple point of view to convey the inner workings of a colonized peasant community. Like Saleem in *Midnight's Children*, Okonkwo in *Things Fall Apart* or Mugo in *A Grain of Wheat*, G. is the central character and yet he does not constantly dominate the narrative. All of these post-colonial novels are concerned with particular societies, and the introduction of the character is meant to help the reader understand the group the character represents. Lamming has explained this point in the introduction to the Schocken edition of the novel:

> And what I say now of *In the Castle of My Skin* is also true of other Caribbean writers. The book is crowded with names and people, and although each character is accorded a most vivid presence and force of personality, we are rarely concerned with the prolonged exploration of an individual consciousness. It is the collective human substance of the Village itself which commands our attention. The Village, you might say, is the central character. (x)

Indeed, G. appears in less than half the novel's chapters. In the other chapters, Lamming portrays the life of a West Indian community in the process of a change that the inhabitants themselves only vaguely comprehend. Not overly concerned with their future, the people of Creighton's Village are involved in living in the present.

In *The Overcrowded Barracoon*, V. S. Naipaul asserts that climate has an important bearing on West Indian life:

> In a warm country life is conducted out of doors. Windows are open, doors are open. People sit in open verandas and cafes. You know your neighbour's business and he knows yours. . . . In England everything goes on behind closed doors. The man from the warm country automatically leaves the door open behind him. The man from the cold country closes it: it has become a point of etiquette. (14)

In *In the Castle of My Skin*, Lamming effectively conveys that open, out-of-door quality of West Indian life. *Island in the Sun*, by contrast, reflects the closed door atmosphere of the colonizers' Club. *In the Castle of My Skin* takes its readers into the streets among the colonized masses, where they experience, as if at first-hand, the discussion among the men at the shoemaker's shop, the "mingled odours" (91) coming from the cart of the food vendor, a street fight between two women which becomes like "a public ball to which everyone had been invited and where there were no restrictions at all" (106), and a schoolboy parade in observation of Empire Day. In these examples, Lamming reflects the life of a colonized West Indian society, which, as he has said, is built upon an "accumulated [colonial] myth, both cultural and political, which an inherited and uncritical way of seeing has now reinforced" (*PE*, 76).

Pa and Ma, like Ngugi's Warui and Wambui in *A Grain of Wheat*, are guardians of the villagers' collective history and ways of life. Pa, who helped build the Panama Canal and knew a time when "money flow like the flood through these here hands" (85), seems to carry a knowledge of the village that spans its entire history. As representative characters, Pa and Ma have observed all the changes occurring in the island community, and both foresee difficult times ahead. As Ma puts it, "'Tis a next Panama we need now for the young ones . . . or there goin' to be bad times comin' this way" (86). Pa also embodies the collective past of his people that goes beyond his own experience. Pa's stream of unconsciousness as he talks in his sleep reveals the depth of his knowledge:

> A man walked out in the market square and one buyer watch his tooth and another his toe and the parts that was private for the coming of a creature in the intimate night. The silver sail from hand to hand and the purchase was shipped like a box of good fruit. The sale was the best of Africa's produce, and me and my neighbour made the same same bargain. I make my peace with the Middle Passage to settle on that side of the sea the white man call a world that was west of another world. The tribes with gods and the one without we all went the way of the white man's money. (210)

As this passage illustrates, Lamming's experimental use of language differs strikingly from Waugh's conventional usage in *Island in the Sun* and puts him in the company of other Caribbean writers such as Earl Lovelace and Erna Brodber. In *In the Castle of My Skin*, Lamming employs dialect, stream of consciousness, and a collective narrative voice to evoke poetically a distinctive West Indian identity.

The old West Indian ways of life which Pa and Ma represent are obviously passing. During the course of the narrative, Ma dies and Pa is forced to leave his home to live in the Alms House. Their passing seems to indicate a movement toward a less stable and less passive way of life in the West Indies, for Pa and Ma's stability is built upon innocence and naivete. Ma, for instance, looks upon Creighton as the villagers' father figure and sees his sway as benevolent paternalism: "we won't ever understan' the kind o' responsibility [Creighton] feel for you an' me an' the whole village" (185). And Pa puts great faith in Mr. Slime's Penny Bank and Friendly Society, institutions which eventually lead to Pa's eviction from his home.

In his review of *In the Castle of My Skin* in *The New Statesman*, V. S. Pritchett wrote: "The view of Barbados seen from the inside is inevitably warmer, fresher, and more humane than anything the most sympathetic settler can give us from the outside" (460). Surely, one way in which Lamming conveys a warm, humane view of Barbados in his novel is through his intimate portrayal of a West Indian family, in this case, the family made up of G. and his mother. Pritchett compares Lamming's portrayal of G.'s relationship with his mother to D. H. Lawrence's portraits of mother-son relationships. The analogy seems limited, however, for G.'s mother is a much more positive, less ultimately threatening figure than, for example, Mrs. Morel in *Sons and Lovers*. *In the Castle of My Skin* presents Barbadian society as clearly matriarchal, dominated by strong women who, without the help of husbands, manage to hold their families together. G. looks upon his family as both representative and non-representative:

> Miss Foster. My mother. Bob's mother.
>
> It seemed they were three pieces in a pattern which remained constant. The flow of its history was undisturbed by any difference in the pieces, nor was its evenness affected by any likeness. There was a difference and there was no difference. Miss Foster had six children, three by a butcher, two by a baker and one whose father had never been mentioned. Bob's mother had two, and my mother one. (24)

Had Lamming intended his novel as a direct response to Waugh's *Island in the Sun*, he could surely not have made a better choice than to filter his portrayal of Barbados through the perspective of a young boy coming of age. Just as it is important for Waugh to center his novel in the character of Governor Templeton, who, at the end of a long, distinguished career, symbolizes Britain's waning colonial era, Lamming's character G. represents a "young" West Indian society gaining independence and coming of age. Before writing *In the Castle of My Skin*, his first novel, Lamming considered himself to be a poet rather than a novelist, and he invests the character of G. with a poetic sensibility. Clearly in the sections which reflect the young boy, as opposed to the mature narrator, G. approaches life with a sense of wonder. Like most children, he accepts the life of which he finds himself a part and feels little need to question his own identity or the situation of his village or his native island:

> Not three, nor thirteen, but thirty. Perhaps three hundred. Men. Women. Children. The men at cricket. The children at hide and seek. The women laying out their starched clothes to dry. The sun let its light flow down on them as life let itself flow through them. Three. Thirteen. Thirty. Three hundred. (25)

Thus from Waugh's Governor-General at the pinnacle of the colonial hierarchy, we move to the opposite end of the spectrum: an indigenous child growing up and accepting unquestioningly the colonial underpinnings of Barbadian society. Like Barbados itself, known as "Little England," G. is the child of Mother England. In the first part of the novel, G. accepts life as he finds it, but later, during his nine-year passage, he increasingly begins to question the life about him, and thus his growth parallels the quickening of consciousness in his village.

In *The Wretched of the Earth*, Fanon says, "The zone where the natives live is not complementary to the zone inhabited by the settlers" (38). In Lamming's novel, the people of Creighton's Village are constantly compared to those living in the white sector, Belleville, the name of which implies the luxurious life enjoyed by the colonizers, like the name of the the Fleurys' plantation, Belfontaine, in *Island in the Sun*. After the street fight between the two women, for instance, a constable upbraids the women and the crowd gathered around them:

> "Why all you can't live like the people in Belleville?" he said, turning the pages of the book. "Every day you fightin' and cursin' and fightin' and give me more work than I care to do. What wrong with you people at all?" (107)

Lamming shows the reader only as much as the villagers see and comprehend themselves. It is, then, revealing that Belleville is never described in the novel. Like his villagers, Lamming's readers are not allowed into that zone of society. They see only "the large brick building surrounded by a wood and a high stone wall that bore bits of bottle along the top" (25). From the village, the landlord is occasionally visible, as if on high, as he entertains guests: "planters whose estates in the country had remained agricultural; or otherwise there were English visitors who were absentee owners of estates which they had come to see" (25).

In *The Pleasures of Exile*, Lamming discusses *The Tempest* as an allegory of colonialism, and he points out "the quality of spontaneity which got poor Caliban into such trouble" (175). In his novel, Lamming shows that the West Indian people have clearly paid a price for their "quality of spontaneity"—their hospitality and willingness to accommodate themselves to the colonizers' way of life. That accommodation begins in the schools, which, of course, operate on a curriculum devised in the mother country. The pervasive colonial influence on all aspects of Barbadian life becomes clear in the Empire Day episode at the school. The highlight of the ceremonies is an address given by an English inspector to the assembly of schoolboys and teachers:

> "My dear boys and teachers, we are met once again to pay our respects to the memory of a great queen. She was your queen and my queen and yours no less than mine. We're all subjects and partakers in the great design, the British Empire, and your loyalty to the Empire can be seen in the splendid performance which your school decorations and the discipline of these squads represent." (38)

The inspector clearly describes the qualities valued by the Empire: knowing one's place in "the great design," loyalty, and discipline. The effectiveness of the colonial indoctrination of the schoolboys is obvious later when a group of them on their way home from school discuss a remark one of the boys has heard an old woman make: "We're all slaves" (70):

> The idea of ownership. One man owned another. They laughed quietly. Imagine any man in any part of the world owning a man or woman from Barbados. They would forget all about it since it happened too long ago. Moreover, they weren't told anything about that. They had read about the Battle of Hastings and William the Conqueror. That happened so many hundreds of years ago. And slavery was thousands of years before that. It was too far back for anyone to worry about teaching it as history. (58)

The men who gather at the shoemaker's shop unconsciously trace the logical outcome of this selective teaching of history at the school, which ignores such figures as Marcus Garvey, whom the men remember as once having given a speech in Barbados. The shoemaker, for instance, remarks: "'Taint no joke . . . if you tell half of them that work in those [schools] they have somethin' to do with Africa they'd piss straight in your face" (104).

Halfway through the novel, G. and his friends decide one night to sneak inside the walls of the landlord's castle to see for themselves the life of "the Great." This episode is a turning point in the novel and in the life of the sleepy shanty-town community. After this point, the earlier stability of the village gives way to change—especially in the relations between Creighton and the villagers. In this episode, too, we might say we have come full-circle from Kipling's *Kim*, in which the Irish orphan secretly observes the off-limits world of another colonial Sahib named Creighton. In Kipling's novel, however, Kim eventually gains entrance into that off-limits world. G. and his friends, by contrast, vaguely realize that they are permanently excluded and unwelcome in the white colonial's castle. As the boys climb the wall and hide behind a rubbish heap to observe a party Creighton gives for some visiting sailors, we see the large house from the awe-struck perspective of G.: "The house looked so much bigger than I had thought. It was like some of the castles we had seen in pictures" (171). Frightened away when the landlord's daughter and one of the sailors come outside to embrace amorously near the boys' hiding place, G. and his friends narrowly escape being caught by the landlord's overseer. Although the actual experience teaches them little, the boys later come to learn an important lesson about the subservient position of the colonized in the colonial world as a result of their nocturnal journey of discovery.

Lamming's exposé of the British colonial subjugation of Barbados becomes clearer when we learn that, following the boys' innocent escapade, Creighton orders an official search to find and punish the three "little vagabonds" who attempted to rape his daughter. The boys have, in effect, been relegated to the position of Caliban whom Prospero punishes for attempting to rape Miranda. The reader learns of this official version of events—the same version of events which determines the history curriculum at school—from the character of Ma. On her way to pay the rent, Ma encounters Creighton on horseback and the two have a brief conversation. Ma is the ideal, sympathetic listener for Creighton because she accepts his paternalistic attitude at face value. The landlord asks her "whether she could explain why things had changed so greatly in the village" (184). When Ma replies that she likes certain changes she sees taking place, Creighton agrees, but adds that "these weren't an excuse for the disrespect which he had had to suffer in recent times" (184). Lamming's satire is evident in his narrative commentary on the discussion between Ma and Creighton: the landlord, the narrator comments, "could bear anything except disrespect. It knocked at the roots of his world" (184).

The natural ascendancy of the colonizer over the colonized, which is central to effective colonial rule, is no less an assumption for Ma than it is for the landlord. The self-denigration resulting from colonial rule is obvious in Ma's relating of Creighton's news to Pa:

> The vagabonds try to force rudeness on the landlord's daughter. . . . The poor chil' they say wus takin' little fresh air. She ain't thinkin' no more 'bout what goin' to happen than the man in the moon, an' then out come those three wicked brutes to tear her to pieces, and 'twus only the grace o' the Almighty God who let the sailor be where he wus, or they would have make a mess o' that child. (188)

It is quite natural for Ma to assume the pure intentions of Creighton's daughter and the sailor and the base motives of the three "little vagabonds," whom Ma transforms into "wicked brutes," following the classic Caliban-Miranda pattern. According to Lamming, however, just such assumptions as these must be called into question before the West Indian people can free themselves from colonial domination.

In *Island in the Sun*, the reader is made to sympathize with Governor Templeton and his plight as the bearer of responsibility for a colonial society about to explode. Templeton is beset with problems on all sides. He must not only work out a solution to the growing rift between the planters and a striking labor force before the latter resorts to violence, but also continually reassure the Colonial Minister in Whitehall that the situation is under control. After the strike erupts into violence and the Minister recalls Templeton, the reader is made to feel that the Governor's situation was an impossible one and that, given the various factors involved, he did the best that he possibly could. Lamming, on the other hand, elicits the reader's sympathy for the poor shanty-town folk by portraying their basic helplessness, which is especially evident in the transfer of power from the colonial landlord, Creighton, to the corrupt politician, Slime. The people regard Creighton as a father-figure and as a protector, and they also trust Slime as a spokesperson for their cause, a leader committed to the welfare of the village. The reader comes to realize that Creighton and Slime have made a deal which benefits themselves at the villagers' expense. Eventually certain villagers also come to suspect that they have been victimized by those in power, but by that time it is too late.

In his allegory of Empire, Lamming chronicles that phase of decolonization in which the island colony's educated middle-class assumes the position of power vacated by the departed colonizer. In *A Grain of Wheat*, Ngugi also portrays this aspect of decolonization: after the Emergency in Kenya, the educated Kenyans take over power and those who actually fought for Uhuru are excluded. In *The Wretched of the Earth*, Fanon describes this phenomenon which took place in numerous Third World countries following independence from European colonial rule: "To [the national middle-class], nationalisation quite simply means the transfer into native hands of those unfair advantages which are the legacy of the colonial period" (152). In Lamming's novel, Slime represents this emergent national middle-class. His metamorphosis from school teacher to labor union representative to powerful politician who controls ownership of the land is a calculated movement toward a position of power once independence is achieved. During the episode of the strike, Slime's intentions, which have been cloaked in mystery throughout the narrative, finally become clear to the reader as well as to a handful of villagers, including the shoemaker, Pa, and G.'s friend, Trumper. Slime's goal, in short, is to move into the castle and to keep the peasantry in a subservient position.

In the episode of the dock workers' strike, we can see Slime's manipulation of the villagers' ignorance. A small group of men collect daily at the shoemaker's shop, and their discussions reflect the level of their awareness of their own lives. Of the group, the shoemaker is perhaps the most aware. Based on his reading of Priestley, for instance, the shoemaker starts "to think of Little England as a part of some gigantic thing called colonial" (99), and gains a degree of insight into the colonial condition of Barbados:

> "[The British Empire is] what we here is part of. . . . But times goin' change . . . and that big British Empire goin' change too. . . . God don't like ugly, an' whenever these big great empires starts to get ugly . . . the Almighty puts His hands down once an' for all. He tell them without talkin,' fellows, you had your day." (103)

The villagers' ignorance, however, about the various forces controlling their lives is made apparent in their dialogue about the pending strike in the nearby port city where many of the males in the village work:

> "'Twill give the landlord something to think 'bout," said the overseer's brother. . . . The men looked at him in bewilderment. They always expected him to say what the average person didn't know. He was the overseer's brother.
>
> "What it got to do with the landlord?" the shoemaker asked.
>
> "He's partner in the firm," said the overseer's brother. "Jones an' Creighton Shipping Company Limited. He's the Creighton part of it." (96)

The realization that Creighton has a financial stake in the strike is a step forward for the villagers. The overseer's brother shows insight, but his information leads him astray: that is, to assume that Creighton and Slime are on opposing sides, and that Slime has the villagers' interests in mind.

In *Island in the Sun*, Waugh portrays the labor strike in Santa Marta as a frightening prospect. Boyeur controls the mindless peasantry, and once he calls the strike, it amounts to an opening up of the floodgates of chaos. Boyeur in effect unleashes the unruly laborers' naturally violent and disorderly instincts, and a brutal murder occurs as a result. Waugh implies that Santa Marta's prosperity depends on its political stability, which means that the latent violence of the indigenous masses must be held in check. By contrast, Lamming depicts the labor strike in Barbados, which is patterned after the actual strike that Lamming lived through as a child, as a staged manipulation of the naive and frightened villagers by a colonial governor and an ambitious indigenous politician, working in close cooperation with each other. In both cases, the peasants are manipulated, but Lamming focuses on what the villagers must learn, their developing consciousness of their situation. Waugh, by contrast, sees the villagers as static, incapable of awareness.

In much West Indian fiction as well as in post-colonial fiction more generally, the poor condition of the indigenous people's homes represents more than their poverty. It also symbolizes their identity, which has likewise fallen into disrepair. In Reid's *New Day*, for instance, the destruction of the Campbells' homestead by colonial military forces during Jamaica's labor riots symbolizes the collapse of the Campbell family itself. Again, in Naipaul's *A House for Mr. Biswas*, Biswas' own fragmented identity is reflected in the dilapidated condition of the house he finally manages to buy, or in Rushdie's *Midnight's Children*, Saleem's shanty in the Magicians' Ghetto reflects the precarious existence of many Indians during the Emergency. In *In the Castle of My Skin*, the ominous situation of the peasantry during decolonization is re-evoked as they are dispossessed from their homes, many of which fall apart when the owners attempt to move them.

When Pa, the guardian of the village's history and traditions, is forced to move to the Alms House, the result of Slime's rise to political power and his systematic manipulation of the naive, trusting peasantry becomes obvious. Pa becomes the first villager to awaken to the role of Creighton and Slime in the people's dispossession from their homes. After Pa receives his eviction notice, he has a visit from the head teacher, who, as one of Slime's accomplices in the transaction with Creighton, pretends to show Pa sympathy. Pa's persistent questioning of the head teacher, however, puts the latter on the defensive and represents the beginnings of a stirring of consciousness among the villagers:

> "I'd like to know just one thing or two. . . . Why first of all did Mr. Slime leave the teachin', an' how an' why he come to buy this land since there wus no love an' harmony 'twixt 'imself and Mr. Creighton? . . . The paper say something 'bout the Bank and the Society. 'Tis with the money o' these two he buy it. . . An' why the landlord go an' sell it without tellin' us?" the old man said. "Why he do that?" (254-56)

Pa's questioning has no effect on the loss of his home, but, perhaps more importantly, it represents a growing awareness on the villagers' part of their common plight, in itself a step toward the attainment of their own castle: a "home," or identity, built upon a solid foundation. It is important, too, that Pa's enlightenment, like that of the shoemaker, involves not only an awareness of the villagers' manipulation by Creighton and Slime, but also a sense of racial pride in his black African descent. This process of enlightenment or journey toward a secure identity within the castle of one's skin is continued by G. and his friend, Trumper, both of whom eventually realize they must leave Barbados to gain self-realization.

In *The Pleasures of Exile*, Lamming writes: "Unawareness is the basic condition of the slave. Awareness is a minimum condition for attaining freedom" (12). In *The Wretched of the Earth*, Fanon also stresses the relation between consciousness and freedom (200-201). The shoemaker and Pa are forerunners of a collective quickening of consciousness that, finally, extends beyond the time frame covered in the novel. Like many post-colonial writers, Lamming describes the difficulties following decolonization and points toward the hope of a future resolution. Although Slime has successfully manipulated the naive villagers and dispossessed them of their land and homes, Lamming implies that the villagers learn an important lesson in the process. And through characters like G. and Trumper, the author points toward a Barbados of the future that will be less susceptible to empty promises. In his guarded optimism concerning the West Indian future, Lamming is similar to other Third World writers: Rushdie, who points toward a better future for India in *Midnight's Children*; Ngugi, who despite his novels' "dark" endings illuminates the path toward a brighter Kenyan future; and Naipaul, who implies through his character Biswas that the West Indian quest for a secure home must continue into the future. All of these post-colonial writers seem to say that to chart a course for the future, Third World countries must cast off the shackles of the past and its legacy of denigration and doubt, and set new priorities for themselves.

Lamming has said that a "man is always resident in the castle of his skin. If the castle is deserted, then we know the Devil has been at work" (*PE*, 75). Throughout most of the novel, G.'s castle is deserted: he knows himself only in terms of his experience in the village, and he finds security in his identity with the village and with his peers. As he grows older and the village begins to change, however, G. comes to accept the basic uncertainty of life. His circle of friends is broken: Trumper goes to America, and Bob and Boy Blue take up jobs on the police force. G. senses the transience of his existence and questions his identity as well as his earlier relationships with his friends:

> When I review these relationships they seem so odd. I have always been here on this side and the other person there on that side, and we have both tried to make the sides appear similar in the needs, desires and ambitions. But it wasn't true. It was never true. . . . The likenesses will meet and make merry, but they won't know you. They won't know the you that's hidden somewhere in the castle of your skin. (261)

Here Lamming seems strikingly similar to Naipaul who, during his trip to India, recorded in *An Area of Darkness*, felt himself apart and paradoxically different from those of his own Indian ancestry (46). Both writers surely reflect the complex inheritance and identity crisis of many West Indians as well as others with a colonized background. The colonial legacy in a country like Barbados results in a feeling of being different and unique, and an attendant difficulty in identifying with any one particular group, since one feels a part and yet not a part of several different groups.

In *The Pleasures of Exile*, Lamming describes his own complex situation as a black man from a formerly colonized West Indian island living in the mother country: "The pleasure and paradox of my own exile is that I belong wherever I am" (150). The position of the formerly colonized thus seems to be that one's "castle" is no longer in one definite place, but rather involves an affiliation with others of one's race or colonial background; in other words, identity is transferred to the inside of one's skin. This is the lesson that G. learns when he prepares to leave for Trinidad and meets Trumper, who has just returned from a three-year stay in America. Trumper has made an important discovery while in America: that he is a member of the black race and that he should be proud of his heritage. In effect, Trumper has cast off the white mask which Fanon describes in his classic study of colonialism, *Black Skin, White Masks*.

Trumper tells G. that "it ain't have nothin' to do with where you born. 'Tis what you is, a different kind o' creature" (297). G. feels confused by Trumper's new assurance, and yet he senses that in Trinidad he may perhaps make a similar discovery. Trumper thus in part functions as a foreshadowing of what will become of G. in Trinidad. As a result of his life abroad, Trumper has a new political consciousness. Whereas G. and his mother only begin to think of Slime as "suspect" (288), Trumper has accumulated experience that enables him to understand the situation with clarity: "I know for a fact that the very money that go in that Penny Bank an' Society buy this land in his name. That's what I know. Nothin' he do ain't surprise me" (288). G. only vaguely comprehends Trumper. When the latter refers proudly to "my people," G. responds innocently, "What people?" (295). What G. does realize through Trumper, however, is the possibility for change. As G. prepares to leave for Trinidad the next day, he realizes that he, like Trumper, is undertaking a journey of discovery.

In *The Pleasures of Exile*, Lamming draws a distinction between the African and West Indian colonial experience. The African, Lamming argues, can derive strength from the "traditional cultures of African civilisation." For the West Indian, however, the colonial experience runs deeper:

> It is not merely a political definition; it is not merely the result of certain economic arrangements. It started as these, and grew somewhat deeper. Colonialism is the very base and structure of the West Indian's cultural awareness. (35)

As a result of the impact of colonialism, the process of identification with an indigenous tradition becomes much more difficult for a West Indian than for an African or Indian. Lamming suggests, though, that the West Indian has a place in something larger than a traditional culture, for "the West Indies—African, Chinese and Indian by mixture— . . . belong to that massive peasant majority whose leap in the twentieth century has shattered all the traditional calculations of the West, of European civilisation" (*PE*, 36). It is thus not by accident that Alec Waugh's treatment of a fictional West Indian island gives us the sense of an ending, the passing of an era, whereas Lamming's novel ends with a representative young man's beginning.

Island in the Sun describes the collapse of an imperial order as perceived by those in power. Waugh's focus on Governor-General Templeton as a fair-minded, able administrator underlines both the importance and difficulty of maintaining order in the post-war, disruptive atmosphere of the West Indies. On another level, Templeton can be seen as embodying the Empire itself: at the end of a long, impressive career of duty and responsibility, he readies himself to step down. The labor strike, which hastens Templeton's "retirement," moreover, represents the potential overthrow of British colonial order and stability. At the novel's end, as Templeton and the others prepare to return to England, the only apparent hope for Santa Marta lies in the ability of the English-educated lawyer, Grainger Morris, to continue the civilized system of law and order established by the British colonizers.

In the Castle of My Skin traces the same process described in *Island in the Sun*, except that Lamming, in conveying the viewpoint of the colonized people, portrays the British colonial order as an exploitative imposition on West Indian life. Lamming posits that the West Indians must first cast off the oppressive vestiges of British colonial rule before they can begin to chart their own course for the future. And his choice of the *Bildungsroman* form helps convey the idea of a West Indian island coming of age and accepting its problematic position as an independent country. Furthermore, Lamming's implicit rejection of the traditional English novel's narrative focus on an individual consciousness and his adoption of the Village as the central character in his *Bildungsroman* signals a step in the throwing off of British colonial influence. Lamming has stated his central theme as Caliban's getting hold of Prospero's weapons and no longer asking for his master's permission. In *In the Castle of My Skin*, the weapon Lamming seizes is the English novel itself, and, like other post-colonial anglophone writers, he uses that weapon for his own ends: to re-tell the story of his country and people in their own terms and from their own unique vantage point.

The hallmark of modern consciousness
is its enormous multiplicity.

Clifford Geertz

Conclusion

In *The Wretched of the Earth*, Fanon discusses the relation between the various countries dominated by French colonization:

> There is no common destiny to be shared between the national cultures of Senegal and Guinea; but there is a common destiny between the Senegalese and Guinean nations which are both dominated by the same French colonialism. (234)

Certainly the same may be said about the various countries dominated by British colonial rule. Although the national cultures of India, South Africa, Nigeria, Kenya, and Barbados may have little in common, the shared history of subjugation under British colonial rule gives them a common past and, as Fanon points out, a common destiny. Their individual national concerns take on a global significance as a result of this shared past. And this commonality is surely evident in the fiction written by both British colonial writers and indigenous, post-colonial writers.

The post-colonial writers' self-appointed mission to forge their countries' national consciousness is largely defined by the Anglocentric portrayal of their culture and people by the earlier British colonial writers. Indeed, the fiction of many Third World writers can only be fully understood through an awareness of its interconnection with earlier British fictional works. Before the emergence of post-colonial fiction, Western readers were given the British view of the Empire, and thus naturally came to see the various colonized lands and peoples as the colonizers saw them. Shakespeare's *The Tempest* and Defoe's *Robinson Crusoe*, perhaps the earliest examples of colonial fiction, give readers the British perspective of the colonization of the West Indies. In his African romances, Rider Haggard valorizes the explorers and adventurers who opened up the "dark continent" of Africa for later colonization. Even though documenting the British imperial era may have been far from these writers' intention, their works nevertheless portrayed people and places with which their readers had little acquaintance. Many readers therefore adopted views of the colonized lands based largely on popular British fiction: it was, in the words of Edward Said, discussing Western perceptions of the Orient, "a textual universe by and large . . . made through books and manuscripts" (52). Haggard biographer Morton Cohen, for example, writes that for many Victorian readers, "Africa was the Africa of *King Solomon's Mines*" (94). Kipling in India, Cary in Nigeria, Elspeth Huxley in Kenya, and Alec Waugh in the West Indies, similarly served as chroniclers for the colonial era in other areas of the Empire.

The fact that much British colonial fiction takes the form of the romance or boys' adventure tale is certainly not accidental. One link among all these British works is a participation in and celebration of the romance and excitement of the imperial venture. The panoramic settings and picaresque structures of Haggard's *King Solomon's Mines* and Kipling's *Kim* certainly convey the sweeping, open-ended grandeur of the British conquest of the vast colonial territories. The lengthy road-building episode in Cary's *Mister Johnson*, in which the Nigerian interior is opened and the bush is tamed, similarly evokes the excitement of the imperial mission in action. Certainly Elspeth Huxley's description of the beautiful, spacious Kenyan Highlands in *A Thing to Love* also communicates the colonizers' feelings of pride and wonder in surveying their colonial possessions. Likewise, in *Island in the Sun*, Alec Waugh paints an attractive picture of the warm, sun-drenched West Indian islands, which for many of his characters serve as a refuge far removed from cold, industrialized, war-torn England. The British sense of national expansion, fulfillment, and destiny, which make up the essential components of the spirit of Empire, is clearly on display in the work of each of these writers.

The British writers' attitude toward both their English and indigenous characters also indicates an overall similarity among them. There are three recurrent aspects of this body of fiction which reflect the British colonizers' attitude toward the colonized people and culture. First, the primary focus is almost always on the British rather than the indigenous characters. The colonized characters, when they appear at all, are usually relegated to the background. Thus Achebe criticizes *Heart of Darkness* for its portrait of "Africa as setting and backdrop which eliminates the African as human factor" (*Hopes*, 12). Second, the indigenous characters are portrayed as isolated individuals with little or no humanizing connection to family or society. And third, the British writers, perhaps unconsciously, frequently use animalistic images in describing indigenous characters. By no means are each of these conditions true in every British colonial work. In fact, these characteristics are found less frequently in later British colonial fiction written around the time of decolonization. Nevertheless, these three characteristics recur with enough frequency to establish a link among the British writers and their conscious or unconscious attitudes toward the colonized people and culture.

Salman Rushdie asserts that "English fiction set in India—Kipling, Forster—has only been about what happened to the West when it went East. The language, contents and tone have never reflected how Indians experience India" (Smolowe, 56). Rushdie might well be speaking not only about English fiction set in India but that set in the other former colonies as well. Perhaps the most remarkable attribute of British colonial fiction is that it is only indirectly concerned with the place in which it is set. First and foremost, the British writers' interest is in their British characters and what happens to them. The concern with the indigenous people and culture comes in only so far as it affects the English characters; and this is as true of Joyce Cary, Elspeth Huxley, and Alec Waugh as it is of Kipling and Haggard. The indigenous characters, furthermore, are rarely given the rounded, multidimensional portrayal which the English characters receive. The colonized characters instead often appear static and stereotypical: like their culture, they are mired in their own backwardness and in obvious need of outside assistance.

Another recurring feature of British colonial fiction is the virtual absence of the indigenous family. The indigenous characters are almost always represented as individuals oddly cut off from a familial or social context. The reader of Forster's *A Passage to India*, Kipling's *Kim*, and Haggard's *King Solomon's Mines*, for example, sees nothing of indigenous family life. When the indigenous family does appear, as in Leonard Woolf's *The Village in the Jungle* and Cary's *Mister Johnson*, it is on the verge of deterioration. The native family in Woolf's novel disintegrates as a result of its sheer purposelessness and inertia; and the marital relation between Johnson and Bamu in Cary's novel is so tenuous that Bamu not only leaves Johnson but also turns him into the authorities who suspect him of murder.

One possible explanation for this curious absence of the indigenous family is that, as colonizers, the British probably had little access to the homes of the colonized people and thus little knowledge of their family life. The emphasis on the indigenous characters' individuality might, furthermore, reflect the British writers' own cultural bias in coming from a country where individuality is emphasized and encouraged. The result, however, of portraying the indigenous people as isolated individuals or as members of a "lost tribe" is that the native peoples seem to have no real culture or history. They are cut off from the cultural and historical mainstream which touches them only upon the arrival of the colonizers. Thus the colonial writers' ignorance of indigenous family life surely also reflects the colonizers' lack of interest in various aspects of colonized culture as well as their tendency to band together into an exclusive enclave, the Club, where they would not have to deal with a foreign society which they could not understand. In this way, the absence of the indigenous family in British colonial fiction further points up the colonizers' essential outsider status. Clearly, these writers set their works in faraway, exotic lands whose culture and history they failed to understand, and thus chose to disregard.

British writers further dehumanized their indigenous characters by frequently casting them in comic roles and by describing them in animalistic terms. Because the colonized people's ways of thinking, motivations, and actions were often perceived by the colonizers as strange and incomprehensible, it was easy for British writers to satirize them as comic figures. Indigenous characters in British fiction therefore often assume the role of buffoon. In this regard, one might think of Kipling's Hurree Chunder Mookerjee, Haggard's Kukuana tribe (who mistake Quatermain's rifle for a magic tube and believe Good has the power to control the sun), and Cary's laughably unpredictable and irresponsible clerk Johnson. Not only do the indigenous characters often assume a comic role, such as that of the irresponsible, inept underling or servant, but they also often seem to resemble animals. The British writers repeatedly describe the colonized people in animalistic terms. Thus Kipling's Teshoo Lama is compared to a camel (234); the African guide in *King Solomon's Mines* has the instincts of a ram (73); Cary's ineffectual and talkative Johnson is likened to a dog (235); and the African Home Guards in Huxley's *A Thing to Love* remind Sam Gibson of "a flock of birds" (249). In this connection we should also remember portraits of the colonized in canonical works not normally considered "colonial" texts, such as that of the West Indian Bertha Mason locked in Rochester's attic in *Jane Eyre*. Jane perceives Bertha as indeterminately "beast or human," grovelling "on all fours [as] it snatched and growled like some strange wild animal" (295). Gayatri Spivak has cited this animalistic portrayal of Bertha as an example of the register between "Europe and its not-yet-human Other" (Gates, 266). Perhaps the British writers did not deliberately set out to dehumanize their indigenous characters; nevertheless, this feature of the fiction accurately reflects the hierarchical nature of colonialism itself, the essential difference in station between colonizer and colonized. Colonialism by its very nature dehumanizes, casting the colonial subject into the mold of the Other, the incomprehensible alien with whom the British could not identify. Although they may not have seen themselves as spokespersons for the Empire, the British colonial writers, as we have seen, shared the colonialist ideology to a greater or lesser degree, and thus, whether willingly or not, gave voice to that self-justifying way of perceiving the colonized people and culture.

Another remarkable feature of colonial fiction is that almost all the British writers were implicitly of two minds about the Empire. Although, on the one hand, each writer participated to a degree in the romanticism of British imperial expansion, on the other hand, each also expressed reservations about the ultimate consequences of colonialism. From Ignosi's warning against further encroachment by the white man in *King Solomon's Mines* to the unnecessarily tragic outcomes of Cary's Johnson and Huxley's Raphaelo, the British writers implicitly recognize with increasing concern that the cost of colonial domination to both colonizer and colonized is at least as high as the supposed reward. It is not accidental that the spirit of adventure infusing early works such as *Kim* and *King Solomon's Mines* gives way to a more sober and even pessimistic appraisal of the ultimate benefit of the Empire by later British writers. Works like Forster's *A Passage to India*, Orwell's *Burmese Days*, Huxley's *A Thing to Love*, and Waugh's *Island in the Sun* chronicle either the end or the coming end of the imperial era, and all express reservations about the Empire's benefits.

Although it may seem that a novel like Waugh's *Island in the Sun* would represent the last word by the British regarding the Empire, English writers have continued to utilize the former colonies as a setting for their fiction, and readers have remained fascinated by the Empire. A more recent novel like Ruth Jhabvala's *Heat and Dust*, for instance, looks back on the Empire as a phenomenon which in spite of its shortcomings still possesses an almost magical, romantic appeal. More recent examples of colonial fiction, such as Paul Scott's *The Raj Quartet* and William Boyd's *A Good Man in Africa*, have also enjoyed considerable popularity. Scott's *The Raj Quartet* represents a more critical look at the Empire than most colonial fiction; nevertheless, it too contains an unmistakable nostalgia for the romantic, imperial past, and clearly conveys the excitement and adventure felt by the colonizers. The continuing appeal of fictional portrayals of the colonies is perhaps even more evident in film. Adaptations of *Kim*, *King Solomon's Mines*, *Mister Johnson*, *A Passage to India*, *The Raj Quartet*, *Heat and Dust*, *The Far*

Pavilions, Elspeth Huxley's *The Flame Trees of Thika*, and Isak Dinesen's *Out of Africa* have been made in the last ten years for cinema and television. Thus Western audiences receive a view of the so-called Third World that is largely unchanged from that put forward by British writers during the colonial era; Edward Said has asserted that due to "television, the films, and all the media's resources," there has been "a reinforcement of the stereotypes by which the Orient [as well as other areas of the so-called Third World] is viewed" (26). Rather than critically appraising the good and bad points of the British Empire, contemporary audiences seem more inclined to relive vicariously this seemingly simpler, romantic time. In this way, the popular reception of both fiction and films provides an ironic commentary on the wide cultural gap which remains between the "developed" and the "developing" worlds. Observing the recent proliferation of British fiction and film set in the colonies and its popular reception, Salman Rushdie concludes that "the refurbishment of the Empire's tarnished image is under way" (*IH*, 91), and he calls such works "only the latest in a very long line of fake portraits inflicted by the West on the East" (*IH*, 88).

Post-colonial writers obviously seek to address what they perceive as an inaccurate or incomplete portrait of their people and culture in British fiction. On the most basic level, the indigenous writers reverse the cultural perspective of the British writers: the indigenous characters move to the foreground and the British characters become background figures. In some cases, the colonizers are presented as flat, stereotypic figures, reminiscent of the indigenous characters in British fiction. Winterbottom, the British district officer in Achebe's *Arrow of God*, is an example of such a one-dimensional, stereotypic colonizer.[1] In general, however, post-colonial writers offer a more balanced portrait of the conflict of cultures than their British predecessors. Although Rushdie satirizes the self-important Anglo-Indian Methwold in *Midnight's Children*, the author also portrays the "subtle magic of Methwold's estate" which lingers long after India gains its formal independence (100). In *Wild Conquest*, Abrahams' treatment of the historic Boer-Matabele conflict is remarkably balanced in its portrayal of both sides. And in *Things Fall Apart*, Achebe shows both the good and bad sides of the British missionaries by contrasting the sensitive Reverend Brown with the absolutist Reverend Smith. Moreover, although Ngugi and Lamming are critical of British colonial domination of their countries, they reserve their harshest criticism for indigenous characters like Karanja of *A Grain of Wheat* and Mr. Slime of *In the Castle of My Skin* who succumb to self-interest and betray the national cause of independence from colonial rule. Part of the reason for the generally even portrayal of both sides in post-colonial fiction could be that most of these writers aim in part for a Western reading audience, and thus are careful not to overstate their own cultural perspective. Unlike the British colonial writers, the post-colonial authors write for readers representing both sides of the cultural confrontation. But perhaps their position in history also gives them a clearer insight into the cross-cultural encounter: they can present their own culture from the inside, and their Western education and knowledge of colonial culture also enable them to understand the colonizers' point of view. For surely the colonized, like the African American slaves, always knew more about their colonial "masters" than their colonizers knew of them.

One of the most remarkable differences between the earlier British and later post-colonial representations of Third World culture is the emergence of the indigenous family in the latter. The majority of post-colonial writers focus on the family as the center of society, and they use this portrait of the family as a way of illustrating the cohesiveness of the pre-colonial, indigenous culture and of the society at large. Whereas the indigenous characters in British fiction often appear alienated and disconnected, the same people in post-colonial fiction are delineated as part of an understandable, familiar family unit and an organized culture. In this way, post-colonial writers re-humanize their indigenous characters and make them part of a knowable cultural, historical context. No longer is the Third World person the strangely alienated "Other"; rather, he or she is portrayed as a member of a family and culture which, from the post-colonial writers' point of view, is suddenly threatened with extinction by the disrupting, outside force of British colonialism.

The post-colonial writers often go back into their country's colonial past to explain and account for the confusing present day. Unlike the British colonial writers' use of the romance and boys' adventure tale as literary forms, a majority of post-colonial writers work in the realist tradition, often blending fiction with history in an attempt to recreate their nations' problematic past. The post-colonial writers also often concern themselves with the collective past of an entire people rather than with the individual past life of a single character. Thus Fredric Jameson argues that "the story of the private individual destiny is always an allegory of the embattled situation of the public third-world culture and society" (69). Rushdie's *Midnight's Children*, for instance, attempts to capture the experience of the entire, populous nation of India through its recent history from pre-independence to the present. Abrahams focuses on the Boer-Matabele conflict to portray the vital turning-point in southern African history when possession of the land passed from blacks to whites. Similarly, Achebe turns to the Nigerian past in *Things Fall Apart* to illuminate the consequences of colonialism for the Ibo people. And both Ngugi and Lamming also focus on significant national events—the Mau Mau Revolt and the 1930s labor riots in Barbados, respectively—to recreate their countries' history from an indigenous insider's viewpoint. In this way, the post-colonial writers show that the present is comprehensible only through an understanding of the past. Moreover, their novels share a didactic intent to show both Western and indigenous readers alike that their countries' past was not, as Achebe puts it, "one long night of savagery from which the first Europeans acting on God's behalf delivered them" (*MYCD*, 59). Patrick Taylor has stated that Lamming and Derek Walcott are both "concerned with the transformation of the colonizer-colonized dualism in a struggle for recognition, a liberating encounter with history" (194). The same could be said for the other post-colonial writers we have examined.

The conflict of cultures brought about by colonialism is a central concern for the post-colonial as well as for the British writers. The effect of that conflict is obviously one of confusion for both sides. The main characters in British colonial fiction—Kipling's Kim, Cary's Rudbeck, Huxley's Patricia Foxley, and Waugh's Governor Templeton—feel torn in opposite directions by events which almost overwhelm them. Similarly, indigenous protagonists, such as Rushdie's Saleem, Abrahams' Dabula, Achebe's Okonkwo, Ngugi's Mugo, and Lamming's G., are people who emerge confused, uprooted, and often defeated by the confrontation between colonizer and colonized. Not surprisingly, the post-colonial writers' narrative frequently ends on a note of tragedy and loss. This tragedy only sometimes involves physical destruction. More often it involves a national identity crisis and a loss of dignity experienced by the colonized people in the wake of foreign exploitation and domination. From the colonized point of view, colonialism results in the implantation of alien standards and values which are nearly impossible to maintain following decolonization. Ironically, the legacy of colonialism, seen from the colonized perspective, involves not the transference of the ideals of civilization, as the colonizers intended, but rather the loss of a cohesive and secure identity on the part of the uprooted colonized people.

Despite tragedy and loss, however, post-colonial fiction often expresses a paradoxical hope for the future. Although Saleem's individual story in *Midnight's*

Children is a tragic one, Rushdie implies that India will continually transform itself and remain adaptable and resilient. Similarly, even though Gubuza is killed by the Boers in *Wild Conquest*, Abrahams' Matabele recover and progress towards their "new day." Achebe's *Things Fall Apart* and Ngugi's *A Grain of Wheat* paint a tragic picture of the consequences of colonialism. And yet, despite the negative outcomes of Okonkwo and Mugo, respectively, all is not hopeless for the Ibo and Gikuyu peoples. Both Achebe and Ngugi convey the importance of adapting in order to remain vital in a rapidly changing world. And Lamming, perhaps most surprising of all given the devastating effect of colonialism in the West Indies, envisions a more open, tolerant society resulting from the displacement of various peoples to the West Indies.

> We [in the West Indies] are used to living with many islands. From the very beginning we were part of the island of China, and the island of Africa and the island of India. . . . We have not solved any racial questions; for prejudice is with us in one form or another; but we have been for a very long time a good example of the evolution of human relations in the future. (154)

Derek Walcott has echoed Lamming's point, calling Port of Spain "one of the most interesting cities in the world" because "every culture is represented": "It is inevitable that if all these various strains of Asian, African, and Mediterranean people are circulating, something is bound to ferment that is very, very fertile" (Moyers, 431). Clearly the post-colonial writers relate that Third World people have been and still are beset by many problems, some of which were created during the colonial interval in their country's history. Nevertheless, through a greater awareness of pre-colonial culture and traditions and an increased appreciation of their important role in the contemporary world, the indigenous people of former colonies are forging new ways to overcome their problems and to face an even more problematic future. In this regard, the task of the post-colonial writer becomes an increasingly important one, for, as Abdul JanMohamed has argued, the new work in "the domain of literary and cultural syncretism belongs not to colonialist or neocolonialist writers but increasingly to Third World artists" (Gates, 104).

In *The Wretched of the Earth*, Fanon writes that the "accession to independence of the colonial countries places an important question before the world, for the national liberation of colonized countries unveils their true economic state and makes it seem even more unendurable" (98). The question Fanon refers to is that of the economic inequity between the so-called "developing" and "developed" nations which is in part the outcome of colonialism. "Humanity must reply to this question," Fanon claims, "or be shaken to bits by it" (98). Although Fanon's solution of redistribution of wealth may be unlikely in the foreseeable future, the immediate need to bridge cultural and national gaps is surely recognized by people everywhere. This bridging of gaps separating "developing" and "developed" nations is one of the implicit aims of much post-colonial fiction. Before recognition of the needs of other countries is possible, there must be an understanding of those countries and their history. The post-colonial writers' re-creation of their nations' past and their portrayal of the bitter fruits of independence represent an important first step in that direction. While working toward a more equitable economic relationship between nations, countries must move toward an ever greater understanding of their differences and a recognition of the similarities which link all nationalities together. I would like to include in my closing a point made by Clifford Geertz in *Local Knowledge*:

> To see ourselves as others see us can be eye-opening. To see others as sharing a nature with ourselves is the merest decency. But it is from the far more difficult achievement of seeing ourselves amongst others, as a local example of the forms human life has locally taken, a case among cases, a world among worlds, that the largeness of mind, without which objectivity is self-congratulation and tolerance a sham, comes. (16)

It is surely toward this goal of greater mutual understanding that the best of post-colonial literature, with its awareness of a problematic past of heirarchy and discrimination and its vision of a future of cultural multiplicity, directs itself.

Notes

Introduction

1. "The British Empire," *Collier's Encyclopedia*. I am indebted to this reference book for background information on the history of the British Empire.

2. See Oliver and Fage, "The European Scramble for African Colonies" in *A Short History of Africa*; Chamberlain, "South Africa" in *The Scramble for Africa*; Denoon, "Imperial Factors" in *Southern Africa Since 1800*; and Lelyveld, "Part of Us" in *Move Your Shadow*.

3. See, for example, *The Black Writer in Africa and the Americas*, ed. Lloyd Brown (Los Angeles: Hennessey & Ingalls, 1973); *Black Time: Fiction of Africa, the Caribbean, and the United States*, ed. Bonnie J. Barthold (New Haven: Yale Univ. Press, 1981); *An Anthology of African and Caribbean Writing in English*, ed. John Figueroa (London: Heinemann, 1982); *PMLA* (January 1990): Special Issue on African and African American Literature.

Chapter One: The Example of India

1. See "The Bisara of Poree" in *Plain Tales from the Hills*.

2. See Michael Kaufman, "Author from Three Countries," *New York Times Book Review*, 13 November 1983.

3. See *Kim*, 87, 89, 95.

4. See "The Mark of the Beast" and "The Sending of Dana Da."

Chapter Three: The Cultural Clash

1. Achebe has stated that a basic belief of the Ibo is that "there is no absolute anything." The Ibo express this belief in a proverb: "Wherever something stands, something else will stand beside it" (Moyers, 333).

2. Sixth Annual South Bank Show Lecture by Achebe before the Royal Society of Arts in London. Radio broadcast on Arts and Literary Affairs program, *The South Bank Show* (host Melvyn Bragg), 1990.

Chapter Four: The Struggle for Independence

1. See Frantz Fanon, *The Wretched of the Earth* (New York: Grove Press, 1968), 136-37, and Percival Spear, *A History of India*, Volume Two, Chapter 16, "Mahatma," 199-200.

2. In *Decolonising the Mind*, Ngugi also refers to Huxley as a "racist" (92). Discussing the literature made available to students as a part of a standard African education, Ngugi lists three categories of works: first, the "great humanist and democratic tradition of European literature" (91), including the Greek tragedians, Shakespeare, Balzac, Tolstoy, Brecht, and others; second,the "literature of liberal Europeans who often had Africa as the subject of their explorations" (91), including Alan Paton, Conrad, Isak Dinesen, and Joyce Cary; and third, the "downright racist literature of writers like Rider Haggard, Elspeth Huxley, Robert Ruark, and Nicholas Monsarrat" (92).

Chapter Five: The Demise of Empire

1. *Abroad: British Literary Traveling Between the Wars*. See "I Hate It Here," 15-23.

2. See Sandra Paquet, *The Novels of George Lamming* (London: Heinemann, 1982), 5-6, and Ngugi wa Thiong'o, *Homecoming* (London: Heinemann, 1972), 110.

Conclusion

1. See Sarah Milbury-Steen, *African and European Stereotypes in Twentieth-Century African Fiction* (New York: NYU Press, 1981) for an interesting discussion of stereotyping in British and African fiction.

Works Cited

Abrahams, Peter. "The Conflict of Culture in Africa." *Phylon* 16, iv, 1955.

__________. *Return to Goli*. London: Faber, 1951.

__________. *Tell Freedom*. London, 1954; rpt. New York: Collier, 1970.

__________. *Wild Conquest*. London: Faber, 1951.

__________. *A Wreath for Udomo*. New York: Alfred A. Knopf, 1956.

Achebe, Chinua. *Anthills of the Savannah*. New York: Doubleday, 1987.

__________. *Arrow of God*. Garden City, New York: Doubleday, 1969.

__________. *Hopes and Impediments*. New York: Doubleday, 1989.

__________. *A Man of the People*. Garden City, New York: Doubleday, 1967.

__________. *Morning Yet On Creation Day*. Garden City, New York: Doubleday, 1975.

__________. *Things Fall Apart*. London: Heinemann, 1958.

Aluko, T. M. *One Man, One Matchet*. London: Heinemann, 1964.

Anand, Mulk Raj. *Untouchable*. Bombay, 1933; rpt. New York: Penguin, 1986.

Annan, Noel. "Kipling's Place in the History of Ideas." *Victorian Studies* (June, 1960).

Anthony, Michael. *The Year in San Fernando*. London: Heinemann, 1965.

Armah, Ayi Kwei. *The Beautyful Ones Are Not Yet Born*. New York: Collier, 1969.

__________. *The Healers: An Historical Novel*. rpt. London: Heinemann, 1979.

Best, Nicholas. *Happy Valley*. London: Secker and Warburg, 1979.

Bhabha, Homi K., ed. *Nation and Narration*. London: Routledge, 1990.

Boyd, William. *A Good Man in Africa*. London: H. Hamilton, 1981.

Brantlinger, Patrick. *Rule of Darkness*. Ithaca: Cornell, 1988.

Brodber, Erna. *Jane and Louisa Will Soon Come Home*. London: New Beacon Books, 1980.

Bronte, Charlotte. *Jane Eyre*. rpt. New York: New American Library, 1960.

Buchan, John. *Prester John*. New York: George H. Doran, 1910.

Carrington, C. E. *The Life of Rudyard Kipling*. London: Macmillan, 1978.

Cary, Joyce. *The Case for African Freedom and Other Writings on Africa*. Austin, 1962; rpt. New York: McGraw-Hill, 1964.

__________. *The African Witch*. London: M. Joseph, 1951.

__________. *Mister Johnson*. London, 1939; rpt. New York: Time, Inc., 1962.

Chamberlain, M. E. *The Scramble for Africa*. Essex, U.K.: Longman House, 1974.

Coetzee, J. M. *Waiting for the Barbarians*. New York: Penguin, 1980.

Cohen, Morton. *Rider Haggard: His Life and Works*. London: Hutchinson, 1960.

__________. *Rudyard Kipling to Rider Haggard: the Record of a Friendship*. London: Hutchinson, 1965.

Conrad, Joseph. *Heart of Darkness*. Norton Critical Edition, ed. Robert Kimbrough. New York: Norton, 1963.

Cronin, Richard. *Imagining India*. New York: St. Martin's Press, 1989.

Crowder, Michael. *A Short History of Nigeria*. New York: Praeger, 1962.

Denoon, Donald. *Southern Africa Since 1800*. London: Longman, 1972.

Desai, Anita. *Clear Light of Day*. New York: Viking Penguin, 1980.

Dinesen, Isak. *Out of Africa*. rpt. New York: Time, Inc., 1963.

__________. *Shadows on the Grass*. New York: Random House, 1960.

Duerden, Dennis and Cosmo Pieterse. *African Writers Talking*. New York: Africana, 1972.

Durix, Jean-Pierre, et al. "Interview with Salman Rushdie." *Kunapipi* IV, ii, 1982.

Fanon, Frantz. *Black Skin, White Masks*. New York: Grove Press, 1967.

__________. *The Wretched of the Earth*. New York, 1963; rpt. Black Cat ed. New York: Grove Press, 1968.

Fischer, Louis. *Gandhi: His Life and Message for the World*. New York: Mentor, 1954.

Forster, E. M. *A Passage to India*. New York: Harcourt, Brace, Jovanovich, 1924.

Foster, Malcolm. *Joyce Cary: A Biography*. Boston: Houghton Mifflin, 1968.

Fussell, Paul. *Abroad: British Literary Traveling Between the Wars*. New York: Oxford University Press, 1980.

Gandhi, Mohandas. *An Autobiography*. Washington, 1948; rpt. Boston: Beacon Press, 1957.

Garcia Marquez, Gabriel. *One Hundred Years of Solitude*. Trans. Gregory Rabassa. New York: Harper & Row, 1970.

Gates, Henry Louis, Jr., ed. *"Race," Writing, and Difference*. Chicago: Univ. of Chicago Press, 1985.

Geertz, Clifford. *Local Knowledge: Further Essays in Interpretive Anthropology*. New York: Basic Books, 1983.

Gilbert, Elliot, ed. *Kipling and the Critics*. New York: New York University Press, 1965.

Gilkes, Michael. *Wilson Harris and the Caribbean Novel*. London Longman, 1975.

Gordimer, Nadine. *The Black Interpreters*. Johannesburg: SPRO/Ravan, 1973.

_________. *July's People*. New York: Viking, 1981.

Grace, Patricia. *Potiki*. New York: Penguin, 1986.

Greenberger, Allen. *The British Image of India*. New York: Oxford University Press, 1969.

Greene, Graham. *The Heart of the Matter*. London: Heinemann and Bodley Head, 1971.

_________. *Journey Without Maps*. London: Heinemann, 1936.

Haggard, H. Rider. *Allan Quatermain*. In *The Works of Rider Haggard, One Volume Edition*. New York: Walter J. Black, 1928.

_________. *Cetywayo and His White Neighbours*. London: Trubner, 1888.

_________. *King Solomon's Mines*. London, 1885; rpt. New York: Penguin, 1958.

_________. *She*. In *The Works of Rider Haggard, One Volume Edition*. New York: Walter J. Black, 1928.

Harrison, James. *Rudyard Kipling*. Boston: Twayne, 1982.

Heath, Jeffrey M. "The Lush Places." *Evelyn Waugh Newsletter* vol. 13, no. 2 Autumn 1979.

Henty, G. A. *Rujub the Juggler*. London: Chatto and Windus, 1893.

_________. *Through Three Campaigns: A Story of Chitral, Tirah, and Ashanti*. London: Blackie, 1900.

__________. *With Roberts to Pretoria: A Tale of the South African War*. New York: Scribner's, 1901.

Herdeck, Donald A. Ed. *Caribbean Writers: A Bio-Bibliographical Critical Encyclopedia*. Washington D.C.: Three Continents Press, 1979.

Higgins, D. S. *Rider Haggard*. New York: Stein and Day, 1981.

Hobson, J. A. *Imperialism*. London: George Allen & Unwin, 1938.

Hodge, Merle. *Crick Crack, Monkey*. Portsmouth, NH: Heinemann, 1981.

Howe, Irving, ed. *The Portable Kipling*. New York: Viking Press, 1982.

Hoyos, F. A. *Barbados: A Short History from the Amerindians to Independence*. London: Macmillan, 1978.

Huxley, Elspeth. "An Edwardian Childhood in Africa." *The Observer* 30 August 1981.

__________, and Margery Perham. *Race and Politics in Kenya: A Correspondence Between Elspeth Huxley and Margery Perham*. London: Faber and Faber, 1956.

__________. *Red Strangers*. London: Chatto and Windus, 1955.

__________. *A Thing to Love*. London: Chatto and Windus, 1954.

__________. *White Man's Country: Lord Delamere and the Making of Kenya*. London: Chatto and Windus, 1956.

Innes, C. L. *Chinua Achebe*. Cambridge: Cambridge Univ. Press, 1990.

Jameson, Fredric. "Third-World Literature in the Era of Multinational Capitalism." *Social Text* (Fall 1986).

JanMohamed, Abdul R. *Manichean Aesthetics: The Politics of Literature in Colonial Africa*. Amherst: Univ. of Mass. Press, 1983.

Jhabvala, Ruth Prawer. *Heat and Dust*. New York: Harper & Row, 1975.

Kaufman, Michael. "Author from Three Countries." *New York Times Book Review* 13 November 1983.

Killam, G. D. *Africa in British Literature 1874-1939*. Ibadan, Nigeria: Ibadan University Press, 1968.

__________. *The Novels of Chinua Achebe*. New York: Africana, 1969.

Kincaid, Jamaica. *Annie John*. New York: New American Library, 1983.

Kipling, Rudyard. *Kim*. New York, 1901; rpt. New York: Dell, 1970.

__________, and Wolcott Balestier. *The Naulahka*. New York: Macmillan, 1897.

__________. *Plain Tales from the Hills*. New York: Thomas Y. Crowell and Co., 1917.

__________. *Something of Myself*. New York: Doubleday, 1937.

__________. *Twenty-One Tales*. London: The Folio Society, 1972.

La Guma, Alex. *A Walk in the Night*. Evanston: Northwestern University Press, 1968.

Lamming, George. *In the Castle of My Skin*. New York, 1954; rpt. New York: Schocken, 1983.

__________. *The Pleasures of Exile*. London: M. Joseph, 1960.

__________. *Season of Adventure*. London: M. Joseph, 1960.

Larson, Charles. *The Emergence of African Fiction*. Bloomington: Indiana University Press, 1972.

__________. *The Novel in the Third World*. Washington: INSCAPE, 1976.

Lelyveld, Joseph. *Move Your Shadow: South Africa, Black and White*. New York: Viking Penguin, 1986.

Lovelace, Earl. *The Wine of Astonishment*. rpt. Portsmouth, NH: Heinemann, 1983.

__________. *The Dragon Can't Dance*. rpt. London: Longman, 1981.

McLuhan, Marshall. "Kipling and Forster." *Sewanee Review* LII (Summer 1944).

Mahood, Molly Maureen. *The Colonial Encounter*. London: Rex Collins, 1977.

__________. *Joyce Cary's Africa*. Boston: Houghton Mifflin, 1965.

Mannoni, Dominique. *Prospero and Caliban*. London, 1956; rpt. New York: Praeger, 1964.

Markandaya, Kamala. *Nectar in a Sieve*. New York: Signet, 1954.

Martini, Jurgen et al. "Interview with Ngugi wa Thiong'o." *Kunapipi* Vol. III no. 2, 1981: 135-140.

Mazrui, Ali. *The Anglo-African Commonwealth*. New York: Permagon, 1967.

Memmi, Albert. *The Colonizer and the Colonized*. New York: Orion Press, 1965.

Meyers, Jeffrey. *Fiction and the Colonial Experience*. Ipswich: The Boydell Press, 1972.

Milbury-Steen, Sarah. *African and European Stereotypes in Twentieth Century African Fiction*. New York: New York University Press, 1981.

Mofolo, Thomas. *Chaka: An Historical Romance*. Morija, 1925; rpt. London: Oxford Univ. Press, 1967.

Monsarrat, Nicholas. *The Tribe That Lost Its Head*. New York: W. Sloane Associates, 1956.

Moyers, Bill. *A World of Ideas*. New York: Doubleday, 1989.

Mphahlele, Ezekiel. *The African Image*. New York: Praeger, 1974.

Mugo Githae, Micere. *Visions of Africa*. Kampala: E. African Literature Bureau, 1976.

Mukherjee, Bharati. *The Tiger's Daughter*. New York: Penguin, 1987.

Naipaul, V. S. *An Area of Darkness*. London: A. Deutsch, 1964.

_________. *Guerrillas*. London: A. Deutsch, 1975.

_________. *A House for Mr. Biswas*. rpt. New York: Penguin, 1969.

_________. *India: A Wounded Civilization*. New York: Knopf, 1977.

_________. *The Middle Passage*. London: A. Deutsch, 1964.

_________. *Miguel Street*. rpt. New York: Vintage, 1984.

_________. *The Overcrowded Barracoon*. London: A. Deutsch, 1972.

Narayan, R. K. *The English Teacher*. Chicago and London: Univ. of Chicago Press and Heinemann, 1945.

_________. *The Guide*. New York: Viking, 1958.

_________. *Waiting for the Mahatma*. London: Methuen, 1955.

Nazareth, Peter. *Literature and Society in Modern Africa*. Nairobi: East African Literature Bureau, 1972.

Ngugi wa Thiong'o. *Decolonising the Mind*. London and Nairobi: James Currey and Heinemann, 1986.

_________. *A Grain of Wheat*. London: Heinemann, 1967.

_________. *Homecoming*. London: Heinemann, 1972.

_________. *Matigari*. Trans. Wangui wa Goro. London: Heinemann, 1989.

_________. *Petals of Blood*. New York: E. P. Dutton, 1978.

_________. *Weep Not, Child*. London: Heinemann, 1964.

_________. *Writers in Politics*. London: Heinemann, 1981.

Oliver, Roland and J. D. Fage. *A Short History of Africa*. New York: Penguin, 1962.

Olney, James. *Tell Me Africa: An Approach to African Literature*. Princeton: Princeton Univ. Press, 1973.

Omotoso, Kole. *The Combat*. London: Heinemann, 1972.

Orwell, George. *Burmese Days*. rpt. New York: Time, Inc., 1962.

_________. *A Collection of Essays*. New York: Harcourt, Brace, Jovanovich, 1953.

Oyono, Ferdinand. *Houseboy*. Portsmouth, NH: Heinemann, 1966.

Parry, Benita. *Delusions and Discoveries: Studies on India in the British Imagination, 1880-1930*. Berkeley: University of California Press, 1972.

Patteson, Richard. "*King Solomon's Mines*, Imperialism and Narrative Structure." *Journal of Narrative Technique* vol. 8 no. 1 (Winter 1978).

Petersen, Kirsten Holst. "Birth Pangs of National Consciousness: Mau Mau and Ngugi wa Thiong'o." *World Literature Written in English* 20, 2: Autumn 1981.

Plaatje, Solomon T. *Mhudi*. Lovedale, South Africa, 1930; rpt. Washington D.C.: Three Continents Press, 1978.

Pritchett, V. S. "A Barbados Village." *The New Statesman* 45. 18 April 1953.

Pynchon, Thomas. *Gravity's Rainbow*. New York: Viking, 1973.

Rao, Raja. *Kanthapura*. London: George Allen & Unwin, 1938.

_________. *The Serpent and the Rope*. New York: Pantheon, 1963.

Ramchand, Kenneth. *The West Indian Novel and its Background* . New York: Barnes and Noble, 1970.

Reid, V. S. *New Day*. New York: Knopf, 1949.

Rhys, Jean. *Wide Sargasso Sea*. rpt. New York: W. W. Norton, 1982.

Roby, Kinley. *Joyce Cary*. Boston: Twayne, 1984.

Ruark, Robert. *Something of Value*. Garden City, N. Y: Doubleday, 1955.

Rushdie, Salman. *Imaginary Homelands: Essays and Criticism 1981-1991*. London: Granta/Viking, 1991.

_________. *Midnight's Children*. New York, 1981; rpt. London: Pan Books, 1982.

_________. *The Satanic Verses*. New York: Viking, 1988.

_________. *Shame*. New York: Alfred A. Knopf, 1983.

Rutherford, Andrew, ed. *Kipling's Mind and Art*. Edinburgh: Oliver and Boyd, 1964.

Said, Edward. *Orientalism*. New York: Vintage, 1979.

Scott, Paul. *The Raj Quartet*. New York: Morrow, 1976.

_________. *Staying On*. London: Heinemann, 1977.

Shakespeare, William. *The Complete Works*. ed. Alfred Harbage Baltimore: Penguin, 1969.

Smolowe, Jill. "Five Winning Recollections." *Newsweek* 4 January 1982.

Snow, C. P. "Atmospherics." London *Sunday Times* May 20, 1951.

Soyinka, Wole. *Season of Anomy*. London: Rex Collins, 1973.

Spear, Percival. *A History of India*. Middlesex: Penguin, 1965.

Stevenson, Robert Louis. *Treasure Island*. Boston: Houghton Mifflin, 1962.

Street, Brian. *The Savage in Literature*. London: Routledge and Kegan Paul, 1975.

Taylor, Patrick. *The Narrative of Liberation*. Ithaca: Cornell, 1989.

Torgovnick, Marianna. *Gone Primitive: Savage Intellects, Modern Lives*. Chicago: Univ. of Chicago Press, 1990.

Vinson, James. ed. *Contemporary Novelists*. New York: St. Martin's Press, 1982.

Wade, Michael. *Peter Abrahams*. London: Evans Brothers, 1972.

Walcott, Derek. *Collected Poems 1948-1984*. New York: Noonday Press, 1986.

_________. *Omeros*. New York: Farrar Straus Giroux, 1990.

_________. *Remembrance and Pantomime*. New York: Farrar Straus Giroux, 1980.

Waugh, Alec. *The Best Wine Last*. London: W. H. Allen, 1978.

_________. *The Early Years of Alec Waugh*. London: Cassell, 1962.

_________. *Hot Countries*. New York: Literary Guild, 1930.

_________. *Island in the Sun*. New York, 1955; rpt. London: Pan Books, 1956.

Waugh, Evelyn. *Black Mischief*. London: Chapman and Hall, 1962.

_________. *A Little Learning*. London: Methuen, 1964.

_________. *Scoop*. Boston: Little, Brown, 1937.

_________. *When the Going Was Good*. Boston: Little Brown, 1947.

Williams, Raymond. *The Country and the City*. New York: Oxford, 1973.

Index

Studies of World Literature in English

The series encompasses criticism of modern English-language literature from outside the United States, Great Britain, and Ireland, concentrating on literature by writers from Canada, Africa, Asia, the Pacific and the Caribbean. Submissions are invited concerning fiction, poetry, drama and literary theory.

Address inquiries to:

Professor Norman R. Cary
Series Editor
Dept. of English Language
and Literatures
Wright State University
Dayton, Ohio 45435